PRIMROSES AND POLYANTHUS

PETER WARD

B. T. Batsford Ltd • London

First published in Great Britain 1997
© Peter Ward 1997

A CIP catalogue record for this book
is available from the
British Library

ISBN 0 7134 8183 8

Printed in Singapore

For the Publishers

B. T. Batsford Ltd
583 Fulham Road
London SW6 5BY

CONTENTS

LINE ILLUSTRATIONS

COLOUR PHOTOGRAPHS

ABBREVIATIONS FOR NAMES OF SOCIETIES

APS American Primrose Society
NAPS National Auricula and Primula Society
NCCPG National Council for the Conservation of Plants and Gardens
RHS Royal Horticultural Society

ACKNOWLEDGEMENTS

Many people and organizations contributed towards this book and I would like to thank all who did most sincerely.

Australia Dr Vincent Clark, Mrs Ann Garton.

Canada Dr John Kerridge, Mrs Maedythe Martin.

Denmark Dansk Primula Klub.

Eire Dr E. C. Nelson.

Germany Klaus Jelitto, Martin Fischer (Ernst Benary), Georg Uebelhart (Jelitto).

Great Britain Bob Archdale, Nick Belfield-Smith (Floranova), Mrs Jennie Bousfield, Mrs Angela Bradford, Brian Coop, Mrs Stella Coop, Mrs S. A. Ecklin (RHS Wisley), John Fielding, John Gibson, Mrs Pam Gossage, Howard Drury, Alan Miles and John Gibson (Colegrave Seeds), David Hadfield, Mark Heath (Samuel Yates Ltd), Mrs R. D. Harvey (John Innes Centre), Mrs Ailsa Jackson, Dr Cecil Jones, Les Kaye, Joe Kennedy, Stiubhard Kerr-Liddell, Mr and Mrs John Langdon (Blackmore & Langdon), the Lindley Library, Geoff Nicolle, Mrs Kay Overton, The Royal Botanical Garden Edinburgh, Derek Salt, S & G Seeds, Mrs Barbara Shaw, Keith Sangster (Thompson and Morgan), David Wales (Royal Sluis), Mrs Val Woolley, Mrs Margaret Webster, Lawrence Wigley, Trevor Wood.

New Zealand Dr Keith Hammett, Geoff Genge, F. M. Tetteroo,

The Netherlands Mike Hull (Sakata), Frederik Jager, Harry Kloppenberg, Mr K. Sahin (Sahin), Jan Sijm (Goldsmith).

United States of America Mrs Cheri Fluck, Mrs Rosetta Jones, Ann and Jay Lunn, Mr John O'Brien Snr, Mrs Dorothy Springer.

If I have inadvertently missed anyone I do apologize to them. Finally may I thank David Tarver for once again producing some excellent drawings.

Peter Ward 1997

INTRODUCTION

The genus *Primula* contains over 400 species, the majority confined to the Himalayas and western China. Europe, by contrast, has only 33, mostly in the Alps, with five native to the British Isles. Amongst these British species are *P. vulgaris* – the primrose, *P. veris* – the cowslip and *P. elatior* – the oxlip. These three plants, including the *P. vulgaris* subspecies *P. sibthorpii* and *P. heterochroma*, together with the diminutive *P. juliae*, from the eastern half of the Caucasus are the grandparents of the many hybrid primroses and polyanthus extensively grown throughout Europe, North America and Australasia. Two other species, *P. megaseifolia* and *P. renifolia* also belong to section Primula but have contributed comparatively little in terms of new hybrids.

Primulas take their name from the Latin name for cowslips and primroses, *primula veris*, translated as 'the first little thing of spring', the Latin *primus* meaning 'first'. In 1753 Carolus Linnaeus published his *Species Plantarum* which set out the bi-nominal system of naming plants and animals. He named the cowslip *Primula veris* and called the common primrose *Primula vulgaris*.

Coloured forms of the primrose, emanating from Europe and the Near East were introduced into England and grown in gardens of the rich and famous. These plants interbred with our native yellow *P. vulgaris*, produced more colourful seedlings, the best of which were selected and passed around, sometimes under a clonal name.

During the late seventeenth/early eighteenth century the florists' gold-laced polyanthus first appeared, followed later in the eighteenth century by the predecessor of the garden polyanthus, believed to be a hybrid between the primrose and the cowslip.

Double primroses were also grown, initially found in the wild as sports of the single primrose. Somehow other colours appeared and also the anomalous forms of the primrose so beloved of the Elizabethans. All these plants were either chance seedlings or the result of placing special plants close to one another and letting nature do the rest.

In 1900 a monumental event occurred when Julia Mlokossjewicz discovered *P. juliae*, which was soon being crossed with the primrose, oxlip and cowslip, resulting in hundreds of new hybrids.

The garden polyanthus was also being developed, initially by Gertrude Jekyll who introduced her Munstead strain of yellows and whites. From these early beginnings the polyanthus multiplied into dozens of strains, with a range of brilliant colours on large robust plants, to become one of the most popular of bedding plants. Some, like the Barnhaven strains, are grown by enthusiasts who prefer them because of the even greater range of colours and types.

Today primroses and polyanthus are at the heart of a massive commercial industry and are produced and sold by the million every year. They are produced mainly for the pot-plant trade and can be found on sale for several months of the year. In these commercial strains brilliant colours and very large flowers are the norm with, in many, primrose and polyanthus blood intertwined.

Despite this trend the more traditional sorts are still extensively grown; by members of the national auricula and primula societies, members of the American Primrose Society and many other keen gardeners.

In this book the story will be told of all the different primroses and polyanthus, a family that remains one of the most popular and rewarding of all garden plants.

1   THE SPECIES

Until recently the primrose, cowslip and oxlip were known as 'Vernales' primulas, being part of section Vernales, and this is the name that most people will recognize. Current nomenclatural law states they are now part of section Primula of subgenus *Primula*, the type species being *P. veris* L. I have primarily followed Richards (1993), but Halda (1992), puts *P. juliae* in its own section Julia with *P. megaseifolia* and *P. renifolia* in section Megaseifolia. Federov (1952) breaks down *P. elatior* and *P. vulgaris* into a number of separate species, now generally considered to be subspecies rather than of specific rank. The primrose, cowslip and oxlip are distributed over a vast area, are very variable, and have been split into a number of subspecies. As mentioned Federov *Flora SSSR* treats some as species.

Primula vulgaris PRIMROSE

The primrose, probably better known to most as *P. acaulis* rather than *P. vulgaris*, is one of our best loved plants. *Vulgaris* means 'common', this referring to abundance since many regard the primrose as one of the most

charming of all primulas. Its descendants, the millions of hybrid primroses and polyanthus, are amongst the most popular garden plants.

Primroses have a largely Atlantic and Mediterranean distribution. They are widely but oddly distributed in Europe, missing in most of Spain, Portugal, Germany and countries to the east. They occur in southern Norway and Denmark but not in the rest of Scandinavia. Although native to Corsica, Sicily and most of Italy, they are absent from Sardinia and Cyprus. Primroses grow in Turkey, the Ukraine, the Crimea, the Caucasus and just south of the Caspian sea in Iran. The primrose is one of only two primulas that are found in North Africa. It spreads into Israel, Lebanon and Syria.

Primroses are widely distributed and common throughout much of the British Isles and Ireland, although less so in parts of East Anglia, northeast Scotland and southern Ireland due to the lack of broad-leaved woodland. Like its compatriots, the oxlip and cowslip, it has suffered a serious decline in numbers, particularly near populated areas, due to habitat changes and the widespread digging up of plants. This became illegal in

1975, and together with amenity planting this change has brought about an increase in numbers. In March and April, colonies are to be seen flowering on the banks of motorways, on railway embankments and on similar sites, as well as in more remote areas. In parts of Scotland they flower as late as June; in Cornwall as early as February. Particularly good specimens can be seen in Cornwall, where growth is luxurious, with finer, larger flowers, probably due to the mild, damp climate. In the narrow Cornish lanes, primroses grow happily on near vertical earth banks.

Seed does not normally set without cross-pollination. In a poor spring seed may be scarce despite plants being visited by a range of insects, including hive bees. Where colonies are close to human habitats cross-pollination with garden primroses sometimes occurs. This is one reason for coloured forms being found in the wild.

The primrose is a plant of open deciduous woodland on a range of soils from heavy and slightly acid to limy. Most grow on north-facing slopes and sheltered banks, preferring broken shade, although sometimes in full sun if near a stream.

Primroses dislike peaty and heavily waterlogged sites and very light soils that dry out in summer. They will also seed themselves in some gardens but are unpredictable in others despite similar conditions. Although the flowers show very little variation (a remarkable fact, given their enormous range), four subspecies are recognized:

Subsp. *balearica* A white-flowered form growing in the mountains of Majorca and parts of Africa, heavily scented.

Subsp. *heterochroma* White tomentose lower-leaf surface with flowers in shades of purple, pink, red, violet, white or yellow. Bordering the Caspian Sea, Iran and Azerbaijan. A major contributor to the coloured hybrid forms.

Subsp. *sibthorpii* Leaves grey-green beneath with flowers in shades of lilac, pink, purple, red, white and occasionally yellow. Found in northern and central Greece (excepting the Peloponnese), Crete, Turkey, the Crimea, Caucasus and Armenia. Like subspecies ***heterochroma*** a major contributor in the raising of coloured hybrids.

Subsp. *vulgaris* Yellow flowers on short stalks, leaves green beneath. The most common throughout the range except for the regions listed previously. Although yellow is normal, other colours are sometimes found.

COLOUR VARIATIONS IN THE WILD

The Reverend J. T. Boscawen, a noted gardener, sent 'a very splendid collection of varieties' of coloured primroses found growing wild in Cornwall to the first Primula Conference in 1886.

On 26 April 1898 J. H. Arkwright of Hampton Court, Leominster, exhibited a plant of 'Evelyn Arkwright' at the RHS, a wild primrose he had found in Dinmore Wood, Herefordshire, 11 years previously. This plant, with flowers twice the size of the normal primrose, was given an Award of Merit. When raised from seed the resultant seedlings had similarly large flowers. Margery Fish mentions this variety in her book *Cottage Garden Flowers* (1965), so it was evidently quite long-lived.

The Bristol Flora, first published in 1912, states that 'pure white and purplish varieties have been met with in woods near Temple Cloud'. Temple Cloud is an old village on the A37 about six miles south of Bristol.

Barnhaven Primroses, using the name 'Harbinger', have been selling seed developed from 'a sport of the wild primrose found more than a hundred years ago in a Cornish wood'. The original clone was awarded a first class certificate by the RHS in 1882. Messrs. H. Cannell & Sons' 1883 catalogue says, 'Harbinger leaves all white ones far in the rear, in fact it is one of those marches past that seldom occurs,' and 'We have many extracts eulogising this wonderfully sweetly-scented Primrose.' The price was 5 shillings a plant, a lot of money in those days.

Cecil Monson, the Irish enthusiast, was sceptical about Barnhaven's 'Harbinger', claiming it was simply a 'fair form' of the single white primrose. According to Monson the true 'Harbinger' was 'a delightfully large, fully single, very white primrose' that had grown in his family gardens for over 150 years. He went on to say, 'The distinctive thing about it is that the sex organs are white too, and this makes it look semi-double at first glance.' Mrs Emmerson of Limavady also listed a 'Harbinger', her plant being a white semi-double.

Many other reports mention pink primroses, especially in West Wales, as well as doubles, jack-in-the-greens and hose-in-hose forms.

When I visited Geoffrey Nicolle in West Wales to discuss his 'Rising Sun' cowslips the subject of the wild primrose arose. It has

been said that the pink form is very common in Pembrokeshire, and very high percentages, up to 90 percent, are quoted. This has led to suggestions that some pink primroses were indeed truly wild and not the result of liaisons with garden escapees. Given the colour variations in the other subspecies it seems perfectly possible, but bees will travel three miles, possibly slightly further – many of these mixed populations are well within this distance of dwellings of one sort or another where cultivated primroses are or were commonly grown.

This is the case in West Wales, even though the area is sparsely populated. Geoffrey has lived there for 30 years and says that, although 'wild' pink primroses are common, they seldom exceed 5 percent of the populations he has seen, the mass being yellow with the odd white. Another piece of information was that it had been common practice in the area for 'special' primroses to be dug up and planted in the grounds of local churches. He has seen many such plants, including pinks and other shades.

My co-author on *Auriculas*, Gwen Baker, tracked down a small mixed yellow and pink population on a farm in Staffordshire in 1985. She was escorted across two fields, down to a little wooded hollow, by the farmer and his wife. The primroses grew on a steep bank by a small pond, shaded by trees and protected from cows by barbed wire. The colony was between 20 and 30 plants in full flower, five or six of which were pink. The farmer told Gwen that the pink ones had been growing there for at least 24 years. A second smaller colony of yellow-flowered plants grew in the same wood and more yellow primroses could be found on the bank of a local reservoir half a mile away. Although Gwen is convinced the plants were truly wild the nearest house is less than a mile away.

In Cornwall, Jenny Bousfield, who runs a small nursery at Launceston specializing in primulas, has grown wild white primroses, originally from an orchard at Polyphant, for some years. At that time no other primroses grew, either in the orchard or neighbouring gardens. These plants have the typical character of the wild form, unlike others, with white, buff or soft pink in a cottage garden near her nursery. The latter show a relationship with cultivated primroses, she suspects the *juliae* hybrid 'Wanda', commonly grown in Cornish gardens. Jenny's whites usually last up to three years and seed produces mostly white forms with the odd yellow and pale pink.

Another point made by Jenny, who grows Barnhaven and other primroses extensively, is that cross-fertilization between cultivated plants and the wild yellow rarely seems to occur. The top of her garden is carpeted with wild primroses yet she has seen little or no evidence of hybridization. An adjacent wood, only a narrow pathway away, has a very dense carpet of wild primroses and, over a period of years, has only once produced a single large-flowered hybrid in a reddish shade.

Many county floras refer to colours other than yellow during the long history of the primrose. Apart from the normal yellow, white, dull red, red, dull reddish, purple, liver-coloured, salmon and various shades of pink have been mentioned as well as anomalous forms. The nineteenth-century writer and journalist, Shirley Hibberd, in his book *Field Flowers* (1870), described 'great circular clumps of wild primroses, sometimes covering as much as a hundred square yards each' in Devon and

Somerset. He described colours of 50 different hues including palest lilac, delicate rose, rich purple and an occasional curious tint of blue. At that time the population of England, Wales and Scotland was less than half the present total. The type of conditions that suited primroses were common and plants abundant. This was more than 30 years before *P. juliae* was discovered but coloured forms of *P. vulgaris* had been introduced from abroad in the early sixteenth century, possibly earlier. Whatever the truth, it is a fascinating subject and worth further investigation.

In spring 1996 when taking photographs of wild primroses at Easton-in-Gordano near Bristol I found three white-flowered plants. The plants were growing on a bank at the side of the road. The largest group was where the first white was found, a large-flowered pin-eyed plant, with two others in a smaller patch 75 m (250 ft) away.

In addition to the white primroses two hybrids were discovered. The first was growing amongst the primroses, 1.2 m (4 ft) from the first white. It had short polyanthus stems and primrose-type flowers of a slightly deeper shade of yellow. I should mention that small groups of *P. veris* were growing on the bank not far from the primroses. Halfway between a group of cowslips and one of primroses was another hybrid on its own, similar to the first except for a brighter colour. I suspect one *might* be *vulgaris* × *veris*, with the second possibly *veris* × *vulgaris*. Both resembled primroses in overall appearance, and there are houses and gardens within 90 m (300 ft).

Primula veris COWSLIP

The cowslip is a well-known European plant

and has accumulated a vast literature over several centuries. It is one of the most widespread of all primulas and extends throughout large areas of eastern and western Europe, Iran, Siberia, Turkey, the upper Amur valley northeast of Mongolia, finally almost reaching the Pacific coast.

The plants grow in well-drained neutral grassy fields or on banks, more open sites than usual for primroses – also in light woodland, up to approximately 3000 m (9700 ft). Cowslips flower in May and are pollinated mainly by bees. Once a common plant in much of England, less so in Devon and Cornwall, it is local in Ireland, Scotland and Wales. Due to habitat destruction and intensive farming cowslips became scarce during this century and were heavily picked, not least for their wine-making qualities. In recent years cowslips have returned in numbers since 'amenity planting' became the vogue. One can see the result of this along motorway verges; large colonies are visible in May on stretches of the M4 and M5 motorways, especially near junctions. There are four recognized subspecies:

Subsp. *veris* The dominant form in most of Europe, though less so in southern Europe. Produces a truss of up to 16 slightly drooping flowers on a stem up to 200 mm (8 in) in length. The stem arises from a stout rhizome with fleshy scales at the apex. The rounded leaves are borne on stalks about one-third the length of the leaf. They are prostrate to slightly erect, coarsely and irregularly toothed. The leaves are slightly hairy on the upper surface, more so underneath. Flowers are golden-yellow, cup-shaped, with an orange mark at the base of each petal.

Subsp. *canescens* In this form the leaves

gradually narrow into the stalk and the flowers are larger. Found in the Alps, Pyrenees and mountains of northern parts of Spain. Flowering February to April.

Subsp. *columnae* Mountainous areas of northern Greece, central Italy, central Spain and northeast Turkey. The leaves are oval with thick white tomentose on lower surfaces. Large flowers that are flatter than the others.

Subsp. *macrocalyx* Southeast Russia and Asia as far as Siberia. Also occurs in parts of Turkey. This has the largest flowers and resembles a small polyanthus. It has been described as lacking the charm of the others.

All four subspecies are grown in gardens. *P. veris* is the least spectacular, more suited for naturalizing in rough grass. Subspecies *columnae* is the most attractive, ideal for the rock garden or indeed for pot culture. Plants in the garden readily hybridize and seed may be of mixed parentage.

Strains of orange and red cowslips exist but are probably garden hybrids. Richards (1993) states that red colours are 'not known' in wild cowslips, although in the past pink, purplish, purple, red, dull red and dark red have been recorded in the wild.

Although not noted so frequently as those of the primrose, aberrant forms are sometimes found.

Parkinson (1629) described and illustrated the '*Paralysis hortensis flore plena*', a double cowslip or 'Paigle' as well as feathered, green-flowered, red-flowered, hose-in-hose, jackanapes on horse back and gallygaskins forms.

The Flora of Wiltshire lists a number of abnormal forms, one with six flowers on long pedicels, one with a leafy inflorescence, another with flowers and pedicels 38 mm

(1 ½ in) long and a plant with a secondary inflorescence. In 1982 Bristol University were given a plant of 'Primula veris double white' by a Mr Frank Lawley. This is the only recorded instance I have found of a double white cowslip.

Primula elatior OXLIP

The oxlip is widely distributed and locally abundant in central and southern Europe, as far east as the Carpathians and central Ukraine, also the Balkans, parts of Turkey, the Crimea and Siberia. As far north, in only one location, as southern Sweden. In the British Isles this primula has a very restricted range but where it grows can be locally abundant and may be increasing. In England oxlips grow in broad-leaved woodland, usually oak, on wet chalky clay soils in East Anglia, centred on the borders of Cambridge, Essex and Suffolk and are rarely found elsewhere. As with primroses and cowslips, habitat destruction has reduced numbers. Hybrids between the primrose and cowslip, commonly called 'false oxlips' and also botanically P. tommasinii, often masquerade as oxlips in other localities. In the false oxlip a distinguishing feature is that the flowers point in different directions like the cowslip. Where mixed populations occur, possibly due to coppicing, few true oxlips are found, most having been replaced by hybrids. In England the oxlip flowers slightly later than the primrose and earlier than the cowslip. Although hybrids with the primrose are common, those with the cowslip are virtually unknown and they rarely grow together. Like the cowslip, oxlips are mainly pollinated by bees. They flower in April in England and set seed freely. Oxlips are abundant in parts of the Alps, where

they flower much earlier, often in melting snow, and are usually confined to limestone formations. In northwest Europe they grow in wet, shaded woodlands, but elsewhere can be found in a variety of habitats. The oxlip tolerates hotter, drier conditions than its relatives, growing at sea level and as high as 4000 m (13,000 ft). A general description is a hairy leafed plant, short crisped hairs, up to 200 mm (8 in) × 70 mm (2 ¾ in), rounded at the tip, finely toothed. The stem rises to 300 mm (1 ft), bearing up to 12 flowers in a one-sided drooping umbel. Flower stalks vary in length up to 20 mm (⅘ in). The flowers are pale to bright yellow or purple in subspecies *meyeri* (formerly known as *P. amoena*), with diffuse greenish to orange throat markings, saucer-shaped to flat-faced, up to 25 mm (1 in) in diameter. There is some confusion over the number of subspecies and many variations have been mentioned in past literature. I have followed Richards (1993), who lists eight:

Subsp. *eliator* The commonest subspecies in Europe, although less frequently in the south where it is replaced by subspecies *intricata*. Narrow-bladed, toothed, hairy leaves. The flowers are sulphur yellow up to 25 mm (1 in) in diameter.

Subsp. *intricata* This is the common form in the mountains of southern Europe, excepting the Alps. The leaves are hairy and gradually narrow down into the stalk, which is the main difference from subspecies *elatior*. The bright yellow flowers, rarely more than seven, are flat and up to 20 mm (⅘ in) in size.

Subsp. *leucophylla* Occurring on limestone formations of the eastern Carpathians in Rumania and the Caucasus. The leaves are deciduous, crenated and gradually narrow into the stalk. The funnel-shaped, pale yellow flowers are few to a stem, up to 16 mm (⅔ in) in diameter.

Subsp. *lofthousei* This subspecies is only found in the Sierra Nevada in southern Spain. Similar to subspecies *intricata* apart from the many-flowered umbels of smaller, butter-yellow flowers.

Subsp. *meyeri* This is a very variable plant which is divided into three separate species by Federov, *P. amoena*, *P. meyeri* and *P. kusnetsovii*. It is usually called *P. amoena*. The colour range varies from violet-blue through lavender to purple shades. A mountain primula growing throughout the Caucasus and the Pontic mountains in Turkey, either in peaty, earthy banks or quite rocky terrain. According to Richards *P. amoena* is interfertile with subspecies of oxlip but not with other relatives. This was an uncommon plant in cultivation, often found to be a hybrid polyanthus masquerading as the species. In recent years several expeditions have collected seed and I have grown plants from three sources. Some flowered well and were crossed with a first generation *juliae* hybrid. The resulting plants are vigorous and have been intercrossed to produce an F2 generation. Some have lovely near-red, purple and lilac shades. Although described by Smith, Burrows and Lowe (1984) as relatively easy to grow, *P. amoena* is considered by others to be difficult. Frequently the plants appear to sulk and refuse to grow, slowly fading away. The three pairs of plants obtained, all from different sources, behaved quite differently. One pair refused to grow and faded away; the second grew vigorously and flowered well. The third pair of plants, *P. amoena JCA 785–152*, have grown slowly and not yet flowered, yet all three are supposedly the same species. The indications are

that the compost may be the key factor, the plant preferring a good measure of either peat or leafmould rather than a gritty alpine mix. Whatever the truth subspecies *meyeri* is a magnificent plant with a great deal of potential for hybridization.

Subsp. *pallasii* Nearly hairless leaves, gradually contracting into the stalk and coarsely toothed. The pale yellow flowers are few to a stem and up to 25 mm (1 in) in diameter. It grows in the eastern part of the range from Turkey and northern Iran to the Urals, the Altai and eastern Siberia.

Subsp. *cordifolia* A small, neat plant with smoother, hairless leaves, of a bronze-green shade contracting into a long, narrow, stalk. The dark stems contrast well with the luminous pale yellow flowers. It occurs in the Caucasus and Armenia, usually at lower levels than Subsp. *meyeri*.

Subsp. *pseudoelatior* Occurring in northeastern Turkey and the Caucasus, this is similar to subspecies *elatior* except that the leaves are heart-shaped and hairier.

The oxlip is a splendid garden plant, particularly suited to rock gardens with subspecies *eliator* the best general choice. The others include some very choice plants that need careful cultivation and are probably better in pots. The best are subspecies *cordifolia*, subspecies *leucophylla* and subspecies *meyeri*, all primulas of distinction.

Primula juliae

This fascinating miniature primula was discovered by Julia Ludvikovna Mlokossjewicz (or Mlokosewitsch) at Lagodekh in the eastern Caucasus on 20

April 1900, 130 km (80 miles) east-northeast of Tiflis, growing in moss amongst wet, dripping rocks close to waterfalls. Julia was the daughter of Ludwig Franzevich Mlokossjewicz (1831–1909) a Polish aristocrat who was born in Warsaw. At the age of 22 he enlisted in the Russian army and was stationed at Lagodekhi in the Caucasus, where he laid out and planted a regimental park and orchard, collecting trees, conifers and exotic plants. In the course of a colourful career he was falsely arrested, after resigning from the army, for allegedly being involved in intrigues and uprisings. In 1879 he was appointed inspector of forests for the Signakhi district and settled in Lagodekhi where he remained for the rest of his life.

Mlokossjewicz explored the Caucasus extensively, sending zoological, entomological and botanical specimens to Russian museums. His reputation blossomed and eventually he was considered the leading authority on the Caucasus. Julia, along with her brothers and sisters, was taken on botanical expeditions from a very early age and grew up to share his tastes, as her discovery of *Primula juliae* illustrates.

The species makes large carpets of creeping rhizomes, with fleshy, reddish scales forming close to the ground. The stalked flowers are a bright, deep bluish magenta – darker and redder around the eye, which is yellow. Richards describes the colour range in the wild as 'red to white'. A *P. juliae alba* is sometimes offered but whether this is a collected form or a garden-bred hybrid is something I have not been able to verify.

The range is fairly widespread, covering the eastern half of the Caucasus, Georgia from Ossetia eastward and Azerbaijan. In cultivation it is not free-flowering and poor forms are common. I have grown plants from several sources and they showed considerable variation in flower size and colour; all, however, are in bluish magenta shades – some light, some darker.

P. juliae is easy to grow in damp, shaded conditions in good, well-drained soil and is suitable for pot culture. Some dispute has arisen as to the actual date of introduction. Barbara Shaw in *The Book of Primroses* (1991) says that the famous gardener and plant explorer, Reginald Farrer, obtained *P. juliae* not long after its discovery, possibly around 1902, and cites Nancy Lindsey, a knowledgeable gardener who ran a nursery at Sutton Courtenay in Oxfordshire, as the source; her family had been friendly with Farrer. Most sources say that *P. juliae* was sent to Kew and Oxford in 1911 by Professor Kusnetsow of Dorpat Botanic Garden. However, an interesting article by Clarence Elliot, of Six Hills Nursery fame, in *My Garden*, August 1935, states that a list of seeds was sent to the Oxford Botanic Garden from Tiflis Botanical Garden in 1911, which included a primula with purple flowers. 'Only Mr Baker of Oxford Botanic Gardens spotted a small important difference in the botanical description. The leaves were given as cordate – heart-shaped – while the leaves of the common primrose are, as everyone knows, ovate or oblong. That was good enough for Mr Baker who wrote off for seeds.' Shortly after its introduction hybridizers began crossing *P. juliae* with other coloured primroses and a torrent of hybrids botanically known as *P.* ×

pruhoniciana resulted. This hybridization was not confined to Great Britain. It was extensive in continental Europe, especially in Germany and Holland, and later in North America. Many hybrid primroses and some polyanthus have *P. juliae* somewhere in their genetic chain.

Primula megaseifolia

This is an interesting primula, not terribly well known, although a distinctive and unusual species. The flowers, not very attractive, are magenta-rose to rose-pink with a whitish eye, but the glossy foliage is most odd, resembling a small Bergenia. Some better forms do exist with well-formed clear pink flowers, although I have yet to see one. According to Halda, *P. megaseifolia* was discovered in May 1866 by Balansa near Rice in the Trabzon district in the Turkish Pontus mountains, at an elevation of 300 m (975 ft), growing in 'moist, shady defiles'. It was introduced into England by Miss Ellen Wilmott in 1901. Distribution is somewhat limited, beir.g confined to an area near the Black Sea coast, over a distance of about 130 km (80 miles) in northeast Turkey and the adjoining province of Batum. The plant is long-lived in shady, fertile, moisture-retentive soils that are well drained. It has been grown in some quantity at the Savill Gardens, Windsor. It resents being disturbed and takes a while to settle after replanting. Few seeds are normally set in cultivation although abundant in the wild. In 1995 two pin-eyed plants flowered in my greenhouse and I was fortunate to obtain pollen from a thrum-eyed plant grown by a friend. From approximately 50 seeds ten germinated, in three flushes, over a period of three to five months. The seed pan was retained and left outside, completely exposed, during the 1995/6 winter. In spring 1996 another 30 germinated. The first seedlings were expected to flower in 1997.

P. megaseifolia HYBRIDS

At least two people in the UK have raised hybrids from this species and two named clones are available, both raised by John Fielding of East Sheen in London. Before continuing, it is interesting to note that George Arends was given an Award of Merit by the RHS on 30 May 1905 for *P. × Arendsii*, 'Raised from *P. obconica* × *P. megaseaefolia* [sic]. Flowers a lovely mauve-pink, freely produced in large umbels, somewhat resembling *P. obconica*, but superior to it. While foliage is nearer to *P. megasaeafolia* [sic]. An acquisition for the cool greenhouse.' It would appear that this cannot be correct, as these species are not compatible.

In 1985 a plant of *P. megaseifolia* was pollinated by *P. juliae*, while other crosses were made with *P. vulgaris* and *P. elatior*. Sown fresh in 1986, only one seed germinated in the winter of 1987/8. By early spring a large-flowering plant had developed with orchid purple (old RHS colour chart 31/1) flowers 23 mm (almost 1 in) in diameter on 100 mm (4 in) stems. The leaves are spinach-green (old RHS colour chart 0960/1), up to 45 mm (1 ⅘ in) long and 40 mm (1 ⅗ in) wide. They are elliptical with a dentate margin, while the petioles are up to 70 mm (2 ⅘ in) long. Plants grow well in plastic pots in John Innes No. 3 compost with added coarse peat and grit. They thrive in the garden in an open organic soil with added leafmould.

A plant was initially supplied to Edrom Nurseries in Scotland, then other specialist nurseries. 'John Fielding' appears to be prolific and is becoming well established. The plants I have seen are interesting rather than attractive. Although they are variable, a feature is the flowering period, which extends over six months

The name 'John Fielding' was bestowed on it by Graham Rice who wrote an article on John Fielding's greenhouse and garden.

'John Fielding' was pollinated by *P. juliae* and by May 1990 two seedlings germinated. One died but the other grew rapidly into a large-leaved plant, producing one flower in the spring of 1991. By December the plant, kept in a frost-free greenhouse, burst into growth developing numerous crowns and flower buds. By the end of January it was in full flower with up to seven blooms on each 100 mm (4 in) stem. The pin-eyed flowers are the same colour and diameter as 'John Fielding' although the tube is slightly longer and the calyx shorter. The similarly shaped leaves are the same shade of spinach-green but appreciably smaller at 30 mm (1 ⅕ in)long and 25 mm (1 in) wide. After flowering the leaves increase in size appreciably. The plant has been named 'Barbara Midwinter' after a gardening friend and neighbour. Both plants have been given preliminary commendations by the Alpine Garden Society.

A plant was supplied to Blackthorn Nursery in Hampshire and the rapid rate of increase – every node roots – should ensure wide distribution quite soon.

Lawrence Wigley, of Carshalton Beeches, Surrey has also made numerous ongoing crosses with *P. megaseifolia*. Lawrence became interested after seeing a plant at C. G. Hollett's alpine nursery at Sedburgh, Yorkshire in 1975. His first plant came from the Savill Gardens the following year and he at once began to hybridize.

P. megaseifolia was used mainly as a pollinator, and the seed parents were two Barnhaven polyanthus, a Barnhaven 'new pink' primrose and a yellow hybrid primrose. The latter was used to pollinate *P. megaseifolia*. The only real success was from the yellow hybrid, 30 strong seedlings, large enough to be potted into 5 inch (125 mm) pots by the autumn of 1977. Foliage was intermediate between the parents and the plants began to flower in November, continuing throughout the winter.

These seedlings proved very prolific flowerers with several polyanthus-type stems on each plant. The stems varied in height between 152 mm (6 in) and 304 mm (12 in) and flowers varied from shades of pink to intense magenta. All displayed the deep orange eye of *P. megaseifolia*.

Further crosses were made with selected seedlings, *P. megaseifolia* itself and various primroses and polyanthus. Although seed was obtained from most of the crosses, the resulting plants lacked quality. By this time the original seedlings had shown a steady decline and by 1981 were discarded.

After a break of several years further crosses were made in 1989, again using *P. megaseifolia* as the pollinator. The seed parents were a bright cerise polyanthus and *P. elatior* subspecies *pallasii*. One seedling germinated from the polyanthus cross, flowering in December 1991. The polyanthus habit was retained, the foliage intermediate between the parents. The flowers were rich cerise with the distinctive eye of *P. megaseifolia*. By 1994 this seedling had declined in vigour and faded away just like the earlier ones.

The seed from the other cross was not sown until 1990 and the seedlings, together with those from one involving *P. elatior*, germinated in December 1991. These seedlings varied in colour from pale yellow to pink and were a mixture of pins and thrums. In some seedlings the one-sided umbel of *P. elatior* was present and the flowers were larger where subspecies *pallasii* was the parent.

Some of these seedlings succumbed to severe frost in an unheated greenhouse and most of the others showed the previous tendency to fade away. A few remain and further crosses with primroses and miniature polyanthus have been made.

Overall these results are not promising except where *P. juliae* was used as a parent.

Primula renifolia

Resembling a smaller version of *P. megaseifolia* but considerably more attractive; only discovered as recently as August 1936, in the foothills of Mount Great Dombai in the western Caucasus by Volgunov. It was growing around waterfalls at about 2000 m (6500 ft) in a mixed beech forest. The flowers are blue-violet with a yellow eye, flat and large for the size of the plant, up to 30 mm (1 ⅕ in) in diameter. There have been suggestions that *P. renifolia* is a form of *P. megaseifolia* but it is now generally agreed that the species is distinct.

Despite early reports suggesting cultivation presented few problems this has not proved the case. The very few who have grown it say that *P. renifolia* is prone to fungal problems and root rot.

The clone remaining in cultivation, introduced in 1982 by an East German collector who was allowed into the home range, is thrum-eyed and so far has refused to set seed.

Ray Edwards, the gardening journalist, obtained some small seedlings from an Australian friend in 1978 and flowered two pin-eyed plants in 1980. Attempts to self-pollinate failed, but he succeeded in obtaining seed when the plant was crossed with a commercial strain of violet-flowered *P. vulgaris*. The fate of these seedlings is unknown but it is presumed they did not survive. Pollen from the thrum-eyed clone has been used on *P. vulgaris* without success.

P. renifolia appears to be hardy, flowering in late March. This is a choice plant but experience so far indicates it will prove difficult to maintain and increase in cultivation. The possibilities of hybridizing with related species, while tantalizing, are similarly uncertain.

It is interesting to note that the Dutch company of K. Sahin, Zadin BV have a long-term hybridizing project with *P. renifolia* and *P. megaseifolia* to produce a new race of house plants.

This concludes details of the primrose species and we now move on, in succeeding chapters, to the fascinating story of the garden hybrids.

Fig. 1. *Primula megaseifolia* and *Primula renifolia*

2 THE SINGLE PRIMROSE

Primroses became popular garden plants towards the end of the fifteenth century. They were common in the wild, collected and planted in gardens for medicinal and sweetening purposes. The herbals of the time, not gardening books in the true sense, were primarily concerned with plants of medicinal value and contain the earliest references to the cultivation of cowslips and primroses.

The word 'primrose' and its older variants, 'prime rolles', 'primerole' and 'prymerose', are derived from the Latin *prima rosa* (first or earliest rose). 'Primerole' is also an abbreviation of the French *primeverole*, Italian *primaverola*, a diminutive of *prime vera* from *flor di prima vera*, the first spring flower. Henry Phillips in *Flora Historica* (1824) wrote that the primrose was 'anciently called Paralisos, after the name of a beautiful youth who was the son of Priapos and Flora'. There are other interpretations although not all refer to primroses.

The earliest reference to coloured primroses was made by John Rea in 1665. He describes more than 20 shades, all classified as 'diversities of red', implying that they were of foreign origin. Twenty-five years

earlier in 1640 John Parkinson had described 'Tradescant's Turkie-Purple Primrose', believed to be the first mention of *P. vulgaris* subspecies *sibthorpii* brought back from the Black Sea coast by Tradescant. John Tradescant the elder was an inveterate plant collector, who travelled widely on the Continent in search of new plants for the garden of Hadfield House, then under construction. This lilac or purple primrose was considered a great rarity and Parkinson said it was especially valued for its early flowering.

By 1648 Jason Bobart the elder was growing blue, purple and white single varieties at the Oxford Botanic Garden, as well as the common 'Feild Primerose'. The blue and purple were presumably forms of *P. vulgaris* subspecies *sibthorpii* although it was not until the late 1880s, more than 200 years later, that G. F. Wilson at Wisley raised the first recognized blue varieties. Miss Gertrude Jekyll, at the April 1916 Primula Conference, stated 'it was from a purple primrose with a colour inclining to violet that Mr G. H. Wilson raised his celebrated blue varieties.' After the culmination of 12 years work, on 8

April 1890, the RHS gave an Award of Merit to Wilson for 'Oakwood Blue' described as 'a deep indigo blue – best yet.'

Nevertheless, until the early 1900s many coloured forms of primrose were grown in gardens. They were either the result of selection, where seed was collected from different forms planted together, or chance seedlings. Line breeding as we know it was unknown and hand pollination little understood. It is incredible that so many good plants were raised by these methods. George Arends attended the RHS shows in 1903 and 1904 and commented in his book on the 'marvellous Primula hybrids from *elatior*, [and] *vulgaris*' that were exhibited. He also wrote that all the garden hybrids of the *acaulis* [*vulgaris*] type were 'much inbred with *P. vulgaris*, *sibthorpii*, and like kinds, giving rise to rich colour variations'.

These coloured flowers rapidly became collectors' flowers, although the single *vulgaris* primrose never attained the status of either the double or anomalous forms. Sacheverell Sitwell in his classic *Old Fashioned Flowers* (1939) wrote 'it seems to have aroused much less interest than the double.'

The new primroses came in shades of red, purple, blue and lilac and were found to be less hardy than the native field varieties. Alice Coats, in another classic work, *Flowers and Their Histories* (1956), quotes the Reverend William Hanbury's reproof to Phillip Miller who had suggested these rare primroses be planted in the wild, saying such action would result in 'the loss of the whole stock thus planted'.

Named varieties appear to have been rare. Sitwell dismisses them in a few lines mentioning only 'Old Irish Single Primrose',

'Miss Massey', and 'Apple Blossom' although he was only referring to older varieties still known to be in cultivation. The 'Apple Blossom' he mentions is presumably the plant from James Whiteside-Dane in Ireland. Roy Genders in *Primroses* (1959), wrote that lack of interest in the primrose during the nineteenth century almost brought about its total eclipse, but by the end of the century nurserymen like the Dean Brothers of Ealing were working on improved strains that could be raised from seed.

On 20 April 1900 a momentous event occurred in the history of the primrose when Julia Mlokossjewicz discovered a tiny primula growing near waterfalls in the Caucasus. This heralded the arrival on the horticultural scene of the miniature primrose that was to have such an impact in the following 50 years.

Named in honour of its discoverer, seed from *P. juliae* was sent to Oxford in 1911 and plants the following year to Kew and Edinburgh. A mystery remains surrounding the miniature stemmed primrose 'Craven Gem', introduced by Reginald Farrer in 1902 and thought by some to have *P. juliae* blood. It seems unlikely that a plant only discovered in 1900 in a remote part of the world would have reached England so soon.

A plant of *P. juliae* was exhibited at the RHS, by Mr W. G. Baker, on 2 April 1912 and was given an Award of Merit. The word soon spread and so did *P. juliae*, with many plant-breeders obtaining plants, both in the UK and Europe, for hybridizing purposes. *P. juliae* did not reach North America until some years later.

As so many were involved, the end result was hundreds of hybrids, initially as the result of crosses with forms of *P. vulgaris*, *P. elatior* and *P. veris*. It would seem that practically every nursery, as well as many amateur gardeners, both in the UK and in Europe, bred hybrids.

It has been suggested that 'Wanda' was the first *juliae* hybrid, but two years earlier, in 1916, Waterer Sons and Crisp Ltd, the famous Twyford nursery, were given an Award of Merit by the RHS for 'Crispii' thus pre-dating 'Wanda' which received an award in 1919. 'Crispii' was the result of a cross between *P. juliae* and 'the common primrose'.

'Wanda', the best-known and most numerous of all *juliae* hybrids, even today, received the Award of Merit on 8 April 1919. The report in the *Gardeners Chronicle*, of 12 April 1919, describes:

> *a handsome hybrid obtained by crossing* P. juliae *with a crimson form of P.* acaulis. *The plant is of neat and robust habit with rounder and shorter leaves than in* P. acaulis. *The flowers are so freely borne that they almost hide the foliage. The individual pips are slightly larger in diameter than a half crown and their colour is deep dark purple blue, with a golden eye or velvety purple with a ruby flushing and an orange yellow eye. Shown by Bakers.*

The RHS Floral Committee description is more precise: 'Flowers of bright, purplish crimson with golden eye, of a large size. The most striking of the many hybrids resulting from this cross so far exhibited.' So barely eight years after the introduction of *P. juliae* to England 'many hybrids' had already been raised.

As well as 'Wanda', Baker's raised many others including 'Felicity', 'Lilac Time', 'Pam' and 'Beamish'. In 1925 they were given an Award of Merit for 'Bunty', another well-known hybrid, which was a 1922 cross between 'Wanda' and 'Wilson's Blue'.

In 1919 the John Innes Horticultural Institute began a comprehensive series of breeding experiments crossing *P. juliae* with *P. vulgaris, P. elatior* and, towards the end of the programme, the polyanthus 'Cloth of Gold'. The work was begun by Miss Pellew and only ceased in 1927 when Mr R. J. Chittenden, who took over the programme in 1922, departed for the Malay States. Although this was essentially a scientific programme it did produce a number of plants of horticultural merit that were grown on for trial and possible commercial introduction. Unfortunately, what happened to these plants is not clear. The present John Innes Centre has no record. It is known that Ingwerson's listed a 'Merton Hybrid' in the 1930/31 catalogue with the comment 'one of the many fine things raised at the JII. Rich Purple.' Merton Hybrid' is the correct name for the plant variously called 'Morton Hybrid', 'Moreton Hybrid', 'Moreton' or 'Morton'.

George Arends, a well-known nurseryman from Wuppertal-Ronsdorf, Germany, while on a visit to England in 1913, purchased *P. juliae*. He flowered it in 1914 and immediately recognized the close relationship with *P. vulgaris*. All the flowers on *P. juliae* were crossed with different coloured *vulgaris*. Plenty of seed resulted – unusual, as he indicates *P. juliae* was the seed parent – subsequently producing hundreds of seedlings. All had the growth characteristics of *P. juliae*, including the much divided, stoloniferous rootstock, but the flowers were larger and better. They were offered for the first time as a hybrid mixture in his autumn 1920 list as *P.* x. *helenae,* after his wife Helene.

From the first group of seedlings a number were propagated and named. 'Purple Carpet' was introduced in 1921, with 'Gem' and 'Jewel' following in 1925. Later more *vulgaris* blood was introduced resulting, in 1931, in 'Blue Cushion' and 'Snow Cushion'. Of these plants, 'Snow Cushion' or 'Schneekissen' is still grown and so possibly is 'Jewel'. 'Snow Cushion' is usually described as being of Dutch origin. Arends raised numerous others, such as 'Frülingsbote'(Spring Messenger), 'Frülingsfeuer' (Spring Fire) and 'Edelstein' (Precious Stone). In his book *My Life as Gardener and Plant Breeder* (1951) he mentions other raisers like W. Dorn, who raised 'March Joy'. Arends was still hybridizing as late as 1949 when he introduced 'Flower Cushion'.

At the same time Frantisek Zeeman began raising hybrids with *P. juliae*. Zeeman was the Head Gardener at the Austrian Dendrological Society's garden at Pruhonice Castle, near Prague, the estate of Ernst Count Silva Tarouca. Born in 1881, he had studied horticulture in Austria, England, Germany and Holland, and on the formation of the first Czech Republic virtually took over the garden under his own name. When the Czechoslovakian Dendrological Society was formed Zeeman was retained as a member of their council with the title of inspector of gardens. Zeeman crossed *P. vulgaris coerulea* with *P. juliae* in 1918 and raised a number of hybrids that he called *P.* x. *pruhoniciana*. Although very hardy, they did not have the range of colours of Arend's hybrids. The Dendrological Society remains active, although the gardens are now at Tschechien, and one of Zeeman's original hybrids is still grown.

Activity in Britain was also hectic. Practically every nursery and many private individuals contributed to the wave of *juliae* hybrids. Clarence Elliot of the famous Six Hills Nursery at Stevenage, Hertfordshire, raised a number and described 'Gloria' as his finest introduction. Elliot also mentions a Professor Bateson as raising others, but the origin of many named plants remains obscure. In February 1920 Dr Rosenheim showed at the RHS the progeny from crosses he made in 1917, first flowering in 1919, between *P. juliae* and *P. elatior*. By 1928 Ingwerson's nursery were offering 18 cultivars and others soon followed suit.

One mystery is the origin of named plants listed as 'raised' or 'obtained from Holland'. The word 'Verwanis' cropped up against some of these plants, 'Sir Bedivere' for example, and led me to wonder if the name had some association with a Dutch raiser or nursery. This proved not to be the case. Mr Klaus Jelitto says, in a letter, that *P. verwanii.hort* is a synonym for *P. pruhoniciana* and that plants raised in England in the 1920s, were given the name prior to *P. pruhoniciana* being accepted. Another new designation, not mentioned in any of the primula books consulted, is *P. margotae*. This relates to hybrids between *P. juliae* and *P. elatior* and includes the larger types. Mr Jelitto says that *P. margotae* came later than *P. pruhoniciana* and was often sold under the latter name. This information was also unearthed by two Dutch members of the

APS, Harry Kloppenberg and Frederik Jager. The Agriculture University of Wageningen suggested to Mr Jager that *P. verwanii* was a combination of VERis and WANda.

A book by Leo Jelitto, *Die Freilandprimeln* (1938), calls the *juliae/elatior* hybrids *P. margotae* C. Schn., and refers to *P. ansoldii* as another synonym, while *P. spaethii* Whn. is described as a cross between *P. juliae* and *P. sibthorpii*. These names, like *P. juliana.hort*, are horticultural synonyms and have no scientific or taxonomical authority.

Jelitto's book listed 35 named forms, mostly of Continental origin. They included 'Garteninspektor O. Sander' ('red violet'), Spaeth's 'Jubiläumsgruss' and 'Olympiagruss' ('cherry-carmine red' and 'pure brilliant lilac blue' respectively) and 'Gartenglück' ('carmine-red with a yellow centre'). Few that are listed became known in the UK.

THE GARRYARD PRIMROSES

Although not initially related to *P. juliae* the Irish 'Garryard' primroses have a fascinating history and are favourites of many primrose lovers. A great deal of misunderstanding exists about them, and published information is frequently incorrect. Thanks primarily to the late Cecil Monson, a well-known Dublin actor and great primrose enthusiast, and Dr Charles Nelson, formerly of Glasnevin Botanic Garden, Dublin, a more accurate account is possible.

I corresponded with Cecil Monson in the late 1960s, and he also wrote a number of articles in both the British and American primula society yearbooks. Dr Nelson researched the subject in the early 1980s, as well as the history of other Irish primroses. He has said that none of these primroses were deliberate crosses – they occurred as chance seedlings. I contacted Dr Nelson when researching this book but he was unable to add anything. He believes that the full truth will never be known as those involved are long dead and left no records.

The first and only true Garryard was discovered growing in his garden by James Whiteside-Dane at Johnstown near Naas, County Kildare. At this time Whiteside-Dane was deputy lieutenant of the county and president of the Kildare Archaeological Society. Considerable confusion exists as to the exact date he discovered 'Apple Blossom', usually written as 'Appleblossom' although the early accounts favour the former. Cecil Monson said that his grandmother had obtained 'Garryard Apple Blossom' from Whiteside-Dane, who was a family friend, prior to 1900. Whiteside-Dane lived at Osbertstown Hill in 1896, moving to Abbeyfield near Naas about 1903. He was first recorded as living at Garryard, which was the name of the house, in 1912, where he remained until 1922, moving to County Cavan after retirement. 'Garry' is the Irish word for 'garden' and 'ard' for 'high' and the primroses grew in a quarry. In March 1920 The National Botanic Gardens at Glasnevin sent out plants of 'Dane's Primrose' to a gardener in County Limerick, although no record exists of them receiving plants from Garryard. They had supplied some primulas to Whiteside-Dane a year earlier and this was the only occasion he is referred to in the records. The reference to 'Danes Primrose' is believed to refer to 'Apple Blossom' but raises further questions. It seems strange that Cecil

Monson should be so far out in his dates. Mrs Gladys Emmerson, another famous Irish primrose enthusiast, said that a friend of hers had seen these bronze-leaved primroses around 1900. One possible explanation is that 'Apple Blossom' had appeared much earlier and plants were taken to Garryard by Whiteside-Dane.

A description of 'Apple Blossom' is of a plant resembling the wild primrose in leaf shape and texture, with bronze leaves and a large head of pink and white appleblossom-coloured flowers, on a stout, red, hairy stem, 125 mm (5 in) in length. It is considered to have been either a putative mutation of *P. vulgaris*, or a hybrid with a red primrose. The real puzzle is where the bronze foliage came from. 'Apple Blossom' seems to have disappeared some time in the 1940s, and although described as 'a robust plant, increasing rapidly' never became widely distributed. The existence of this bronze-leaved cultivar remained little known until the late 1930s, by which time 'Guinivere' had also been introduced, and Miss Eda Hume, amongst others, began mentioning them in articles. It has been said that 'Apple Blossom' still existed in the USA in 1984, but I understand that the plant grown is an American introduction.

The next to appear was a plant that was pictured in black and white in *Gardening Illustrated* on 6 April 1935 as 'Garryard'. This is thought to be the first illustration of 'Guinivere' which Cecil Monson said was raised by Mrs Johnson, the introducer of 'Kinlough Beauty' and 'Lady Greer'. Possibly the plant depicted was that shown by Mrs Page Croft at Dublin in the same year. The earliest references I have found to 'Apple Blossom' always refer to the plant as 'Apple Blossom' and never as 'Garryard Appleblossom'. Could this indicate that 'Apple Blossom' had been raised some years prior to Whiteside-Dane's move to Garryard?

'Guinivere', usually called 'Garryarde Guinivere', is the most widely distributed Irish raised primrose-polyanthus and has spread well beyond the United Kingdom and Ireland. It is a wonderful plant and presumably the parent, probably as a pollinator, of many of the later Garryard and Buckland varieties. The *New Flora and Silva*, Vol. IX. No. 4, July 1937, page 235, has the following description:

> *Partly Polyanthus partly primrose is the exquisite new hybrid Garriarde [sic]. Raised in County Fermanagh, it does credit to a famous old garden there. The pale-pink flowers are as large as those of a fine type of polyanthus and very fragrant. They are borne on a stout stem which rises from the midst of olive-tinted foliage which betrays its origin,* Primula Juliae.

This is one of the first descriptions of the plant that has become well-known as 'Garryard Guinivere'.

Not long after 'Guinivere' came 'Julius Caesar' from Miss W. F. Wynne, an *acaulis*-type plant with flowers of deep claret and an orange eye. It had the bronze foliage from either 'Apple Blossom' or 'Guinivere' but the seed parent was a famous old primrose, 'Miss Massey', said to be the single form of 'Madame Pompadour'. I saw 'Julius Caesar' some years ago but it is now believed to be extinct. I have never seen 'Miss Massey' –

very scarce in 1959 but, amazingly, still surviving in a few places.

'Tawny Port' is another Irish cultivar with bronze foliage, a sport of 'Garryard' raised by Colonel Graham of Sallins, County Kildare. 'Tawny Port', an excellent miniature polyanthus, is still in cultivation despite several other primroses masquerading under the name. These plants – apart from 'Victory', raised by Winnifrid Wynne ('richest paeony purple'), and two other seedlings from Cecil Monson, one of which he named 'Dottie Monson' – are the best-known cultivars raised in Ireland with Garryard blood.

Many other bronze-leaved cultivars now appeared. Mrs Emmerson wrote 'there are now all sorts of primroses on the market which are hybrids between Garryards and *juliae*.' *P. vulgaris* subspecies *sibthorpii* and *heterochroma* were also involved in some of these crosses.

Earlier I mentioned the Buckland varieties, raised in Devon by Mr Hugo Jeffrey of the Champernowne Nurseries at Buckland Monachorum, Devon. In the 1968 catalogue of East Coast Primrose Gardens, Roy Genders' primrose nursery, are listed six primrose-polyanthus with the Buckland prefix. They were 'Belle' ('violet-blue flowers with a crimson flush and paler foliage than the others'), 'Canterbury' ('pearly grey, flushed with cream and with brown veinings'), 'Enchantress', 'Primrose' and 'Wine' (all described elsewhere) and 'Scarlet' ('the blooms are of brilliant crimson scarlet and are completely circular, with a clearly defined centre of gold').

'Buckland Belle' was introduced in 1952; 'Buckland Wine' and 'Scarlet' in 1965.

Interestingly, in the 1955 catalogue of Champernowne 'Buckland Belle' is described as a single primrose, 'Victorian violet of juliae parentage'. Genders describes it as having 'short polyanthus stems'. In the same Champernowne list is 'Garryarde' – 'very beautiful with bronzy-green foliage and lavender pink flowers'. This is probably 'Guinivere' but who can say for certain ?

Another nursery that listed a number was Townsend's, who offered seven different sorts, including 'Enid' ('deep pink'), 'The Grail' ('brick red') and 'King Arthur' ('deep burgundy red').

Genders' catalogue (received in 1966) listed as Garryards 'Edith' ('darkest mahogany-red') and 'Hillhouse Red' ('clear burgundy-red') as well as several of the above. In his book *Primroses* (1959), 'Hillhouse Pink' ('pale pink with distinct orange eye') and 'In Memoriam' ('memorian purple flushed with crimson') are listed as Garryards.

This is not the full list by any means, 'Lopen Red' and 'Wisley Red' are two others with bronze-coloured foliage but once again the *juliae* connection is obvious, especially with 'Wisley Red'.

While many were excellent plants, few survive. Cecil Monson, who must be considered the leading authority on the subject, thought that 'Apple Blossom' and the Buckland varieties 'Canterbury' and 'Enchantress' were the only plants entitled to be called Garryards.

Much of this argument is academic and only serves to put the matter in perspective. It seems reasonable that offspring from plants with a direct link to 'Apple Blossom', 'Guinivere' and 'Enchantress', are classed as

'Garryards' or failing that 'Garryard type'. I think of the seedlings I am currently raising as 'New Garryards', because the original seed parent was 'Enchantress'.

In Ireland Joe Kennedy has been raising seedlings of this sort for many years, while the quarterly journal of the APS has had several illustrations of plants of Garryard breeding raised by well-known enthusiasts like Cyrus Happy and Peter Atkinson. 'Guinivere' has been extensively used for hybridizing by American primrose enthusiasts.

These bronze-leaved cultivars should not be confused with the Barnhaven 'Cowichan' polyanthus, generally a larger plant with eyeless flowers.

Earlier I mentioned my 'New Garryards', a breeding line started several years ago with 'Enchantress'. Roy Genders described 'Enchantress' as 'amongst the best dozen garden plants', strong praise indeed, and perhaps something of an exaggeration, but it is a beauty nevertheless. The blooms, a deeper pink than 'Guinivere', with most attractive darker veinings, are very distinctive. Several seedlings show the same veining but with more suffused colouring.

PRIMROSES IN NORTH AMERICA

In America work did not begin until the mid-1930s, with Florence Bellis and Dr Matthew Riddle raising the first American *juliae* hybrids. Florence Bellis used *P. juliae* as a pollen parent because her plants, 'in too much shade along the creek', produced few blooms. She never succeeded in getting any seed from *P. juliae*. In order to overcome the dominant magenta colour and produce new colours, yellow-flowered seed parents were used. Various shades of blue *vulgaris* and polyanthus were crossed with *juliae* to get true blue shades that eventually came true from seed. In the early stages some plants were named, including 'Millicent'. Seed was offered in a number of specific crosses. The 1946/7 catalogue lists 10 with 'Schneekissen' and 'Dorothy' the favoured seed parents, crossed with a range of others. In 1954/5, 25 individual crosses were listed featuring a wide range of named plants. This eventually led to the excellent Barnhaven juliana seed strain.

In the January 1945 *APS Quarterly* (Vol. 2, No. 3), Mrs Lou Roberts, a founder member, listed 69 varieties, the majority available from 'the trade' in the United States and British Columbia. Twenty-eight were purple shades, eight red, twelve light red and rose, six pink, eight lavender and orchid, two near-blue, one yellow and five white. Where known, the raiser and country of origin were given, although some are incorrect. Several American raisers feature, the most prolific being Mrs Roberts herself, who raised 'Lakewood', 'Roberta' and 'Margo'. Others are Nevill, a nurseryman from Washington State ('Valiant', 'Nevill's Hybrid', 'Purple Splendour', 'Ayleen'), and Fred Borsch, an Oregon nurseryman, with 'Wanda' 'Borsch var' (later renamed 'Amy'), 'Chief Multnomah', 'Sonny Boy', 'Rae', 'Hose-in-Hose', 'Crimson Glow', 'My Irish Girl' and 'Springtime'. 'Verwanis' is listed against five plants. A German nursery, Pfitzer, is shown as the introducer of 'Helen Müller'. Twenty-four of the named plants originated in North America, with the majority coming from

England, followed by the Continent.

Dr Riddle raised and named numerous plants including 'Red Riddle' and 'Red Velvet'. He delighted in very tiny forms and called one 'Thumbelina', small enough to fit into a thimble. 'Red Riddle' was a sensation when first exhibited at the 1949 National Show. Florence Bellis wrote in her catalogue '… it inspired our development of "Miniature Polyanthus" as a new race of primroses.' As well as 'Red Riddle' and 'Red Velvet', a number of Dr Riddle's other introductions were listed by Barnhaven including 'Joy' ('soft heliotrope'), 'The Dove' ('a soft apricot palomino shade'), 'Bounty' ('mauve-pink') and 'Frolic' ('shiny, plum-red floral umbrellas').

A contemporary was the Vancouver nurseryman William Goddard and many of his plants were also available from Barnhaven. They included 'Gold Jewel' ('large, brilliant, gold'), 'Snow Maiden' ('a snowy, elfin blanket'), 'Lavender Cloud' ('pink-lilac haze'), 'Dainty Maid', 'Firelight', 'Maiden's Blush', 'New Dawn', 'Pearly Gates', 'Bouquet' and 'Paisley'. Goddard supplied plants to various growers in England, including Roy Genders and Dr J. M. Douglas Smith. In the case of Dr Smith this included 'Dorothy' leading to suggestions it originated in British Colombia. It seems probable that Goddard obtained 'Dorothy' from Florence Bellis who always said it was an English plant.

PRIMROSES AFTER 1945

The Second World War and its immediate aftermath slowed things down in England, but by the early 1950s a number of nurseries were offering an increasing range of primroses, including many *P. juliae* hybrids.

Roy Genders' 'East Coast Primrose Gardens', Townsend, Champernowne, Blenheim, Chalmers, Hillview, Mrs McMurtrie, Mrs Emmerson in Ireland and Margery Fish all issued substantial lists while many others offered some named primroses.

E. B. Champernowne of Yelverton, Devon, mainly Daffodil growers, were notable for raising the 'Buckland' varieties. They were bred by Mr Hugo Jeffrey, who had worked at Dartington Hall before becoming manager in 1955. The nursery had been bought in 1944 by the Argyle family, who owned Dartington Hall, and they have it still. It has been wholesale for more than 20 years and grows no primroses.

The Buckland plants were Garryard hybrids, considered to be the best, especially 'Canterbury' and 'Enchantress'. They raised several others, probably all bred by Jeffreys, and a number of *juliae* and polyanthus hybrids including 'David Green', 'Afterglow', 'Anita', 'Czar', 'Veronica' and 'Tiny Tim'. Few survive, mainly two or three of the 'Buckland' types.

T. A. Townsend of Forest Town Nursery, Mansfield, had a huge list. As well as substantial numbers of doubles, hose, jacks and named polyanthus, more than 100 single primroses were grown. Townsend, in a foreword to his catalogue wrote that 'there are two of us, the one seventy-five, the other twenty-four, and we love what we produce and sell.' At that time 205 varieties were cultivated with new ones constantly being added. The list is enough to make a collector drool but, alas, like all the others the nursery disappeared some time in the late 1950s or early 1960s.

Roy Genders' Scarborough Nursery listed over 80 singles but was short-lived and closed about 1968. The ladies lasted longer than most, and Mrs Emmerson was still trading a few years later. Even where lists continued to be issued, the number of available plants steadily declined.

During the 1970s and 1980s many people who had been bitten by the primrose 'bug' continued to seek the elusive and fast-disappearing named varieties. I knew several of these collectors. Some are still with us, and without exception they suffered great frustration and lack of success. Why did the plants vanish? John Richards says in *Primulas* (1995) 'many are now rare or extinct due to virus.' The truth is slightly more complex. Seed strains, producing plants superior in many respects to the named clones, became widely available. Many 'juliana' seed strains appeared, plants that were vigorous and easier to grow. The long-term trend towards drier summers was also a factor. Vine weevil, the current bugbear, cannot really be blamed as, although known to primrose growers, it wasn't the menace it has become. Changes in fashion are another factor, with so many new gardening plants becoming available.

Since then interest in named clones, if subdued, remains. The mass growth of the large-flowered pot primrose has continued apace. The plants have been developed to a point where they bear little resemblance to the species or indeed the many hybrids. As a result interest in these older sorts has returned with three National Collections (see Appendix 2) and several nurseries offering named clones.

In North America enthusiasm remains high and a large number of varieties have been raised in recent years. Many new ones have been introduced by Dorothy Springer, Cy Happy, Ann and Jay Lunn, Herb Dixon and others members of the APS, some of them commercial growers, some amateurs. As in the UK, naming problems are rife, but it does appear that a few older varieties, extinct in the UK, may be alive and well.

More are being raised and the potential for raising yet more is considerable.

3 DOUBLE PRIMROSES

The earliest recorded mention of the double primrose is by Tabernaemontanus, who described the double yellow in 1500.

Clusius, in his *Rariorum Plantarium Historia* (1601), mentions a *P. veris vulgaris albo flore pleno*, a white double and *P. veris vulgaris rubra flore pleno*, a shade of red. The assumption has always been that Clusius was referring to plants of polyanthus type, hence his use of 'veris'.

Gerard, *Herbal* (1597), gave us the immortal phrase 'Our Garden Double Primrose, of all the rest is of the greatest beautie.' He referred to the double white, illustrated in his first edition in polyanthus form. In his *Catalogue of Plants* (1599) he also lists the double green primrose. In a later edition of his *Herbal*, Johnson (1633) portrays the double white as a primrose.

Parkinson published his *Paradisus Terristris* or *The Garden of Pleasant Flowers* in 1629, describing 21 forms of the primrose and cowslip, 'all these kindes as they have been found wilde'. Amongst this plethora of unusual forms are several double cowslips and primroses. The primroses are 'The double greene primrose', 'Master Heskets

double Primrose', 'The ordinary double primrose' and 'The small double primrose'.

The double green primrose 'is in his leaves like the former single greene kindes'. Parkinson then wrote 'it beareth upon every stalke a double green flower, of a little deeper green colour than the flower of the single kinde… of two rowes of short leaves most usually… of an equal height above the husk.' Several double green primroses have been grown since and despite claims to the contrary, are mostly of more recent origin.

'Master Hesket' or Hesketh's double primrose was found in a wood three miles from Settle in Yorkshire by the aforementioned gentleman. Parkinson called it *Primula veris Hesketi flore multiplici separatim diviso*! It is described as 'very like unto the small double primrose', carrying flowers of both primrose and polyanthus type. In the latter case, with stalks of different thickness and height bearing malformed flowers, 'being of a white or pale primrose colour, but a little deeper'. These are extracts from a lengthy description.

The ordinary double primrose was the pale yellow double form of *P. vulgaris* still sometimes found. Parkinson makes the comment that the leaves 'are very large, and like unto the single kind, but somewhat larger, because *it groweth in gardens* [authors italics]'. This has been taken to mean that the double yellow primrose was already a common garden plant.

The final double *Primula veris flore duplici*, would appear to have been a miniature version of the ordinary double 'altogether like unto the last double primrose… it is smaller in all things'.

John Rea in his *Flora* (1665), speaking of the double yellow primrose, said 'were it not so common in every Country-womans garden, it would be more respected' then went on to describe it as 'a sweet and dainty flower… chiefest of all our English kinds'. Rea mentions the double red primrose although he knew it only by repute and 'so much seed hath been sowed in hope to obtain'. He died in 1681 but his son-in-law, Samuel Gilbert a clergyman, Rector of Quatt in Shropshire, published his *Florists Vade Mecum* in 1682. In it he doubted the existence of the double red. He had bought some and as the bloom was 'of a dull horse flesh hue' had no use for it.

Phillip Miller, in 1731, wrote of both the 'Double Red' and 'Double Crimson' and made the intriguing statement there were 'a great variety of these at present in the gardens'.

Curtis, in the *Botanical Magazine* for 1794 describes the following:

> The Double white, rarely met with.
> The double deep red or velvet, the blossoms of this will sometimes come single.
> The double pink or lilac, here figured a plant much admired.
> The double crimson, a new variety, which, in brilliancy of colour, far surpasses all the others.

The above, as written, was followed by the comment that 'The red, commonly called the Scotch primrose, less ornamental than any of the preceding: besides these, we have observed a variety with blossoms of a dingy yellow inclining to red, not worth cultivating.' The lilac, *'Primula Acaulis Fl.Pleno Carneo',* is illustrated and is assumed to be the plant still grown today as 'double lilac' or 'lilacena plena'.

Articles by Loudon and others up until the mid-1850s refer to a whole variety of coloured doubles including 'blush', 'buff', 'carmine', 'crimson', 'crimson purple', 'copper', 'dark purple', 'dingy', 'deep yellow', 'flesh colour', 'purple', 'straw colour', 'red', 'rose', 'pink', 'violet' and 'salmon' as well as the normal yellow and white. From available evidence it would seem they were of primrose form and must have occurred, incredible as it seems, spontaneously. As only yellow, green, white and dingy pink doubles have been recorded growing wild, most must have arisen from coloured forms of *P. vulgaris* in gardens. Another point about this early period is that no names are known until 1879, plants being until then identified by colour, when the name 'Madame Pompadour' is first recorded. This famous plant is the only known example of an early double primrose to be given a proper name. It has been suggested that 'Madame Pompadour' was in fact the 'double crimson' mentioned by Miller in 1731. The practice whereby 'double crimson', 'double sulphur', etc became 'Double Crimson' and 'Double Sulphur' was probably started by accident and these names have no validity.

At this point I will discuss the occurrence of double forms in the wild. From Parkinson and others it is clear that the early yellow doubles, and possibly whites, were found growing wild. Perhaps some other colours were, because we know that primroses were abundant and many county floras refer to colours other than primrose yellow. Could it be that these unusual colours were sought out, dug up, and transferred to gardens on a large scale? Geoffrey Nicolle has told me that it was a common practice in Pembrokeshire for unusual primroses to be collected in the wild and planted in the grounds of local churches. If this were done over a long period it might have resulted in the yellow colour becoming dominant: virtually the same effect as deliberately breeding out the aberrant colours. Today, while the numbers of wild primroses are only a fraction of what must have been, pink and white forms are rare and most populations are yellow. Even when found, many of the wild 'coloured' forms are obvious hybrids with garden plants.

Throughout the history of the primrose, doubles have been found growing wild. It should be stressed that these occurrences are rare and many primrose lovers have never seen one.

Examples can be quoted from the late 1800s to the present. *The Gardener's Chronicle* 14 May 1881 has the following: 'Mr Boscawen sends in flowers of the double yellow primrose, found wild in Cornwall, of great size and Beauty. Some of the flowers measure 2 inches [50 mm] across and they are very double.' *The Flora of Wiltshire,* as well as other kinds, mentions 'a form with double flowers' but gives no details. This flora is the only one I have consulted that refers to a wild double, although most describe anomalous forms of the cowslip and single primrose. Roy Genders wrote, in several of his many books, that 'natural "sports" in yellow and white are quite common.' He also referred to the 27 June 1975 issue of *Country Life* where a photograph appeared of double whites growing in a wood in Kent. In his book *Primroses*, he wrote 'they may be found in a particular wood in Dorset,' and goes on to say that he had found double primroses growing wild at Great Everden, near Cambridge.

The Devon group of the NCCPG have published a book about Devon plants, *The Magic Tree* (1989), later reissued as *The Devon Plants*. In it is an interesting account of the discovery of a wild yellow double. The plant was found in 1967, 'quietly growing in a leafy lane' close to the A38 and the nearby Pridhamsleigh caves at Buckfastleigh. It was discovered by Mrs Charles Hillard nestling between two granite boulders. The plant was rescued before bulldozers moved in to widen the road. The initial flowers are single but the second flush, a little later than the ordinary primrose, are fully double. Plants were sent to Kew and Wisley but failed to survive. Even in gardens in Devon the plant has proved unreliable, flourishing in some and dying in others. Where suited, large clumps develop that divide easily.

Geoffrey Nicolle found a double yellow primrose growing alongside the track on the main Paddington line near Rosemarket about 1975, but the most interesting and unusual account is by Barbara Shaw.

Mrs Shaw says that the variety 'Elizabeth Dickey', named after its finder, was found by an eight year old girl about 1930, growing near her home at Ballymoney in Northern Ireland. The plant grew in her mother's garden for 30 years before coming to the attention of the famous Irish gardener Dr Molly Sanderson. She named it and sent a plant to David Chalmers. The plant flourished and was distributed for some years until the nursery closed in 1990.

Dr Sanderson sent another double yellow that was found growing in the Boyne Valley on a 'bank with a great population of primroses, nearly all double'. This incredible find is the only recorded example of such abundance.

Dr Charles Taylor, in the 4th edition of his Glazeley Garden's catalogue, *A Book about Double Primroses*, undated but published in the late 1950s, listed five forms of yellow doubles, all foundlings, and said that 'We have half-a-dozen quite distinct varieties *of our own collecting*' [authors italics]. He continued 'and [we] know of two districts in this neighbourhood where it has recently been found.'

Peter Coates in *The Story of Plants and Gardens Through the Ages* (1970) relates that, as a child, he remembered a bank by the River Coil, in Ayrshire, on which a lilac-coloured double primrose grew for many years, although he seems to think it might have been a naturalized garden form.

Finally I must mention 'Sue Jervis', a pinkish double distributed by Bressingham Gardens in the 1980s. This is said to have been found in the wild, and named after the finder's niece. In his book *Herbaceous Plants* (1995), Graham Rice poses the question 'can it really have been found growing wild in a wood in Shropshire?' I recently obtained 'Sue Jervis' and must say that, apart from the dingy-pink colour, the physical resemblance to the double white is striking.

We now return to the garden doubles. In *Primroses and Polyanthus* (Genders and Taylor 1954), Major Charles Taylor, a key figure in modern double primrose history, listed 24 different colours that he had identified as being recorded between 1597 and 1875. Double primroses had become common garden plants and were mass planted. Richard Dean, a London nurseryman and one of the famous Dean brothers, wrote in 1879 'the white, lilac and yellow are much grown... for market purposes... planted out in beds.' He continued by saying 'hundreds of these plants are purchased every Spring and planted out in an improper manner... where they soon die.' Although then considered easy garden plants one can see the beginnings of the problem that has dogged double primroses ever since, difficulty in cultivation.

The second half of the nineteenth century saw a vast increase in the population of the UK. With it came a huge expansion of housing, and consequently of gardens. In this period many new plants were introduced and fashions changed. We have seen what happened to the florists' flowers and to some extent this affected the double primrose. Nevertheless, it seems evident that a few varieties, in particular the double white and lilac, remained common garden plants well into the 1930s.

What happened to the other coloured varieties listed by the early writers? In the final quarter of the nineteenth century interest waned with attention switching to the many hardy primula species introduced from abroad. At the RHS Primula Conference of 1886 no mention was made of double primroses, either verbally or in papers read. Only one class out of 22 was devoted to them and this attracted two entries.

Major Taylor, in *Primroses and Polyanthus* wrote that examination of the *Gardeners Chronicle* between 1894 and 1910 found not one reference to the double primrose, although references had been fairly frequent in previous years. Similarly, the famous gardening magazine *The Garden*, which had featured double primroses extensively, confirms the decline in popularity. H. Cannell & Sons' *Floral Guide* of 1883 offered only seven for sale, although listing 25 'best exhibition' gold-laced polyanthus. The doubles were 'Cloth of Gold', 'Crousseii Flore Pleno', 'Lilac', 'Platypetala Plena (Arthur Dumollin [sic])', 'Rose', 'Sulphur' and 'White'. They were priced from sixpence to 3 shillings, with 'White' – the cheapest – at 3 shillings per dozen. The other primroses and gold-laced polyanthus were generally more expensive.

I have mentioned 1879 as the date when the first named double is recorded. From then on names began to appear, but it is interesting to note that the majority of plants were of polyanthus form. The reason for this is simple. The number of hybridizers raising doubles was small and they mostly used a double polyanthus, introduced from Belgium about 1880, called 'Arthur du Moulin' or, more commonly, 'platypetala plena', as the pollen parent.

The famous double 'Marie Crousse' was raised by the Crousse nursery in France and given an Award of Merit by the RHS in 1882. This variety is supposedly still in cultivation although there are at least two 'clones' and Major Taylor, amongst others, suggested the plant he and others grew was not the original. Other varieties from the same period include 'Buxton's Blue' (1901), 'Crimson King' (1897), 'Curiosity' (1899), 'Derncleughi'(1899), 'Golden Ball' (1898), 'Golden Pheasant' (1898), 'Harlequin' (1888), 'Jacques Lienhart' (1888), 'King Theodore' (1884), 'Mont Blanc' (1881), 'Paddy' (1897) and the famous 'Prince Silverwings' (1897). Many others are listed in the gardening journals of the time, especially *The Garden*.

The work of Mr Murray Thompson and the Cocker brothers has been rightly given prominence in the post-1900 history of the double primrose. However, George Arends in Germany raised doubles earlier. In 1888 he started his nursery with his brother-in-law, and a collection of doubles was established, purchased from Holland and England. The varieties comprised double white, lilac, sulphur, cream-yellow, aurea-plena, dark yellow, purpurea-plena, purple-red, 'Croussei-plena', lilac-red, negro-plena, black-red, sanguinea-plena, brilliant red, 'Crimson King' and crimson dark red. You will note most are still described by colour and do not have proper varietal names. Arends sold them in bunches of cut flowers and they were popular at the markets. The plants were grown in cold frames due to their 'doubtful hardiness' and a particularly hard winter destroyed the entire collection. German winters are much colder than those endured in all but a few locations in the UK.

Discouraged, he temporarily gave up and developed a range of *P. elatior* hybrids, calling his mixture *P. elatior grandiflora*. Another fierce winter, in 1908/9, saw the loss of this collection, but he noted that the garden hybrids of the *vulgaris* type survived relatively unscathed.

This started him on a new quest for doubles using the hardier *P. vulgaris* hybrids to instil the same quality into the doubles. He purchased 'all former mentioned varieties' and found traces of pollen in a few plants. From this beginning several hundred plants were raised by hand pollination of selected *vulgaris* hybrids. Every seed of the F1 generation was collected and a further 1500 seedlings flowered. 'A few hundred' plants flowered completely double in 'every possible colour variation… delicate rose to dark yellow, dark purple to carmine. But no whites.' Other crosses were made to raise further generations but he found that the number of double seedlings declined and so did the quality. The best plants were divided and increased but this was just prior to 1914. During the First World War neglect, mainly through lack of assistance, led to the loss of all these plants. Later, in 1925, he attempted to raise doubles again, using *P. juliae* as well as his *P. helenae* hybrids. Hundreds of promising seedlings were raised, vigorous and hardy, but the Second World War brought this to an end and it would seem he did not attempt to raise doubles in the years afterwards.

In the UK work on producing new double primroses was begun by P. Murray Thompson about 1900, originally when living at Downshill, Hereford. Later he moved to Omachie, Angus, in Scotland. In the first instance he used a single white primrose pollinated by the pale purplish-lilac double polyanthus 'Arthur du Moulin', or 'platepetala plena'. His first generation, containing no whites, were all single, but the seed from these F1 plants, not artificially pollinated, produced a good number of doubles, although the percentage is not known. Murray Thompson had read about Mendel's experiments and continued on these lines. It has been suggested that this is the first recorded instance of the parentage of a double primrose.

By 1911 his varieties were becoming known and were exhibited at a show in Edinburgh. He named at least 16 and possibly more, of which 'Downshill Ensign' is the best known. Major Taylor gave the introduction of this plant as 1930, which is odd considering it was supposedly raised at Hereford. 'Bluebird', 'Cambridge Blue' and 'Plum' were all given Awards of Merit in 1930. Some of his hybrids were described as 'appearing to have *juliae* blood'.

The 'Downshill' group were not long-lived and 'Ensign' was almost the only one remaining in catalogues of the 1950s. William Chalmers's 1947 catalogue has a typed list added with 'scarce varieties'. Amongst them is 'Downshill Flag-Signal' where one plant was available at 10 shillings. I have seen no other reference to this variety. One other catalogue, the 1954 one from the short-lived Blenheim nursery in Devon, lists 'Ronald' and 'Vanity', as well as 'Ensign'. Major Taylor visited the district in which they were raised but found no trace of surviving plants or indeed any information on them.

Double seed, supplied by Murray Thompson, was offered by two commercial firms, one of which was Stormont, between the wars. Several named varieties came from this seed including a deep blue 'Maid Marian', raised at Waithman's Nurseries.

It was Murray Thompson who persuaded the Cocker brothers, of the famous Aberdeen rose nursery James Cocker & Sons, to start breeding double primroses. This was done at their old nursery at Morningfield by William Cocker, who was the rose grower. As a sideline or hobby he spent much of his time raising double primroses. The resulting plants were given the prefix 'Bon Accord' which is the motto of the City of Aberdeen. Like Murray Thompson, the Cockers used the single primrose 'Wilsons Blue' and later introduced *P. juliae*. The pollen parent was again the reliable 'platypetala plena'. Using information from Murray Thompson a large number of double seedlings were raised and referred to as 'polyantha-primroses'.

On 25 April 1911 the *RHS Journal* recorded the following:

> *A large number of flowers of double polyanthus and primroses which they [the Cockers] had raised from seed. Colours from primrose yellow, white to purplish-blue shades, but were not, as a whole, very bright. They were raised by crossing the Wisley Blue primrose with the well-known polyanthus platypetala plena. In the second and third generations numerous dbl-flowered forms appeared with a wide range of colours.*

Cockers were granted a Certificate of Appreciation and the 'Bon Accord' doubles had arrived. The number of those actually named and offered for sale was less than 20 and probably no more than 16. Mrs McMurtrie said there were 137 double seedlings in the nursery between 1915 and 1918. Many were not worth naming and lack of stock prevented some good ones being named and distributed.

The 'Bon Accords' have survived better then the 'Downshill' varieties and a few exist today. In the early 1960s Glazeley Gardens listed nine, while in the 1950s Blenheim had ten and Townsend nine. East Coast Primrose Gardens still had ten in 1967: Fiona Stark listed four in 1990. The 1995/6 *Plantfinder* lists three, with three deletions from the previous edition. Three of the plates in Barbara Shaw's book, illustrating plants in her National Collection, are of Bon Accords 'Cerise, 'Lavender' and 'Purple'.

The First World War and the following depression affected the double primrose like other specialized plants. The number available, never abundant, declined and many varieties disappeared.

Up to now I have not mentioned the role of Ireland. Sitwell, in 1939, wrote: 'It is... safe upon general lines to state all the rest of the Double Primroses have claims to be considered as Irish in origin, or flourish there, at least, more than anywhere else; although, in parts of Scotland... they grow nearly as well.' He went on to say:

> *Before the War they grew in Ireland in great profusion. One Primrose grower writes that, before 1914, old plants could be bought by the dozen and in limitless quantity. There are persons who remember, in their youth, seeing whole quarter-acre plantings of the rarer forms, many of which are now extinct and unobtainable.*

Who were the growers of these plants? The famous Daisy Hill Nursery at Newry, introducers of 'Our Pat', 'Prince Silverwings' and others was the best-known commercial concern. The vast majority though were grown in the gardens of rectories, farms and the larger houses by amateurs and semi-commercial small growers, many of them ladies, who supplied plants to nurseries in England. The legend of the 'little old primrose ladies' of Ireland was still given credence as late as 1984. Dr Charles Nelson wrote how he was 'chastised' for suggesting they were extinct. Some of these ladies were the famous Miss Winnifrid Wynne of Avoca, Mrs Barlee of Dundrum, County Dublin, Mrs Johnson of Kinlough, Mrs Scott of Castleburg, that prolific writer Miss Eda Hume and later Mrs Gladys Emmerson of Limavady. There were many others but they gradually disappeared and by the late 1960s Mrs Emmerson and Cecil Monson were the sole remaining sources of plants. In her many articles, in the yearbooks of the NAPS, Mrs Emmerson often told little anecdotes that illustrated the disappearance of the Irish primrose growers. Many plants have been given the prefix 'Irish' or 'Old Irish' but Dr Nelson was of the opinion that most of the plants grown in Ireland had arisen as chance seedlings, while the origin of others was unknown.

The efforts of Murray Thompson and the Cockers have been well recorded but there were other enthusiasts who helped to maintain double primroses. They included the Dean Brothers of London, the Reverend Mules, who wrote an article for *The Field*, part of which was included by William Robinson in his *English Flower Garden*, Dr

John McWatt, author of *The Primulas of Europe*, the Reverends William Murdoch and John McMurtrie, both of whom lived in Aberdeenshire, the Misses A. and M. Cadell of Longniddry, East Lothian, and William Chalmers of Stonehaven. Both Dr McWatt and the Misses Cadell exhibited doubles at RHS shows.

The Reverend William Murdoch, writing in the 1935 report of the NAPS southern section said that 'during the last few years quite a number of new varieties... have been appearing.' While bemoaning the fact that many of the older varieties had lost their constitutions, he commented unfavourably on some of the newer sorts. He also had this to say; 'I have had doubles submitted to me for inspection... and the claim made that they are very old. These doubles showed the influence of *juliae* blood... this at once dated them.'

In the 1936 Diamond Jubilee report of the NAPS southern section is an article by H. G. Moore of Dorchester which summarized the double situation. He listed nearly 100 but made the comment 'I am afraid many... do not exist today.' Moore complains about the misnaming of plants and makes a plea for some form of registration of named varieties 'in order to improve the position which is chaotic'. All the famous names are listed together with many other less well-known sorts. He mentions several 'new' varieties, including some with *juliae* blood which indicates that some hybridizers were still active. This article was reprinted in the 1952/3 journal of the NAPS northern section and Major Taylor asked to comment. In a long critique he made the point that many of the names had no validity and included the remark 'I very much doubt if more than one-fifth… could be obtained today.'

Perhaps the last word on this prewar period should be left to Sacheverell Sitwell. He expressed some disenchantment with double primroses, 'much money spent and much labour taken have yielded… excessively poor results.' According to Sitwell only about 25 were still known 'of which fifteen are Cocker's Bon Accord'. The double polyanthus are treated with rather more reverence; 'Rex Theodore', 'Derncleughi' and 'Prince Silverwings' ('rarest and most beautiful'). Descriptions are glowing and take up several paragraphs. I once saw a 'Prince Silverwings', and we have the painting in Barbara Shaw's book as a reference. On this basis I would find it hard to agree with him.

One puzzling point is that a handful of double primrose varieties remained common garden plants. My father gardened in private service most of his life and has told me many times that the double lilac and double white were plentiful in the 1930s.

By the 1950s Major Taylor had begun his campaign to resurrect the double primrose. He grew thousands at his nursery in Shropshire, lectured to the RHS in 1956, and wrote many articles. Once he described how 40 or 50 plants of 'Marie Crousse' were increased to 5000 in five years. In *Primroses and Polyanthus*, he related how, in 1949, he discovered a number of double primroses growing in turf in a long-derelict cottage garden. From it were rescued 15 distinct plants which he concluded were seedlings. There were no other doubles and no indication how the plants had arisen. His view was that a strain of primroses had once

been grown there with a tendency to doubling.

The plants found in the cottage garden were introduced as the 'Glazeley Double Primroses' and identified by colour. In the 4th edition of his double primrose catalogue eight are listed: 'Grey', 'Peach', 'Mauve', 'White', 'Cream', 'Silver', Lilac and 'Old Rose'. They never became widely available and few were offered by other nurseries. Genders makes no mention of them in *Primroses*, published five years after his collaboration with Major Taylor. This probably reflects a deterioration in their relationship, which is hinted at by Major Taylor in a letter he wrote to Dr Cecil Jones.

In this later period several small, specialist growers, most of them enthusiasts, who spent considerable time and effort looking for old varieties, offered a selection of plants. They included William Chalmers (who, on his death in 1955 was succeeded by his son David), the Daisy Hill Nurseries, Alan Vandervelde of Hillview, Mrs Beevor of Great Yarmouth, T. E. Townsend of Mansfield, and the Champernowne Nurseries of Yelverton. The famous Somerset gardener Margery Fish, Mrs Mary McMurtrie, wife of the Reverend McMurtrie, and of course Mrs Gladys Emmerson were also part of this group. I am sure there were others but these people, together with amateurs like Captain Hawkes of Nantwich, ensured that double primroses remained in being.

William Chalmers raised many new double primroses in the last years before his death in 1955. Mrs McMurtrie described them as 'beautiful' and said there were 39 in the small Stonehaven nursery, of which 30 were still in cultivation in 1957. Many were named; 'Alexander Bowhill', 'Rev. W. M. Murdock', 'Blackbutts Glory' and 'Supreme' are examples. One of the most interesting was the 'Rev. W. M. Murdoch', described by Townsend as a 'Double-flowered Hose-in-hose. Colour a fine crushed strawberry. It has three corollas instead of two.'

The nursery was continued by his son David and was offering a limited range of primroses, including rare doubles, until final closure in 1990. Both father and son were great double enthusiasts and amongst the most skilful of growers. It has been said that the Chalmers were able to grow doubles that most others found hopeless. The Stonehaven plants were taken over by Fiona Stark at Torphins with initial success, and a substantial list was issued – over 60 primroses, including 19 doubles. Unfortunately, it appears this was short-lived and most, if not all, seem to have been lost.

DOUBLES IN NORTH AMERICA

The history of doubles in North America stems from 1945. That doubles were grown earlier was illustrated in an article by Izetta Renton, a long-time member of the APS, in the 50th Anniversary edition of the *Quarterly* (Fall 1991). Mrs Renton, who ran a nursery, moved to the Snoqualmie valley in Oregon in the 1920s. As well as saying that primrose gardens were plentiful, she mentions a double yellow *acaulis* [*vulgaris*] grown by her friends, the Reimstetters, who owned Flower Acres, a nursery specializing in, amongst other plants, primroses.

In the 1946/7 Barnhaven catalogue

Florence Bellis wrote that only four doubles 'are to be had', listing three of them, 'Double White', which she refers to as 'Cottage White', 'Double Lavender' (Quaker's Bonnet), and 'Marie Crousse'.

The show reports of the APS in the 1945–50 period are full of descriptions of polyanthus and *juliae* hybrids but there is a little on double primroses. The July 1945 *APS Quarterly* (Vol. 3, No. 1) has a report on the fourth exhibition. In it are mentions of 'new double plum-coloured primroses' as well as 'new double yellow polyanthus Juanita, brought down from Washington'. The same report says that 'Yellow, lavender and white doubles… were prominent'. The famous Mrs A. C. U. Berry had a large separate exhibit which included 'something never before seen… a double lavender juliana hybrid'.

At the same time William Goddard, at his Flora-Vista Gardens in Colquitz, near Victoria, British Columbia, introduced a double light yellow polyanthus that he called 'Moonlight'. This, together with a lilac-coloured double 'Enchantress', was sent, amongst other primroses, to Dr J. N. Douglas Smith in England in 1948.

Peter Klein was a self-educated farmboy from northeast Illinois. A widower, he moved to Tacoma in 1937. He worked for a landscape contractor and came to know primroses at first hand. At some stage he joined the APS and attended a lecture given by Florence Bellis; he has in fact been described as one of her 'disciples'. In 1949 he became interested in doubles, reading all the literature he could find. A natural hybridist, he discovered pollen on a plant of 'Quaker's Bonnet' and used this to begin his breeding programme, resulting after a few years in his 'Tacoma Doubles', which caused a stir at APS shows. Like many American enthusiasts he ran a small nursery and went on, until his death in 1957, to create many more beautiful doubles, including double *juliae*s and some of the first, if not the first, double jack-in-the-greens. Peter Klein is regarded with reverence by many of the APS enthusiasts, especially the few remaining who knew him, and his influence was considerable, possibly second only to Florence Bellis's.

Other raisers included John E. Walker of Sherwood, Oregon who won the 1960 APS Hybridizing Award for double polyanthus. Walker was an amateur who joined the APS 'after a gentle shove from Florence Bellis'. His initial efforts with doubles were mixed, but eventually pollen was found in a single plant of 'Quaker's Bonnet' growing on a very dry bank. The half-starved plant had a mass of small ragged blooms, all with pollen. Previous attempts to find pollen in dozens of thriving plants of the same variety had been unsuccessful. The pollen was used on some semi-doubles he acquired and the seed produced 14 poor doubles – out of 300 – in the F1 generation. He continued and by 1960 had raised a good strain of double polyanthus in a wide range of colours, except blue. Unfortunately, he died in 1963 and his strain appears to have died with him.

Others who raised doubles include Ruth Bartlett at her Spring Hill nursery at Gig Harbour, Washington. Several years after Peter Klein's death she was advertising plants from his 'Tacoma' strain, as well as those of her own breeding. Dr Jones corresponded with her, exchanging seed, and in a letter to him in 1983, some years afterwards, she says

that the thing that caused her most sadness in her gardening life was the theft, on three separate occasions, of her double breeding stock!

MODERN RAISERS

In England interest in doubles remained high, if isolated, and Dr Cecil Jones in Llanelli and Dr E. Lester Smith in Hastings were prominent, recording progress in the NAPS southern yearbooks. While Lester Smith, who had close contacts in the USA, did raise a number of doubles, the efforts of Cecil Jones made him the leading amateur grower in the UK. Not only that but his extreme generosity, in sending seed literally all over the world, helped others as well.

Cecil Jones became interested in primroses after reading an article by Mrs Emmerson in *Amateur Gardener* in the late 1950s. He soon borrowed a copy of the Taylor and Genders book from the local library and this started him on a lifelong path of hybridizing double and other primroses, gold-laced polyanthus and – in brief flirtations – auriculas.

Shortly afterwards he wrote to Captain Hawkes and was invited by Mrs Hawkes to visit them at Nantwich in Cheshire. Thus began a friendship that lasted until Captain Hawkes's death.

At about this time Cecil joined the northern society and visited the shows at the old Corn Exchange in Manchester. Although a long journey from West Wales, this was combined with visits to relatives in Yorkshire. At a northern show he met Dr Duncan Duthie who told him about Winnifrid Wynne, from whom he obtained a jackanapes, double green and the striped auricula 'Mrs Dargan'. Cecil also wrote to Florence Bellis, who sent him articles on hybridizing primroses, and corresponded with Ruth Bartlett, exchanging seed.

Hybridizing began in earnest in 1962 after he discovered a single double white primrose bloom on a small, dejected-looking plant in an elderly relative's garden. That evening, before discarding it, he idly unpicked the flower petal by petal and discovered a single anther of unripe pollen. That afternoon he had collected a quantity of kipper boxes prominently labelled 'Bon Accord' and feels this may have had some psychological effect! Cecil was galvanized into action, and after placing the remains of the flower in a thimbleful of water, read all his available literature on the subject.

The following day the anther was inspected with a magnifying glass and revealed the fluffy appearance that indicates pollen is ripe. It then struck him that he had no suitable seed parent so dashed into the countryside and collected two pin-eyed wild primroses. At the end of July two ripe pods of seed were collected and sown immediately. From this sowing three dozen seedlings germinated and were pricked out – Cecil admits to being somewhat superstitious – into one of the Bon Accord kipper boxes.

The seedlings were planted out under cloches – to persuade them to bloom the following spring – and he ordered 24 'Double Mauve' primroses from four different sources after reading that Peter Klein had discovered pollen in this variety. He also acquired two plants of the known pollen producer 'Arthur du Moulin', as an insurance policy, not really wishing to use

them because of the semi-polyanthus habit.

About half the seedlings bloomed towards the end of April, all yellow and almost identical to the wild parent. Three pin-eyes were potted up and pollinated from the 'Double Mauves', six from one source having pollen, the rest none.

By the spring of 1964 29 F2 seedlings bloomed, 14 of which were double. Four were yellow, two white, two mauve and the rest a mixture of these three colours. The singles were a similar mix of colours. The doubles were a bit rough, lacking symmetry, but were fully double, vigorous and free-flowering. From this beginning Cecil went on to raise many hundreds of doubles and also generously distributed seed far and wide. For a time he supplied a commercial grower with seed for resale, and a customer raised the double white jack-in-the-green 'Dawn Ansell' from this seed. This plant, one of the finest of primroses, has been micropropagated and is grown throughout North America, New Zealand and Australia, as well as Europe.

The majority of the early doubles were in yellow and cream shades and I remember seeing them at London shows, where they created tremendous interest. This was before the Barnhaven doubles appeared and Cecil's plants were a novelty, as doubles had become very scarce in the preceding years.

Plants that were used as pollen parents in these early crosses included the semi-double 'Harbinger' from Mrs Emmerson and 'Red Harlequin', a 'Prince Silverwings' seedling from Major Taylor. 'Our Pat' was also used in the quest for blue doubles and a 'Double Pink *Juliae*' from Mrs Fish. A red single from Barnhaven was the seed parent for a line of red doubles, while the single blue came from Dr E. Lester Smith.

The major problem encountered, never solved, was the lack of longevity of his doubles. This we know is a problem and Cecil never introduced *P. juliae* into his hybridizing, unlike Rosetta Jones in the USA. Many plants were sent to well-known growers like David Chalmers and Major Taylor but soon faded away. The one exception was 'Penlan Cream', described by Chalmers as 'an outstanding new large cream polyanthus' and priced, in the 1970 catalogue, at an astonishing 25 guineas. In the 1990 list of Fiona Stark the price was still very high at £10. A letter from David Chalmers in April 1995 to Dr Jones mentions that 'Penlan Cream' had 'gone downhill' fading away after doing well for some years.

Although Cecil produced many hundreds of beautiful doubles – both primrose and polyanthus types – in shades of red, yellow, blue and white, he could not keep them, so eventually became discouraged. When the Barnhaven doubles arrived a new challenge was needed and he began a quest for double jacks. I recall Cecil Monson writing in a letter to me that he thought this unlikely, but he was soon proved wrong.

One day Cecil was inspecting a batch of 150 seedlings containing about 20 percent doubles. He noticed one of the doubles had greatly enlarged sepals. Although not a particularly good specimen it was found to have pollen which soon found its way on to several of the F2 seedlings. He awaited the flowering of the resultant seedlings with great expectation, indeed he has described it as 'the most eagerly awaited event of his

gardening life'. Hopes were realized with the blooming of both single and double jacks as well as plain singles and doubles. Following on from this cross, beautiful jacks in shades of red, yellow, white and the much coveted blue have been raised but, alas, with the exception of the tissue-cultured 'Dawn Ansell', have shown the same lack of stamina as the others.

Cecil's latest creation is the flaked double, raised by pollinating yellow and red singles with pollen from 'Prince Silverwings' via 'Red Harlequin'. Once again he has generously distributed seed to, amongst others, Kay Overton, who showed a lovely example at the 1995 Saltford Show.

In recent years Cecil has gone through a difficult period following the loss of his wife. Happily he has now remarried and is regaining his old enthusiasm although no longer living at 'Penlan', where he had a much larger garden. Perhaps we shall soon see some more superb plants bearing the 'Penlan' name.

Although there are several enthusiasts in America who have raised doubles, the leading raiser is undoubtedly Mrs Rosetta Jones of Shelton, Washington State.

Rosetta had been interested in doubles for some time but, in her own words, 'had only played around with them'. In 1970, then living in Kent, Washington State, she judged a show and was struck by the weakness of the flowering stems on the old variety 'Quaker's Bonnet'. This decided her to try to produce something better. She was also interested in breeding a good yellow as none were available. Her overall aim was to get a hardy strain with good form in a wide range of colours. The initial seed parent was a 'washed out' rosy lavender showing a few extra petals; the pollen parent a muddy magenta with weak, floppy stems. From these unpromising parents a mixed lot of seedlings bloomed, in various shades of lavender and magenta. Some had good double blooms but floppy stems. She continued to pollinate the best singles but had difficulty in finding good pollen-bearing doubles. In 1974 the first breakthrough occurred. Amongst the seedlings was a pale yellow *acaulis* (*vulgaris*) with strong stems, a compact nosegay form with lots of pollen.

Using this plant (No. 11–4) as the pollen parent produced 'astonishing' results. It is the grandfather of her present strain although it was not until 1978 that she was able to sell plants and seed. I should add that Rosetta ran a small nursery for many years.

As she was also crossing *juliae* hybrids she applied pollen from 11-4 to some of them, including a red jack-in-the-green 'Jay-Jay'. Although she was unaware of it, 'Jay-Jay' was a by-product of Peter Klein's double jack hybridizing programme and carried the double gene. When the F1 seedlings were pollinated, again by 11-4, the resulting F2 plants produced 25 percent doubles in both jacks and ordinary sorts, stalked and cushion forms, in magenta, red, lavender, near pink and a few yellows. All were larger in leaf and bloom than 'Jay-Jay' and some had the stoloniferous root system of *P. juliae*.

The F2 seedlings were intercrossed, using pollen from the doubles on the singles. This resulted in many more doubles with further separation of colours, pinks, clear reds, yellows, two-toned (yellow with red centre), lavenders and purples.

During this period Rosetta corresponded with William Holt, a primrose enthusiast who lived in Somerset. Holt, who was a cowman on a farm, built up a collection of doubles, but soon became disillusioned with the old sorts. He advertised extensively for plants in both the UK and Ireland and wrote dozens of letters but found what others had discovered – the old doubles were largely history; the few remaining were disappointing in quality. At this time he heard of Rosetta, contacted her and grew plants from her seed. He called his plants 'The Laurels Collection' and built up a large stock, listing 141 different sorts in 1980 – mostly by colour. Amongst the named plants are several of the current micropropagated varieties. Later he moved, plants and all, to Scotland, but this did not work out and he soon relocated to the East Midlands. Unfortunately, he died shortly afterwards. It was Holt who pointed out in a letter that 'more and more of the doubles have julie roots'. Rosetta hadn't noticed this as she grew her plants in pots and wasn't looking for this feature.

In subsequent years 'Rosetta Jones Doubles' have acquired a worldwide reputation and seed has been available both direct, and from various seed companies.

After selling the nursery she moved to her present home in Shelton and continued to produce seed. Due to space restrictions she is now cutting back. Despite this, her enthusiasm remains undiminished and a new project is the raising of typical *juliae* doubles.

THE BARNHAVEN DOUBLES

The most significant 'double' event in the last 35 years was the 1965 launch of the Barnhaven strain. While the achievements of people already described should not be under-estimated they cannot compare with the impact made by this commercial seed strain. Effectively, at a stroke, very fine doubles in a huge range of colours became widely available.

Florence Bellis had grown and sold named doubles for some years but it wasn't until 1957 that she embarked on a hybridizing programme. Starting with pollen found on 'Marie Crousse', she used it on some of her *acaulis* plants. Eight years later, in spring 1965, 344 doubles bloomed in a wide range of colours. The doubles were launched at the April Coliseum Show in Portland, Oregon, where they caused a sensation.

Shortly afterwards Florence retired and the business was transferred to England's Lake District where Jared Sinclair continued to improve the strain. These plants, much superior in form, size and colours to the older doubles caused an equal impression in other parts of the world. I remember seeing many fine doubles at the shows of the NAPS. It should be said that Cecil Jones's plants were equally as good, although with a smaller colour range. One of my earliest recollections is of a beautiful pale pink double flecked with white, while pollen from a cream Barnhaven seedling produced some of my best doubles. In the 10–15 years after the launch many fine plants were raised. Although some flourished, the majority were not long-lived. Towards the end of the Sinclairs' tenure the quality deteriorated and the standard was not as good. This may have been due to the problem that Mr Sinclair complained about, lack of pollen. As the double flowers became larger and fuller, pollen tended to become scarce or non-

existent. I had a similar experience with a lovely batch raised from the Barnhaven cream and 'Dawn Ansell'. I could not find a speck of pollen so the strain died out.

Apart from Rosetta Jones's strain, a good deal of publicity was given to what were described as 'New Zealand Doubles', introduced by Hopley's Plants of Much Hadham, Hertfordshire, in the early 1980s. Barbara Shaw wrote that 65 plants were brought back from the South Island of New Zealand, and by 1984 Hopley's were offering 43 for sale. They have had much publicity and some were given awards by the RHS. Twelve are illustrated in *Perennials* volume 1 by Phillips and Rix.

Dr Keith Hammett of Auckland, in a letter, says that the plants were originally selections from Barnhaven seed made by Mrs Muriel Davison of Maple Glen Gardens. According to Dr Hammett, they were supplied by Topline Nurseries who are no longer trading. Mrs Davison was somewhat embarrassed when she learned that these plants were promoted as a New Zealand development.

I was unable to obtain any information on the present position of the Hopley doubles but only five were listed in the 1994/5 catalogue.

With the move to France, double seed is still on offer from Barnhaven, but the most significant event has been the production of micropropagated doubles. In the early 1980s a number of Barnhaven doubles were tissue-cultured by Martin Stokes at Microplants, then located at Longnor, near Buxton, Derbyshire. Later more doubles were obtained from various sources and others, usually under number, sent in by specific customers to be produced exclusively for them. Apart from the handful of recognized older sorts, it has been assumed that all the remaining micro doubles, excepting 'Dawn Ansell', were of Barnhaven breeding. This may be incorrect, and some may have been wrongly identified in the list of named varieties. There were other doubles being raised apart from Barnhaven by some amateurs. However, Rosetta Jones has been supplying seed into the UK for 22 years and it seems certain that a few thousand doubles have been grown from her seed. It is very likely that some of the micropropagated plants are Rosetta's strain rather than Barnhaven.

Since the late 1980s millions have been sold and are common in nurserymen's catalogues and at garden centres. These plants are on sale in North America, New Zealand, Canada, Australia and continental Europe. In recent seasons the number of varieties on offer seems to have declined although very large quantities are still sold annually.

These new doubles need careful cultivation to make them flourish, and planted in unsuitable conditions they soon die. During the hard winter of 1995/6 several northern nurserymen suffered severe losses of pot-grown plants.

Dr Keith Hammett raised a number of doubles in New Zealand that were offered for a while by Parva Plants. The availability of tissue-cultured plants brought this to an end.

In Australia Dr Vincent Clark, who has been establishing a specialist primula nursery for the last four years, grows doubles raised mainly from Barnhaven seed and other specialist growers. He is now hybridizing and raising many seedlings of a range of primroses and polyanthus types. Some years ago Goodwins offered double polyanthus seed from plants raised by the veteran plant breeder Fred Danks. In an article in one of the NAPS yearbooks Mr Goodwin described them as 'positively the best double polyanthus in the world'. Seed was available in the 1980s from Thompson and Morgan and plants still thrive in the collections of Australian enthusiasts.

What is the future of the double primrose? Amateurs like myself are still raising new seedlings and this is the route to follow, although some hybridizers have been discouraged because of the ready availability of tissue-cultured plants. A recent attempt to have some excellent new seedlings tissue-cultured foundered due to lack of interest. I have no doubt tissue culture is the only reliable way of keeping many double primrose clones. It would be nice though if some new varieties could be added to those currently offered.

Very recently I have heard that Goldsmith Seeds are working on the development 'of a uniform double primrose'. It is said that the plant is compact with densely clustered cream flowers. This has been developed for the Easter market and will be available eventually in a range of colours via Colgrave Seeds of Banbury, although likely to be expensive. We await this with interest.

4 ANOMALOUS PRIMROSES

Unusual primroses and polyanthus are normally referred to as 'anomalous'. *Collins Concise Dictionary and Thesaurus* gives a variety of meanings for this word including 'aberrant', 'abnormal', 'bizarre', 'odd', 'peculiar', 'unusual' and 'rare'. Sometimes anomalous plants are described, more attractively, as 'Elizabethan' primroses, because of their popularity in the Elizabethan period.

Reginald Farrer in *The English Rock Garden* said 'from the days of Parkinson, freaks, reduplications and virescent forms have been frequent, and particularly valued among gardeners in the various species of vernales primulas.' These rare odd forms have occurred throughout the history of the primrose and are a source of fascination to many.

It would seem that the primrose, and to a similar extent the cowslip, tend to produce aberrant forms. *Hortus floridus*, a florilegia by Crispin de Pas (1614), has two illustrations of anomalous cowslip forms, *Primula veris anglica pleno flore*, a double, and *Primula veris flore gemino*, a hose-in-hose. Parkinson in his famous *Paradisus Terrestris* (1629), described and illustrated 15 different types of primrose and six cowslips, including doubles, the

---

Illustrations from Parkinson's *Paradisus* (1629)

Fig. 1. *Primula veris flore albo.* The single white primrose

Fig. 2. *Primula veris flore viridante & albo simplici.* The single green and white primrose (jack-in-the-green).

Fig. 3. *Primula veris flore viridi duplici.* The double green primrose.

Fig. 4. *Primula veris Hesketi flore multiplici separatim diviso.* Master Heskets double primrose.

Fig. 5. *Primula hortensis flore pleno vulgaris.* The ordinary double primrose.

Fig. 6. *Paralysis flore viridante simplici.* The single green cowslip.

Fig. 7. *Paralysis flore germinato odorato.* The hose-in-hose cowslip.

Fig. 8. *Paralysis flore germinato inodora.* The hose-in-hose oxlip.

Fig. 9. *Paralysis flore & calice crispo.* The curled cowslip or gallygaskins.

Fig. 10. *Paralysis minor flore rubro.* The red cowslip or 'red birds eyes'.

Fig. 11. *Paralysis hortensis flore pleno.* Double Paigle or Cowslip.

Fig. 12. *Paralysis flore fatuo.* The 'Franticke or Foolish' cowslip or jackanapes-on-horseback.

Fig. 13. *Paralysis flore viridante sive calamistrato.* The green or double green feathered cowslip

majority of which can be classified as 'anomalous'. He went on to refer to 'All these kindes as they have been found wilde, growing in divers places in England...'

The Bristol Flora, first published in 1912, mentions both hose-in-hose and jack-in-the-green forms; 'A sport with the calyx converted into leaves was found in 1883 by Miss M. Mayou, near Easton, and near Shepton Mallet, 1900 by Miss Roper.'

The author of the flora, J. W. White, a lecturer in botany at the University of Bristol, found a 'primrose monstrosity', a hose-in-hose form, in a field at Backwell Hill in March 1905. The floras of Gloucester and Wiltshire mention several aberrant forms and many others quote examples of aberrant or unusual plants, although it must be stressed that such discoveries represent a tiny fraction of the wild populations.

Old gardening magazines and the journals of the RHS yield much interesting information.

The RHS journal for 12 May 1891:

> *Miss Woodward sent in a new and remarkable form of a primrose which accidentally appeared in a cottage garden at Belton near Grantham. Its peculiarities consist in the corolla lobes being red below and yellow above, as well as it possesses a sweeter and more powerful perfume than others.*

14 March 1911:

> *Mr Till of the Frythe Garden, Welwyn, showed a well-grown plant of the long known primrose with virescent petals. In*

the present instance the petals showed rather more of the leaf like character than usual, the venation being very distinct. Found growing wild near Welwyn, 1909.

25 April 1911:

> *Flowers of seedling polyanthus with flowers inside one another, each having both calyx and corolla, and so differing from the ordinary hose-in-hose form.*

In the same issue:

> *Green primrose with stamens foliar and green. The original found in Ireland and has been grown by sender for 11 years, but had always until 1911 been single. It had been growing in the same position for three years without doubling. Now even divisions of the original have more or less doubling.*

Geoffrey Nicolle found a primrose-flowered jack-in-the-green near Rosemarket in West Wales in 1990 and I found one in an old garden in Hendon many years ago. Many have reported similar experiences and no doubt numerous others have gone unrecorded. I have not mentioned wild double forms of the primrose which will be covered in the relevant chapter.

One of the problems that has arisen with these aberrant forms is the difficulty in classifying them. The descriptions of the old gardening writers vary and can be contradictory. It is fairly easy to identify the standard hose-in-hose and jack-in-the-green and immediate derivatives, but after that confusion reigns. Some writers have shied away from doing so but I shall now attempt a description of the different forms with qualifications where necessary:

Hose-in-hose This comes in both primrose and polyanthus forms, including the cowslip. The calyx is petaloid giving the appearance of two identical flowers or corollas, one inside the other. Gerard called them 'Two-in-Hose' while Parkinson said 'they remind one of the breeches men do wear.' Other names are Duplex or Cup and Saucer primroses. Most of the original named hose-in-hose were derived from *P. vulgaris* and were sweetly scented, the two blooms seeming to enhance this.

Jack-in-the-green Also known as jack-in-the-pulpit. Both primrose and polyanthus forms exist, single or double. The flower may be any colour and the calyx is enlarged, a ruff of green leaves. The size of the leafy portion varies from quite small, so that it is hardly noticeable, to very large, with the flower sitting in the middle.

Pantaloon Also called jack-in-the-box, a form of the hose-in-hose where the calyx is partly petaloid. The basic colour is green but is striped with the colour of the flower or corolla. The width of the coloured stripes can vary, from narrow to wide, so that, when they are wide, the calyx appears to be striped with green. *An Illustrated Dictionary of Antique Art and Archaeology* by J. W. Mollet says 'pantaloon' is from the Italian *pianta leone* meaning 'plant the lion'. The Venetian standard bearers (of the lion of St Mark) being so called, who wore tight hose, the name came to be given to hose in general. In ancient pantomimes, Pantaloon was always a Venetian.

Jackanapes An interim form between jack-in-the-green and hose-in-hose where the calyx is striped with the colour of the flower or corolla. This form is sometimes seen with the tuft of small, narrow, green leaves at the point where the footstalks or pedicels join the main stem. This latter condition was described by the late Bernard Smith as a 'polynapes'.

Galligaskins, gallygaskins or gallygascoynes So named because of the resemblance to the wide breeches worn by Tudor and Stuart gentlemen. Mollet's book says, 'Broad loose breeches; 16th Century'. Both primrose and polyanthus forms have been recorded although it is more often of polyanthus type. This is the 'Curl'd Cowslip' of Parkinson, where the calyx is enlarged and distorted. In appearance a variant of the jack-in-the-green or possibly an overgrown cowslip.

Jackanapes or jack-a-napes-on-horseback Parkinson's 'Franticke, or foolish Cowslip', this is a form of jackanapes where both the calyx or flower, and the tuft of leaves at the top of the stem, are striped with the flower or corolla colour.

Clowns Of either primrose or polyanthus form with a flower, of any colour that is striped and/or spotted with white.

Feathers or shags A polyanthus with an elongated calyx, cut up fine like a fringe surrounding the flower. According to Sacheverell Sitwell they were known to the Elizabethan and Jacobean writers as the Scattered Polyanthus. Richard Bradley FRS, in his *New Improvements of Planting and Gardening* (1717), gave a different description. He said: '…feathers which seem by nature to

Fig. 3. Anomalous primroses (1)
From Cannell & Sons 1883 catalogue

Pantaloons

Duplex
Polyanthus

King of
Hose-in-Hose

Fig. 4. Anomalous primroses (2)
From Cannell & Sons 1883 catalogue

Jack in the Green
Polyanthus

White and Yellow
Hose-in-Hose

Galligaskins

be at first designed for hose-in-hose have their blossoms so split and curled that they somewhat resemble bunches of feathers… and there are many varieties….'

Other abnormalities have been described in past literature. Margaret Webster uncovered an old paper on the *Morphology of the Primulaceae*, Masters (1877), that mentions two other aberrant forms. In one of these the petals have an abnormally deep division of each petal so there appear to be ten petals instead of five. The other has petaloid stamens, but with three or more small petals in place of each stamen and described by Masters as being from a variety of polyanthus known in gardens as the 'Nigger'.

The collecting of such unusual forms has always been a 'cult' amongst primrose enthusiasts and continues to be so. Few of the old named ones survive, 'Wanda hose-in-hose' and 'Tipperary Purple' are the notable exceptions, although neither are outstanding plants.

One of the earliest catalogues I have seen is that of H. Cannell & Sons 1883, an elaborate production lavishly illustrated with black and white engravings. They include several anomalous forms of both primroses and polyanthus including a laced hose-in-hose and jack-in-the green polyanthus with the polynapes tuft. The plant is called 'King of Hose-in-Hose' and described as 'Colour bright rich rosy deep chestnut, evenly and beautifully laced, outer flower growing direct from the centre of the inner bloom like a telescope.' The price was 12 shillings, a very considerable sum in those days and contrasts sharply with some of the prices for double primroses, from sixpence to a few shillings

each.

Other plants included a yellow hose-in-hose called 'Golden Gem', a white hose-in-hose and both gallygaskins and pantaloons.

Several hose-in-hose polyanthus are listed; 'Golden Prince', 'Irish Cowslip' and 'Queen', all described as golden or bright yellow while 'Charlotte Jones', 'Crimson Queen', 'Camondo' and 'Magenta Queen' are magenta or red shades.

Like the *juliae* primroses little information on the origin of the old named forms exists. Sacheverell Sitwell wrote: 'They come in greatest number from the six counties of Ulster, from Limerick, from near Dublin, or from the perennially green and damp County Kerry, where they have stayed unmolested, since the time of Thomas Moore's Irish melodies.' He was talking about old primroses in general but singled out three 'exquisitely pretty' hose-in-hose, 'beyond question of cowslip descent', which were 'Lady Dora', 'Lady Lettice' and 'Lady Molly', and said they were available from several sources in Ireland. Others he mentioned included 'Erins Gem', 'Sparkler', 'Old Vivid', 'Salmon Sparkler', 'Prince of Orange' as well as several unnamed plants, again from Ireland.

Jack-in-the greens, jackanapes and gallygaskins were mostly described by colour and Sitwells mentions blue, pink, deep red, crimson with a gold edge 'and other colours'. The only named variety is 'Miss Jones', a jack-in-the green, 'red with a white edge'.

All these plants have gone and so have many others listed by primrose enthusiasts like the Misses A. and M. Cadell of East Lothian, Scotland. In their short catalogue, *Primroses in Excelsis*, several anomalous varieties were offered with only the hose-in-hose mentioned by name: 'Ashford' ('pink'), 'Canary Bird' ('deep yellow'), 'Lady's Favourite' ('golden yellow'), 'Lady Lettice' ('creamy white') and 'Sparkler' – synonym 'Old Vivid' – ('a rare colour, red').

Somewhat later, around the early 1950s, Mrs Mary McMurtrie of Kintore, Aberdeenshire, was still offering 'Canary Bird', 'Lady Lettice' and 'Sparkler' and these plants and a few others were sold by several small growers who were enthusiasts rather than professionals. Mrs Gladys Emmerson in County Derry, Northern Ireland, and Mrs Beevor of Great Yarmouth are typical examples, while the famous gardener Margery Fish of East Lambrook Manor, Somerset, offered a few amongst an extensive list of primroses.

The period between 1950 and the late 1960s saw the peak of interest in the named varieties of primrose and polyanthus. While this was mainly devoted to *juliae* hybrids and double primroses, the main primrose nurseries offered a range of anomalous forms.

T. A. Townsend in about 1954 listed 19 named hose-in-hose, including 'Alabaster' ('Semi-polyanthus habit. Unsullied white'), 'Brimstone' ('New. Large Sulphur yellow'), 'Leeke Red' ('a new introduction from Ireland'), as well as several of the old favourites like 'Sparkler' and 'Lady Lettice'. Townsend also listed six named jacks, which included 'Donegal Danny', 'Eldorado', 'Salamander' and the still-extant 'Tipperary Purple'.

Another major primrose nursery, E. B. Champernowne, offered only 'Canary Bird', 'Tipperary' and 'Pink Beauty' as named plants. Instead a range of seedlings were sold

in colour groups. The polyanthus hose-in-hose, 'which are finer in every way than those we have come across in general cultivation', were in ten shades, while the polyanthus jack-in-the-green, 'outstanding for their robust constitution and large flowers', came in white, yellow, pink, crimson and purple.

During my researches I discovered another primrose nursery, previously unknown to me, with a substantial list. This was Blenheim Nursery at Bovey Tracey in South Devon. The 1954 catalogue of this short-lived concern included four jack-in-the-greens and eight hose-in-hose.

Some two years after I became interested in primroses, in about 1967, I obtained plants from Roy Genders at his East Coast Primrose Gardens. With the exception of Townsend his list was the most extensive and included 12 hose-in-hose and four jack-in-the-greens. The hose were most of the old favourites like 'Ashfort' (previously listed as 'Ashford' by the Misses Cadell), 'Canary Bird', 'Lady Molly' and 'Sparkler', with only 'Canary Bird' sold out. Of the four jacks listed he could only supply 'Tipperary Purple'. Soon after, in common with most of the others, this business closed, and while Mrs McMurtrie and Mrs Emmerson continued for a few years, the number of available varieties steadily decreased.

Meanwhile in America Florence Levy (Florence Bellis) of Barnhaven had been sent seed of old varieties from Captain Comely Hawkes of Nantwich, Cheshire, and she began to hybridize. By 1949 she was offering seven different seed mixtures of various hose-in-hose and jack-in-the green crosses with gold- and silver-laced polyanthus in some of them. They were described as novelty strains and continue to be offered, although they were referred to by Jared Sinclair and are referred to now by Angela Bradford as Elizabethan primroses, in a single 'Traditional' mixture.

The Barnhaven plants are mainly of polyanthus form, deliberately so, as the flowers of the *vulgaris* types have a tendency to trail on the ground, due to the weight of the adornments round the flowers. Some excellent plants have come from this seed. Unfortunately, they do not seem to be very long-lived but have proved excellent parents, either as pollinators or seed bearers.

Geoffrey Nicolle first became interested in anomalous forms about 25 years ago when he found a copy of Parkinson's *Paradisus* in that Mecca of second-hand bookshops, Hey-on-Wye in Herefordshire. He later managed to obtain an old hose-in-hose polyanthus, of unknown origin, with small yellow flowers not much larger than those of the cowslip. This was pollinated by a plant of *P. veris*.

Geoffrey's home and garden are in the tiny hamlet of Nolton Haven, a few miles outside Haverford West on the west coast of Wales. His bungalow was originally a pub called the 'Rising Sun' and is now 'Rising Sun Cottage'. Geoffrey and his wife told me they bought the property because of the stream which dissects the garden, running down a long gully into the sea. It is a wildlife paradise with a wide range of birds and animals. Both cowslips and primroses grow wild and it was one of these wild cowslips that was the pollen parent.

Geoffrey credits Dr Cecil Jones with much of his success. Early in his primula career he made himself known to Cecil and was invited to 'Penlan' where, in his own words, 'Dr Jones generously showed me his methods and revealed his secrets.'

Starting with this original cross he has raised many fine plants, mainly of cowslip habit. Apart from the seedlings the only other plants brought in were further wild cowslips and red and orange forms.

From the crosses he has raised several forms of hose-in-hose, galligaskins and pantaloons. The colour range varies from yellow through orange to red.

In 1989, to Geoffrey's surprise, after about five years of crossing and recrossing, double cowslips or 'paigles' appeared. An early seedling was of jack-in-the-green polyanthus type but he did not pursue this line preferring to concentrate on cowslip forms. The first two doubles were respectively red and yellow and the red was awarded 'best double' at the spring London show of the NAPS. In 1990 five more doubles bloomed, all true yellow cowslips but with different degrees of doubling.

The very best of these double cowslips was named 'Katy McSparron' after a granddaughter, a plant that gained considerable acclaim when exhibited at NAPS shows. The doubling is very full with excellent form and it is a really wonderful plant. At the time I suggested he ought to contact a major commercial grower as it deserves wider recognition and distribution. This he did and the nursery chosen, a very famous one, showed great interest and enthusiasm. A plant was supplied more than three years ago and after extended problems the nursery has finally succeeded with tissue culture. Providing everything proceeds smoothly 'Katy McSparron' should soon be introduced commercially and is bound to be a great success.

Several other double cowslips were raised, very similar to 'Katy McSparron' – all truly delightful plants, but they are difficult to maintain after initially vigorous growth.

Unfortunately, Geoffrey has never been able to find any pollen in these doubles but maintains his strain through annual crossing. He is exceedingly modest and claims no real knowledge of genetics or breeding, attributing his success to 'luck'. He is undoubtedly one of those gifted amateurs who instinctively does the right thing.

Margaret Webster was born at Bessbrook, near Newry, and as a child was fascinated by the hose-in-hose primroses her mother grew in the family garden. She later graduated as an art student and after her marriage in 1971 moved to Killay, Swansea, in South Wales, opposite a brickworks. Close by were a row of old cottages and in a hedge that bordered the gardens were several jack-in-the-green primroses, all pale yellow shades similar to the normal wild primrose. They may have been wild mutations or possibly may have been grown by the original inhabitants of the cottages.

In 1980 she moved with her husband and two children, to Winford in the Chew valley, south of Bristol. She brought two or three of the jack-in-the-greens and planted them in the garden. At the time she was ignorant of the technicalities of plant-breeding, and wishing to maintain the primroses, which were proving very slow to increase, tried to obtain seed. Unfortunately, all were thrum-eyed and attempts to self-pollinate failed. She then met Dr Chris Grant, a lecturer in genetics at Bristol University who lived

locally. Chris told her that thrum-eyed plants were self-sterile and she needed a pin-eyed plant to complete the cross. Soon afterwards Don Everett, a well-known nurseryman from Backwell, Bristol, following a talk to the Winford gardening club told her that jack-in-the-greens and hose-in-hose primroses were rare and sought-after. Margaret found the address of the late Mary Mottram who ran a small nursery in North Devon specializing in old-fashioned flowers. From her she obtained a yellow-flowered pin-eyed hose-in-hose.

During this period she was bringing up a young family; after moving to Winford her third child was born, and flowers sometimes took second or even third place. However, Dr Grant, who was now a good family friend, suggested she take a course at Bristol University. Whenever she saw him, she plied him with questions about genetics and associated problems and this led to her taking, in 1986, a two-year part-time course (Certificate of Science/Biology) at Bristol University. Her project was 'Observations of and Breeding Experiments with Morphological variants of Primula Species'. The plants used in the experiments were wild pin and thrum primroses taken from a hedge in Winford, thrum hose-in-hose grown from seed obtained from the outcrossed Mary Mottram plant, and pin and thrum jack-in-the-greens, derived from the thrum-eyed jack brought from Killay, and subsequently interbred with wild Winford primroses.

On completion of the project her examiner, Dr Quentin Key, was so impressed he suggested publication and sent a copy to Dr John Richards. The resulting paper was co-written with Dr Grant and published by the Genetical Society of Great Britain in 1989, entitled *The inheritance of calyx morph variants in Primula vulgaris (Huds.)*. John Richards refers to this paper in *Primula*. A degree in botany followed on an extended study course and Margaret became a BSc.Hons graduate in 1993. She became interested in molecular genetics and took every available course on the subject. Her final year project involved primula DNA. The knowledge she has acquired makes her a leading expert in this particular sphere, certain elements of which have had little previous research.

Margaret's overriding interest is, as will have been gathered, the scientific study of the anomalous or mutant forms of primrose and polyanthus. At the 1995 and 1996 shows of the National Auricula and Primula Society she exhibited a wide range, some of which had rarely if ever been seen before. Photographs of some of these appear in the book, and although her interest is that of a botanist rather than gardener, many are very attractive. I have visited her on a number of occasions and seen her plants, the majority of which are maintained in pots. She has plants that have been kept going, both in the garden and in pots, for ten years. Margaret grows them in Levington Multi-Purpose compost, a soilless mix based on peat, but is now trying a peat-free mixture. The plants are grown in plastic pots and repotted annually in early autumn to combat the ever-present threat of the vine weevil.

At present she is working on producing laced red jackanapes, with the lacing similar to that of the gold-laced polyanthus, although the flowers are larger. Several plants

I saw in autumn 1995 and spring 1996 were most attractive. Another achievement is a true-breeding strain of yellow hose-in-hose. After a considerable effort, involving raising large numbers of seedlings, the cross from selected pin and thrum parents gives 100 percent hose-in-hose. These plants, if crossed with the wild type, give 50 percent hose-in-hose. Experiments with the green primrose are under way and she has two forms, one single and one semi-double. Somehow – she won't reveal the secret – pollen was obtained from the green primrose and I saw a number of small seedlings 'true-breeding hose x green primrose'. Other fascinating seedlings were her 'twins', pairs of seedlings that had emerged from the same embryo, although they have since died! I have seen the photographic evidence confirming this phenomenon, something I had never heard of previously. She has also used pollen from the double jack 'Dawn Ansell' but was not happy with the progress of the seedlings. I am sure that many more fascinating plants will emerge from her garden in the next few years.

Peter Atkinson of Renton, Washington State, is a leading American grower and raiser of anomolous primroses. He has succeeded in creating many of the old forms including the very rare 'feathers' or 'shags', a jack-in-the-green polyanthus with a calyx of leaf formation but with the corolla shaped into long narrow petals.

Peter began his hybridizing with a ragged white *vulgaris* plant that had jack-in-the-green characteristics. The initial cross was with a hose-in-hose *juliae* hybrid, of an unattractive faded purple. After raising several generations many interesting progeny have emerged. As well as white hose-in-hose of sturdy upright habit, they included polyanthus-type jack-in-the-greens with calyxes of different width, feathers or shags and jackanapes-on-horseback. Photographs of several have appeared in the *APS Quarterly* and, exhibited at the various shows of the APS, they created great interest.

Many others have raised anomalous primroses, one of whom is Brian Coop of St Neots who raised a series of attractive hose-in-hose in the 1980s while a close neighbour of mine in the Vale of Glamorgan. Two that were named were 'Belle' and 'Fairfield Gem'. Brian no longer raises hose-in-hose but 'Fairfield Gem' is still grown by his mother Stella, another primrose enthusiast, at Harrogate.

Another well-known grower of anomalous forms is Mrs Jacqueline Giles, whose garden at Windyridge, Percy Bolton, in Yorkshire is home to large plantings of Barnhaven primroses and polyanthus, as well as many other primroses and cowslips. Mrs Giles is particularly fond of anomalous primroses and grows a large number, mainly from Barnhaven seed. She also collects seed from her plants and has raised many more. Her garden is open to visitors under the National Gardens scheme.

I should add that anomalous forms of the gold-laced polyanthus have been shown at several NAPS shows in recent years. They include hose-in-hose, jack-in-the-green and miniature doubles.

All the anomalous sorts can be grown in the garden and include many very attractive plants as well as a few of botanical interest only.

5 NAMED VARIETIES OF PRIMROSE AND POLYANTHUS

The lists of named primroses and polyanthus in the late Roy Genders' books are the main sources on which most subsequent listings, even recent ones, have been based. His book *Primroses* was published in 1959, so the information is nearly 40 years old and very outdated. Since then things have altered dramatically and it is a difficult task to compile a list that could be described as accurate, for reasons that I will explain. With this qualification, perhaps these new lists can be a starting point for the future with additions and corrections noted, when they are verified. One of the frustrating discoveries made during research for this book was the lack of information on many named plants, either regarding origin or description. A high percentage have only a clonal name – linked, usually, to a brief description. Colour, especially, is subject to vastly different interpretation, magenta being a prime example. In future I would hope that

new varieties will be described in a similar fashion to that of the Alpine Garden Society, where careful descriptions are given of award plants, sometimes with colours matched to a recognized colour chart. This is something that the three British auricula and primula societies and the American Primrose Society could easily accommodate. Of the many hundreds of named *juliae* hybrids raised in or introduced into the United Kingdom and Ireland, between about 1918 and 1960, only a handful remain. Of those that do survive a few are plentiful, 'Lady Greer', 'Wanda' and 'Snowcushion' being prime examples, although impostors circulate under these names. Some others, like 'Guinivere', which I believe has *juliae* blood, are also freely available. For whatever reason be it neglect, hot, dry summers or virus most have vanished. This does not seem to be quite the case in North America, although many named clones have disappeared.

My starting point was *The Plantfinder*, the now well-recognized 'bible' of commercially available plants. The first problem was soon apparent. Primroses and polyanthus are scattered at random throughout the 14 pages of primulas, in dual columns of small print, covering a huge number of species and hybrids. It would be beneficial if something could be done to remedy this in future editions.

I soon noticed that the same plant can appear several times under slightly different names. A number of plants are listed that are seed-raised and not clonal forms, but this is not clearly stated. Finally, some names are incorrect – they are names of plants that have been extinct for years. This is another pitfall for the unwary primrose enthusiast. Misnaming is a problem that has been with us since time immemorial. You will find people writing in the 1930s complaining about wrongly named plants. The National Collection holders have all experienced great frustration over this.

From *The Plantfinder* a list of 126 varieties, including doubles, was culled. In addition I listed deletions, which came to 68. This was on the assumption that some would return. Amongst the deletions were quite a number of plants believed to be extinct; perhaps this had been brought home to the sellers. Another problem is that a significant percentage of the plants, listed as commercially available, are not universally recognized named varieties.

I then obtained lists of plants grown by each of the National Collection holders and consulted *The Pink Sheet*, produced by the Conservation Society (NCCPG), listing rare and endangered plants. *The Pink Sheet* lists 99

primroses and polyanthus, although – looking at the names – I suspect many vanished long ago. Using these sources as a starting point, two basic lists were prepared, one for singles and one for doubles. Genders' book had separate lists for jack-in-the greens (6), hose-in-hose (20), *juliae* primroses (92), Garryard primroses (10), varieties of polyanthus habit (28) and double primroses (60) – six lists totalling 216 in all. A major difference is the large number of plants from North America, whereas Genders only listed a small number from British Columbia.

Today we have far fewer in the UK, despite *The Plantfinder* listings. Named hose-in-hose and jack-in-the-green are comparatively few, most of those grown are unnamed seedlings. Large-flowered, named polyanthus are also rare. While a good number of the named hybrids are of polyanthus form, they are generally small and better described as stalked primroses. Where plants are unknown quantities, or are probably extinct, they have not been included, although I have exercised some discretion in this respect.

It was decided to include plants grown in Australia and New Zealand as well as North America, all areas where primroses are very popular. As far as I have been able to ascertain, only a few home-raised plants are grown in either Australia or New Zealand with clonal names.

The situation in North America is very different. My feeling is that there are far more named clones grown in America, mainly the Pacific Northwest region, Alaska, the eastern areas of the USA and parts of Canada, primarily British Columbia. A tremendous number of hybrids were raised from 1940 onwards and to some extent this is still happening. Unfortunately, the problem of identification is not unique to the United Kingdom. In 1992 the APS asked Mrs Dorothy Springer, a long-standing expert on *juliae* hybrids, to compile a registry of named plants, because of the existing confusion. Details of plants were requested from members, together with a photograph. The response has been mixed but a recent count recorded more than 80 named plants plus, in her words, 'a bunch of yet to be identified ones'. Amongst the 'named' plants are three different versions of 'Wanda', two of 'Crispii' and nearly 20 more she considers incorrectly named! This would appear to be the tip of the iceberg, as I feel sure many others are waiting to be discovered. The intention is to establish a North American equivalent of our National Collections but it is proving an uphill struggle. Mrs Springer has kindly shared much of the information she has compiled, and it has been incorporated in the lists.

In Europe, where over the years many hybrids were raised, particularly in Germany and Holland, some named plants are still grown. Details are hard to find, and the Dutch *Plantfinder* only lists a few primroses, mainly micropropagated doubles.

I refer to specific books in some descriptions. Coloured illustrations of named primroses and polyanthus are uncommon. Three books I am familiar with have a number; they are *Primroses* by Genders, *Alpines in Colour and Cultivation* by T. C. Mansfield and *Perennials* (Vol. 1) by Phillips and Rix. The first two are long out of print but can sometimes be obtained from second-hand booksellers. *Perennials* is current.

Another great help, for identification purposes, is *The Book of Primroses* by Barbara Shaw. This contains more than 60 botanical paintings by the author. Mrs Shaw is of the opinion that the only accurate way of identifying plants is through botanical paintings. Apart from those she has produced I know of few others, so while she may be right, it is not a practical solution. As early as the 1930s writers on primroses, like Miss Eda Hume, questioned the naming of so many similar plants. She wrote they needed a 'great sorting out'.

With the above reservations and qualifications, the following lists have been compiled.

SINGLE PRIMROSES AND POLYANTHUS

Adelaide (USA, Dorothy Springer, 'Snow White' x 'Jay-Jay') The ruff and foliage are bronze green. Cushion form, with flowers a similar shade to 'Guinivere'.

Alejandra (Canada, John Kerridge) Described as a 'Wanda-type hybrid with rich red flowers on 6" to 8" [150–200 mm] stems'. Introduced commercially in 1977 via tissue culture.

Amy (USA) A 'Wanda' impostor widely grown throughout the Pacific Northwest. It is a refined 'Wanda' with smaller leaves and brighter flowers, each one having a white fleck on the petals. Roy Davidson, a well-known Northwest plantsman, obtained it from a lady in Everett, Washington State. It was then known as 'Borsch seedling', as it was raised by Oregon grower Fred Borsch. In about 1947 Davidson renamed the plant 'Amy' after his mother. At that time it was extensively grown and fell into the hands of several commercial growers who marketed it as 'Wanda'.

Assiniboine (Canada) Introduced by Holes' Nursery, Alberta. Described as a 'very heavy-blooming primrose with salmon-apricot flowers developed in Manitoba for Canadian winters'.

Ballyrogan 'Cream Edge' A *vulgaris* form with a cream edge round the leaves. It was introduced by Ballyrogan Nursery in Ireland.

Barrowby Gem A famous old polyanthus noted mainly for its fragrance. The pin-eyed flowers are a clear, bright yellow with a small greenish centre. Impostors are frequently sold, often similar in appearance but lacking the scent of the true plant. Miss Sinclair-Rohde, in her book *The Scented Garden* (1931), although she refers to it as a primrose, wrote that it was raised in Scotland by a Mrs Coll, but Barbara Shaw says it originated at Barrowby Hall in East Yorkshire.

Bea (USA) Raised by Ruth Bartlett of Spring Hill Farm, a thick petalled cream with large round flowers, cushion form. One of Dorothy Springer's favourite *juliae*s.

Beamish Foam An older polyanthus primrose with delicate pink blooms splashed with pale yellow.

Belvedere Reputedly an old primrose with large lilac-coloured blooms.

Betty Green A variety from Holland with velvet-red, medium-sized blooms and attractive apple-green foliage. Thrum-eyed with a rounded yellow eye. Impostors have been sold under this name.

Blue Riband Raised in Scotland by Mr George Murray. Deep green leaves with amethyst-blue flowers. The small yellow eye is ringed with crimson, making it easily identifiable. Thrum-eyed. Often sent out from nurseries as 'Blue Horizon', which seems to be extinct.

Blue Velvet An early-flowering plant with deep purple-blue, velvety, flowers.

Blutenkissen German for 'Crimson Cushion'. Crimson flowers with ochre eye, over-rounded-type *juliae* leaves.

Bright Eyes (USA) A large-eyed purple shade, origin unknown. One of the older hybrids.

Buckland Primrose Raised at the Champernowne Nurseries, Buckland Monachorum, Devon. A beautiful polyanthus primrose of Garryard type. Dark green foliage with large trusses of rich creamy-yellow flowers. Sometimes called, erroneously, 'Buckland Cream'.

Buckland Wine Introduced in 1965 by the Champernowne Nurseries. It has dark green foliage and rounded, wine-red blooms with a small circular, yellow eye. Thrum-eyed. Another with Garryard blood. This was the only primrose in the Champernowne wholesale list of 1974/5. There is some dispute over identification. The painting in Mrs Shaw's book does not match the plant described – obtained from Roy Genders – that I used to grow. A book on Devon plants, published by the NCCPG, originally called *The Magic Tree* but now renamed *The Devon Plants* (1989), has a coloured photograph. This agrees with my description.

Butterball (USA, Susan Watson hybrid) A creamy yellow with a tiny yellow eye. Susan Watson was a past *APS Quarterly* editor who lived in Oregon, later moving to British Columbia in the late 1940s or early 1950s. Scarce.

Candy Pink (USA) Also known as 'Skyhook Candy Pink'. Grown by Alice Hills Baylor at her Skyhook nursery in the early 1970s. It is a stalked pink with small foliage and is occasionally referred to as 'Pink Lady Greer'. Dorothy Springer obtained her plants from Skyhook nearly 30 years ago. A very hardy plant, increasing rapidly.

Caroline's Dorothy (Alaska) A striking large-flowered, pale yellow polyanthus originally thought to be the well-known *juliae* hybrid 'Dorothy' until it was realized it was too large. Originating in Caroline Jensen's garden at Juneau it is now referred to as 'Caroline's Dorothy'.

Cherry A compact dwarf polyanthus with very short stems bearing blooms of cherry red.

City of Bellingham (USA) Discovered in a garden in Bellingham, Washington State. by the late Ross Willingham of Seattle over 40 years ago. He gave it the name as nothing was known about it. A plant of cushion form, increasing rapidly, with lavender flowers and a strong yellow eye. In 1994 a commercial grower started distributing it as 'Lilac Wanda'!

Craddock White Large dark green leaves with bronze veins, bearing large, strongly scented, frilled white flowers with a yellow eye. Found in Miss Marker's garden at Yondercott, near Uffolme, Somerset and named by Margery Fish in the 1950s. There was also a very similar plant with pink flowers called 'Craddock Pink'.

Craven Gem Similar to Lady Greer and *might* be the original plant introduced by Reginald Farrer in 1902. Possibly a *juliae* x *veris* cross although *P. juliae* was only discovered in 1900. Given the remote area where *P. juliae* was found and the then means of transport, it seems unlikely that *P. juliae* could have arrived in England so soon.

Crimson Queen Glossy green foliage with large magenta-red flowers.

Crispii A mauve-pink primrose introduced by Waterer, Sons and Crisp Ltd. in 1916, therefore pre-dating 'Wanda' by at least two years and one of the very first *juliae* hybrids, although it is described by Genders as of '*acaulis* [*vulgaris*] habit'. Almost certainly extinct in the UK, a plant under this name is grown in Alaska. Mrs Cheri Fluck of Juneau lists two forms of 'Crispii'. The colour of one she describes as 'pearly-red'.

Dark Rosalie (Northern Ireland, Joe Kennedy) The culmination of Joe Kennedy's hybridizing programme, as he has now dispersed his plants and taken up painting. Originally developed from 'Kinloch Beauty', this is a small bronze-leaved plant with thrum-eyed, almost eyeless flowers, dark red with broad stripes of a lighter shade – a true striped primrose. I understand it is vigorous and increases rapidly. A sensation at the Irish Spring Show in 1997.

David Green A Champernowne introduction. Emerald-green foliage with intense crimson flowers and small deep yellow eye.

David Valentine Introduced by Louise Vockins of Foxglove Nursery at Newbury. Soft mauve flowers on miniature polyanthus stems, fleshy foliage. Obtained from an aunt who had grown it for some while.

Dr Molly Raised by Cecil Monson at Roscommon, Eire and named after Dr Molly Sanderson, a well-known Irish gardener. Of Garryard breeding with bronzed foliage and magenta-pink flowers on *acaulis* stems.

Dorothy A miniature, pin-eyed, polyanthus-primrose with some similarities to Lady Greer, although the flowers are larger with more pink in them. The origin of 'Dorothy' is shrouded in mystery. A 'Dorothy' is mentioned in Mansfield's book published in 1942, but in Genders' book is described as a primrose rather than a miniature polyanthus. According to Barbara Shaw it originated in British Columbia, but this seems doubtful as it is probable that William Goddard received his plants from Florence Bellis, who maintained that it came from England. Nevertheless, 'Dorothy' is abundant in the northeastern United States, in British Columbia and in Alaska. In 1995 John Kerridge, then president of the APS, found a large number of plants growing robustly in borders in the garden of the Governor's mansion in Alaska. The staff did not know what they were but John identified 'Dorothy'. One description of the Alaskan plant says it has fluted light cream flowers with bottle-green leaves.

Duckyls Red Raised by Mrs Hazel Taylor of Duckyls, East Sussex. A medium-sized polyanthus of Barnhaven type. It appears identical to the Barnhaven 'Cowichan' garnet strain and has been micropropagated in large quantities. Although some descriptions call it 'outstanding', very similar plants are raised from packets of Barnhaven seed. Typical 'Cowichan' flowers with 'bee-type' centre, thrum-eyed, of a luminous, bright red.

Early Bird (USA) From Jay and Ann Lunn, a 1988 hybrid between *P. vulgaris* subspecies *sibthorpii* and *juliae* hybrid 'Snow White'. A very early flowering cushion form, with medium-sized flowers similar in colour to *sibthorpii*.

Early Girl (USA, Earl Welch hybrid) A 'Gracie' x 'Guinivere' cross with white flowers and dark foliage. Stalked form and a good parent.

Emily (USA) A highly regarded hose-in-hose stalked primrose raised by Cyrus Happy of Tacoma and named after his daughter. This plant, described as having 'pale greenish-yellow blossoms with lime centres', has won many prizes at APS shows. It is from a cross between a hose-in-hose cowslip and a Clarkes' pink hose-in-hose-*juliae*. Rather larger than the normal *juliae* type.

Enchantress A gorgeous Garryard-type polyanthus raised by Mr Hugo Jeffrey at Champernowne. The pin-eyed flowers are larger than those of 'Guinivere'; a much deeper shade of pink and heavily veined. The dark, bottle-green leaves are crinkled and most attractive. Possibly the most striking of the so-called Garryard primroses. Illustrated in Phillps and Rix.

Enid A similar plant to 'Guinivere' except that the flowers are a deeper shade of pink and more heavily veined. Pin-eyed. Illustrated in Mansfield.

E. R. Janes This famous small *juliae* hybrid is almost certainly extinct in the UK, despite being offered by at least two nurseries in recent years. In each case a different plant was supplied, either 'Kinlough Beauty' or 'Wisley Red'. Some enthusiasts in the USA are still growing plants as 'E. R. Janes', although the plant is not yet confirmed as true. It was illustrated in colour, a rare occurrence in those days, in both Mansfield's and Genders' books and this undoubtedly stimulated interest in what has been one of the most sought-after varieties. The unusual colour, salmon-pink flushed orange, is unique amongst *juliae* hybrids, again an attraction for the collector. E. R. Janes was raised by a Mr T. A. Lawrenson of Gosforth, Newcastle-on-Tyne in the early 1930s. He crossed a *P. vulgaris* seedling with *P. juliae* and exhibited the plant at the November Show of the Newcastle Horticultural Society where it attracted great attention. Later, after increasing the stock to several hundred plants, he sold them to Messrs. Maurice Pritchard & Son of Christchurch, Hampshire. Pritchards sold out almost immediately at the then very high price of 5 shillings each, equivalent to several pounds today. An Award of Merit was given at Wisley on 1 April 1938, the plants being submitted by Pritchards. The description accompanying the award is; 'Plant compact, of *P. juliae* habit bearing flowers either on single stems or six to ten flowers on one stem. Florets 1 ¼" [32 mm] in diameter, rich rosy salmon with cupreous sheen, yellow eye of medium size, pin, free flowering.'

Etha (USA, Dorothy Springer, 'Bea' x 'Stoplight'). Named by Mrs Springer after Etha Tate, a friend and fellow APS judge who died in 1995. The plant was raised several years ago and has thrived ever since. White flowers with a touch of pink compliment the cushion habit. Attractive green foliage. 'Stoplight', a bright red jack-in-the-green, was one of Mrs Springer's early hybrids and is now extinct.

Evonne (Canada, John Kerridge) Described as a 'real breakthrough in the Polyanthus form'. A selected seedling from John Kerridge's breeding programme aimed at producing a large-flowered gold-laced garden polyanthus. Flowers are described as 1 in (25 mm) across, deep red with bright gold edge on 6 in (150 mm) to 9 in (225 mm) stems. Introduced commercially via tissue culture in 1997.

Francesca (Canada, John Kerridge) Described as a 'beautiful light-green and fringed-flowered Polyanthus'. Flowers are clustered on 200 mm (8 in) to 250 mm (10 in) stems. Introduced commercially via tissue culture in 1997.

Friday (USA) Origin unknown, a dark purple cushion type.

Frühlingzauber Large, flat, purple blooms held well above the foliage. Raised in Germany.

Gartenmeister Bartens German origin, *P. juliae* habit with crinkly edged leaves; purple-blue flowers.

Gareth A new polyanthus raised by John Fielding, a cross between 'Guinivere' and a red 'Cowichan'. It is illustrated in Graham Rice's *Herbaceous Perennials*. The flowers are dark red and the plant has a distinct 'Cowichan' look about it.

Gigha or **Gigha White** A neat white form of *P. vulgaris* from the island of the same name in the inner Hebrides.

Gina (USA) Origin unknown. A late blooming, miniature, jack-in-the-green of *juliae* habit. The pin-eyed flowers, crimson-magenta in colour, are almost eyeless and the foliage is bronze-green with a luminous sheen.

Gloria Described by Genders as 'one of the first *juliae* hybrids'. The flowers are of crimson-scarlet with white markings on the inside edge of the petals.

Gloriosa Similar to 'Wanda' except that it is larger in all respects.

Gracie (USA, Earl Welch hybrid) A cushion form with very light cream flowers. A good parent when trying to breed whites.

The Grail Another of Garryard type with dark crimson foliage and flowers variously described as 'purple-red' or 'tudor brick-red'. It has a large, near-circular yellow eye and is pin-eyed.

Groenekan's Glorie This is the correct spelling for 'Groeneken's Glory', probably raised by Copijn of Groenekan, founded 200 years ago and still going. Mauve-pink blooms with a unique green eye.

Guinivere Usually referred to as 'Garryarde [sic] Guinivere' but more correctly the prefix should be dropped. Almost certainly 'Apple Blossom' was one of the parents, the other unknown. I believe it has some *juliae* blood. A polyanthus primrose with bronze-green foliage and flowers of an unusual shade of pale dusky pink. According to Cecil Monson, 'Guinivere' was raised at Kinlough, County Leitrim, by Mrs Johnson. This is a very popular and common plant and has been micropropagated so is universally available. Some variation in micropropagated plants has been noticed.

Harry Adams Raised by the late Harry Adams at Teignmouth in Devon about 1981, by crossing 'Guinivere' with *P. vulgaris*. It is not known which was the seed parent. It is a vigorous plant of primrose habit with typical *vulgaris* leaves, except for a slight bronze tint inherited from 'Guinivere'. The pin-eyed flowers, with slightly overlapping, crinkled petals are similar in colour to 'Guinivere', a soft pink, with a strongly marked centre with shades of 'egg yolk and pale yellow'. The calyx is purple. The long-lasting flowers emit a delicious scent, tending to fade to almost white if exposed to long periods of sunlight. Illustrated in *The Magic Tree*.

Helge Raised by J. Lintner. Typical *P. juliae* foliage with cream flowers on polyanthus stems, similar in habit to 'Lady Greer'.

Hubert Calvert (New Zealand) A selected gold-laced, dark-ground, polyanthus bred by Dr Keith Hammett, listed by Parva Plants.

Ida (USA) Origin unknown. A cushion form with long slender stems. The colour is similar to *P. juliae*. Miniature foliage with tubular flowers. Another good parent and often crossed with 'Guinivere'.

Interface (New Zealand) A large-flowered laced polyanthus from Dr Keith Hammett's breeding programme. Flowers are nicely formed with even silver lacing, contrasting with deep maroon colour against a contrasting golden eye.

Irish Gem (USA) Origin unknown. A low cushion form with dark foliage and wine-purple flowers. It is not certain that this plant was raised in America.

Irish Green (see **Viridis**) Three different green-flowered primroses were grown in Ireland, one with very pointed petals, another with ordinary rounded petals and a third with a welted calyx. Several forms are still in cultivation both in the UK and North America.

Iris Mainwaring A compact plant with deep green foliage and flowers of a very pale blue, flushed pink.

Jay-Jay (USA, P. Klein) This famous plant was raised from seed labelled '*juliae* x Jack', found amongst several vials of seed left after the death of Peter Klein. 'J. J.' stands for 'Juliae Jack' and is considered to be one of the most reliable and prolific primroses in the Pacific Northwest. It has dark green, crinkled foliage, and the creeping habit of *P. juliae*. The flowers are dark magenta-red, similar to

'Wanda'. 'Jay Jay' arose as a by-product of Peter Klein's double *juliae* hybridizing programme. This is the plant used by Rosetta Jones with such success and the most famous of the American hybrids. An excellent parent.

J-One (USA, P. Klein) From the same vial of seed as 'Jay Jay' arose this sister plant. Although not a jack-in-the-green, nor having so bright a colour, it is a vigorous grower and prolific bloomer.

Jeanne Renshaw (Alaska, circa 1972) A vigorous small-leaved *juliae* hybrid with pinkish flowers and the typical *P. juliae* creeping rootstock. It originated in Juneau, Alaska.

Jewell, Jewel or Juwel (G. Arends) Another small plant with crimson-purple flowers.

Jill A dainty little primrose with deep green crinkled foliage, pin-eyed deep mauve flowers. Genders described the small centre as 'greenish-white' but it appears more yellow in the illustration in Mansfield's book. A plant under this name is grown in New Zealand, described as having 'deep violet flowers with gold eyes'.

Katy McSparron Raised by Geoff Nicolle and named after his granddaughter. A magnificent cowslip with well-shaped, fully double, rich yellow flowers. It has been tissue-cultured and may be introduced commercially in 1998.

Kay (USA) Described as a very small, charming, juliana with dark, clear blue flowers.

Kinlough Beauty A miniature polyanthus, otherwise of *juliae* habit. This is one of the most distinctive and popular of the *juliae* hybrids with easily recognizable flowers, thrum-eyed, salmon-pink, with a cream stripe down each petal. It was found growing in her garden by Mrs Johnson, in Kinlough, County Leitrim. I have seen several plants where the striping was missing or very faint. Possibly they were seedlings as the true plant has distinct stripes. It has been incorrectly distributed, by a famous English alpine plant nursery, as 'E. R. Janes'.

Knocklayd Raised by Joe Kennedy, Ballycastle, in 1979 and named after the local mountain. A *juliae* x *vulgaris* hybrid, pin-eyed, of primrose habit with wine-red flowers. The plant has a creeping habit with crinkled, olive-green leaves.

Lacey Lu (USA, Dorothy Springer) A Robert Putnam 'blue silver lace poly x *P. juliae*'. This hybrid has narrow silver lacing on flowers that are an unusual blue-purple. It is of cushion form and multiplies well.

Lady Greer Another plant introduced by Mrs Johnson at Kinlough. With 'Wanda', probably the most abundant *juliae* hybrid of all; a delightful miniature polyanthus with typical *juliae* foliage of bottle-green. Small, fragrant, pale lemon-yellow, funnel-shaped blooms. Readily available as it has been micropropagated. Doubts have been expressed that plants in circulation are true to type.

Lambrook Lilac Raised by that great lover of cottage garden plants Mrs Margery Fish, at Lambrook Manor, Somerset. A lilac-coloured polyanthus primrose.

Lambrook Pink Another from Mrs Fish, a pink-flowered polyanthus primrose.

Lavender Cloud (Canada) Raised by William Goddard, although another source suggests it came from England. It is a medium-sized polyanthus with pale lavender-pink flowers. The foliage is bronze-tinted and the plant appears to have Garryard blood.

Lilac Lady (USA) Superficially resembles *P. vulgaris* subspecies *sibthorpii* but with smaller, star-shaped flower of a lilac shade. May have originated at Rice Creek Gardens in Ohio.

Lillian (USA, Earl Welch hybrid) A stalked primrose with dainty, lavender pink flowers.

Lingwood Beauty Another miniature polyanthus with flowers of rich red. There is another plant under this name described as 'silver-edged'.

Little Gem (USA) Raised by M. B. Stewart of Washington State prior to 1945. It is a late-blooming bright cherry-red, initially of cushion form, but later blooms are on short stalks.

Lois Lutz (USA) Origin unknown. A very nice plant of cushion form with purple flowers.

Lopen Red A plant that was named by Mrs Fish, found growing in a friend's garden, at Lopen in Somerset. The bronze-green foliage suggests Garryard blood and the large blooms are a deep red.

Macwatt's Claret Raised by Dr J. Macwatt, the author of *The Primulas of Europe* and a well-known primrose enthusiast. The plant is another miniature polyanthus of typical *juliae* habit with small dark claret-red blooms.

Macwatt's Cream Another miniature polyanthus with small blooms of pale cream, very similar to Lady Greer. Raised by Dr J. Macwatt.

Mahogany Sunrise (Canada, John Kerridge) A typical gold-laced polyanthus of exhibition type with small 12 mm (½ in) dark ground flowers. Introduced commercially in 1997 via tissue culture.

Margaret Titlow (USA, Dorothy Springer). A dark red 'Cowichan' x *P. juliae*. A compact form of *juliae* habit with dark, eyeless, 'Cowichan'-like flowers. Vigorous grower.

Marilyn O'Brien (Alaska, John O'Brien Snr) Named after Mr O'Brien's wife. Pink flowers with an apricot flush.

Mauve Queen A primrose with pale mauve blooms.

Millicent (USA) Raised by Florence Bellis and named after her daughter. She thought this her best hybrid. Tall dark stems and flowers of a 'crushed strawberry shade'.

Millicent 2 (USA) Origin unknown, although it has been suggested that Ralph Balcom may have raised a plant with this name. Similar to 'Dorothy' in form and colour. Green foliage, with paler flowers having a tinge of lavender on the edges. Said to be a good parent.

Miss Luck Introduced by Veryan Plants of Okehampton Devon. This is a new variety given a Preliminary Commendation by the RHS in March 1996. In appearance it is midway between its parents, 'Guinivere' and 'Lambrook Lilac'.

Miss Massey A legendary old variety raised prior to 1900 by Miss W. F. Wynne at County Wicklow in Eire. Of dwarf habit with bright ruby-red flowers over bright green leaves. Thought to be nearly extinct in 1958 but plants are grown in the National Collections that are said to be this variety.

Mrs McGillivray An early flowering primrose, of compact habit, with purple-pink flowers over a long period.

Mrs Wick (USA, Dorothy Springer 1985, 'Bea' x 'Guinivere') Named after a neighbour Marilyn Wick. A cushion form with long stems and yellow flowers.

Nettie Gale (USA) Introduced by Ella Torpen, a *juliae* hybrid of creeping habit covered by pink-tinted white blossoms in late winter and early spring.

Nora McConnell (Cecil Monson)
Although no description is available, I
understand it is still in cultivation in Ireland.
Raised by Cecil Monson and named after
Mrs McConnell of Shankill, County Dublin.

Old Port This plant was first offered in
Mansfield's catalogue in the 1950s, in more
recent times by a Scottish nursery. Some
confusion has arisen between it and 'Tawny
Port'. The Royal Botanical Garden,
Edinburgh, received a plant in 1945, from Sir
Steven Renshaw of East Wareham, Norfolk.
The main difference is that, whereas 'Tawny
Port' is of polyanthus habit, 'Old Port' is
primrose. The plant has small, bronze-tinted
leaves with dark red flowers, which have a
small yellow eye.

Perle von Bottrop Described by Genders
as a 'super Wanda', an early flowering plant
with large, bright purple-flushed crimson
blooms, almost eyeless.

Pinkie (USA) Probably originating in
Alaska. The colour is described as 'not quite
pink'.

Primrose Lodge (USA) Originating in
Illinois, this is a miniature polyanthus with
purple-crimson flowers and bronze foliage.
Very early flowering. Most plants of this
variety appear to suffer from virus infection.

Purple Splendour A free-flowering plant
with dark foliage and purple blooms.

Putnam (USA, Dorothy Springer) Sister
plant to 'Lady Lu'. A Robert Putnam 'blue
silver laced polyanthus x *P. juliae*'. The colour
is an unusual dark blue-purple without
lacing. A strong compact plant, of cushion
form.

Red Velvet Also introduced by Louise
Vockins, similar comments to 'David

Valentine'.

Roberta (USA, Lou Roberts) An older
variety. Mrs Roberts was an active member
in the early days of the APS. A cushion form
with clear bright lilac flowers, of good
substance. An impostor is being sold under
this name with a tiny red line around the
eye.

Rosalinda (USA, Dr Matthew Riddle) This
is one of the few survivors from the many
plants raised by Dr Riddle. A stalked form
with flowers of a lavender shade.

Romeo A prolific grower in its youth with
very large, flat, vivid mauve flowers. The
plant currently grown may not be the true
form.

Royal Velvet (USA, Dickson 1965) A cross
between a large-flowered 'Pacific' red
polyanthus and *P. juliae*. A larger stalked type
with big, dark velvety-red blooms.

Sea Foam (USA, Dorothy Springer). A
white seedling x 'Snow White'. A cushion
form with round, green foliage and white
flowers.

Show Stopper (USA, Dorothy Springer,
Barnhaven red juliana x 'Jay Jay') A stalked
form with dark bronze ruff and foliage. The
eyeless flowers are of a glowing red. This
variety was Best Plant in Show, Best Julie and
Best Jack-in-the-Green at the 1995 APS
National Show.

Silver Lining (USA, Orpha Salzman)
Introduced by Dorothy Springer this is
'Rosalinda' x 'Snow Maiden' x 'Sibthorpii'. A
stalked form with flowers of a pale silver-lilac
shade. Habit similar to the American form of
'Dorothy'.

Sir Bedivere Raised in Holland prior to
1940. Dark red eyeless flowers are
complemented by the long, cucumber green,

crinkled leaves. Thrum-eyed. Illustrated in Mansfield's book.

Sir Galahad A plant of Garryard type with dark green foliage and blush-white flowers with attractively frilled petals.

Snow Cushion (Arends) Frequently called 'Schneekissen' and described as of Dutch origin. In fact raised by George Arends in Germany in 1931. A small plant with distinctive *juliae* foliage and white pin-eyed flowers.

Snow White A dwarf, early-flowering plant with pure white flowers.

Spring Sunrise (USA, H. Lincoln Foster) A large cushion form with peach-pink flowers. Very cold-hardy. The raiser was a famous American gardener.

Springtime (USA, Fred Borsch) Described as a 'pink *sibthorpii*'. An older variety of cushion form. This plant is often confused with *P. sibthorpii*.

Tawny Port One of the best, a miniature polyanthus introduced by Colonel Graham, Castlesize, Sallins, County Kildare. Received an Award of Merit in 1934, possibly 'Garryard' x *juliae*. The small leaves are bronze-green and the dainty blooms, of deep port wine, have a faint white mark on each petal. Although distinctive it has been confused with 'Wisley Red'. The illustration in *Perennials* (Vol. 1) by Roger Phillips and Martyn Rix, identified as 'Tawny Port', is 'Wisley Red' which is of primrose habit.

Tetchley's Red A plant with this name is in one of the National Collections. It emanates from Abriachan Nurseries in Scotland.

Tipperary Purple A small-flowered, light purple jack-in-the-green presumed to have come from County Tipperary, Ireland.

Tomato Red This is a relatively modern variety that was thought might be 'E. R. Janes'. It was introduced by Lady Anne Palmer of Rosemoor in North Devon who was given the plant by Captain 'Cherry' Collingwood-Ingram. We are fortunate in having two good illustrations in colour of 'E. R. Janes', one in Mansfield and the other in Genders. They show 'E. R. Janes' to be pin-eyed whereas 'Tomato Red' is thrum-eyed. On first introduction it was called 'Tomato' but the name was changed after intervention by the RHS. The colour is near identical to the illustrations of 'E. R. Janes', an unusual shade of orange-red.

Velvet Glow (New Zealand) Another from Dr Hammett introduced by Parva Plants. Described as 'A superb polyanthus of 'Cowichan' type with large scarlet, almost eyeless flowers'.

Velvet Moon (Canada, John Kerridge) John Kerridge has been crossing 'Cowichan' polyanthus for some years and this selected seedling is one of the results. It has very deep red, eyeless flowers 25–50 mm (1–2 in) across, on 200–250 mm (8-10 in) stems. Introduced commercially via tissue culture in 1997.

Victory Another Garryard with bronze crinkled foliage and large purple-red flowers on a polyanthus stem. The plant is thrum-eyed with a medium-sized, yellow centre. Raised by Miss Winnifred Wynne.

Viridis or **Forma *viridiflora*** Druce (see also **Irish Green**) The green-flowered primrose of which several forms exist. A curiosity mainly of botanical interest.

Wanda Probably the best-known and indeed most famous of all *juliae* hybrids. More misinformation has been printed about this plant than any other and it has often been erroneously described as the oldest *juliae* hybrid. In fact 'Wanda' was raised at Bakers Nursery near Wolverhampton circa 1918 and was named after one of the director's wives. Plants in circulation, described as 'Wanda', are frequently other magenta-coloured hybrids, of which there were and are many. The situation has been further confused by the commercial introduction of the so-called 'Wanda hybrids', either as plants or seed strains, bearing no resemblance whatever. A very vigorous, pin-eyed plant, bearing masses of flowers of glaring magenta, that seems to thrive in most situations.

Wanda Hose-in-Hose Almost identical to Wanda apart from the hose-in-hose flowers, one corolla inside the other.

White Swan (USA) Origin unknown. A stalked form with large, clean white flowers with a yellow eye. A *juliae* x polyanthus cross, resembling a miniature polyanthus.

Wilbur Graves (USA, Dorothy Springer, 'White Sakata' seedling x 'Jay-Jay') A jack in the green cushion form, with bronze foliage. Flower colour is a paler 'Guinivere' shade.

William Genders An old variety of polyanthus habit, raised by Roy Genders and named after his father. Described as similar in style to Kinlough Beauty. The colour is violet-pink, candy-striped with white.

Wisley Red This is a very fine variety thought to have originated at the RHS garden at Wisley. Whether it was raised there or discovered growing in the garden is not clear as Wisley have no record. I saw a large patch many years ago, just after the then 'new' rock garden had been completed. It was growing towards the bottom of the hill and the clump was fully 450 mm (18 in)

across. This is a most unusual little primrose with dark 'milk chocolate'-coloured foliage and typical *juliae* habit. The small burgundy-red, almost eyeless flowers are pin-eyed. This plant has been confused with 'Tawny Port' but apart from other dissimilarities is of primrose habit. A 'Wisley Crimson' has also been listed and is, I believe, the same plant. However, I saw plants of 'Tawny Port', growing at the Savill Gardens, Windsor, some years ago, that were labelled 'Wisley Crimson'.

Yellow Dawn (USA) Origin unknown. Another *juliae* x polyanthus cross. A stalked form with large, soft yellow flowers. Similar to 'White Swan' in size and habit.

Yellow Stocking (USA, Dorothy Springer) Tiny green foliage with equally small yellow hose-in-hose flowers.

DOUBLE PRIMROSES

Alba Plena The famous Gerrard's 'double white', said to be centuries old. It is likely that similar plants have carried the name and that the present one dates from the 1800s – extraordinary, even so. A plant of primrose habit with *vulgaris*-type leaves. The pure white flowers are fully double on long thin footstalks, which causes them to trail. In North America known as 'Cottage White'.

Allan Robb A pale orange double raised from Barnhaven seed and freely available due to micropropagation.

April Rose A rich dark pink raised from Barnhaven seed.

Arthur du Moulin An old polyanthus double of a pale lilac shade. Variously described as having been introduced from either Belgium or Ireland at the end of the nineteenth century, although the Irish link is thought unlikely.

Belle Watling Velvety red, another micropropagated plant from Barnhaven seed.

Big Red Giant From the micropropagators, described as having 'large red flowers'.

Blue Sapphire Micropropagated plant described, optimistically, as 'vivid blue'.

Bon Accord Cerise An old variety, raised early this century. A vivid rose, a shade brighter and purer than 'Gem', with thin lacings of white. Scented and free-flowering.

Bon Accord Elegans Originally considered the finest of the Bon Accords with large, circular flowers of phlox-purple, flecked heavily with white and just a trace of yellow in the centre. Of distinct primrose habit.

Bon Accord Gem The most vigorous of the Bon Accords. Huge leaves of cucumber green topped with flowers of a bright rose shade, faintly touched with lilac. Very similar to 'Cerise', which is dwarfer.

Bon Accord Lavender Dauphin's violet (039/3) on the old RHS colour chart. A distinct orange and yellow star surrounding the centre with faint white edges to the petals.

Bon Accord Lilac A light shade of rosy-lilac, a brighter colour than the double lilac.

Bon Accord Purple Described as 'velvety imperial' made more distinct by a definite shade of blue on the reverse of the petals. Of true polyanthus type and considered one of the more difficult.

Buttercup (New Zealand) From Barnhaven seed offered by Bay Bloom Nurseries, golden yellow flowers.

Captain Blood Another Barnhaven seedling of a blood-red shade.

Charlotte (New Zealand) From Bay Bloom, a double 'glowing magenta'.

Chevithorne Pink A polyanthus type with shaggy, orchid-pink blooms, very free-flowering. Raised by Mrs Elison Spence, Stewartstown, County Tyrone around 1950 and passed to Mrs Emmerson who named it, to Mrs Spence's displeasure. Considered one of the easier of the older doubles. It is illustrated in colour in Genders' *Primroses*. Not related in any way to the probably extinct 'Chevithorne Purple'.

Chocolate Soldier Unusual colouring of chocolate purple with a slight gold edge.

Claret New Zealand, from Bay Bloom 'double rich claret red'.

Corporal Baxter Scarlet, shading to crimson, another from Barnhaven seed.

Cream Princess (New Zealand) Another Barnhaven from Bay Bloom, 'vigorous double cream'.

Crimson Beauty Of New Zealand origin introduced by Hopley's Nursery. Described as 'low growing, with compact dark green foliage and deep red flowers'.

Dawn Ansell This is a beautiful large-flowered white jack-in-the green primrose raised from seed of Dr Cecil Jones of Llanelli, the most prominent UK hybridizer of doubles. It has been micropropagated and is widely distributed wherever primroses grow. This is one of the finest of all modern doubles.

Double Sulphur This name covers a number of plants and often means double forms of *P. vulgaris* found growing wild.

Easter Bonnet A lavender colour, a lighter shade than 'Quaker's Bonnet'.

Elizabeth Dickey A sport of the wild

single primrose with double yellow flowers. Discovered circa 1930 outside Ballymoney, County Antrim by a young girl whose mother, noticing it was double, dug up the plant. It was given to Dr Molly Sanderson who named it for mother and daughter, both having the same name. Introduced commercially by David Chalmers of Stonehaven in the 1970s.

Emily (New Zealand) Another Barnhaven described as having flowers of 'old fashioned pink'.

Ethel M. Dell Another Barnhaven, dusty rose-pink.

Eugenie From the micropropagators, 'vivid blue'.

Fife Yellow Said to have originated in Fife, Scotland, a yellow-flowered double whose blooms darken with age. Illustrated in Phillips and Rix.

Freckles Another micropropagated double, possibly from Rosetta Jones seed. Dark red flecked white.

Glenshesk A *vulgaris*-type primrose with double, sapphire-blue flowers flecked with white on both the petals and petal margins. Raised by Joe Kennedy in 1978 from a single-flowered Barnhaven seedling and named for one of the nine glens of Antrim. A colour illustration appeared in *Garden News*, 25 June 1988.

Granny Graham Violet Blue, of Barnhaven breeding.

Jubilee Another Hopley's plant, free-flowering in shades of pink, purple and mauve.

Ken Dearman Another Barnhaven with pretty flowers in shades of orange, red, yellow and copper.

Lavender Plum (New Zealand) Described

as an old variety with large well-formed flowers of a deep lilac colour, somewhere between lavender and plum.

Lilacena Plena The companion plant to *alba plena*, more commonly known as the 'double lilac' or 'Quaker's Bonnet'. Similar in habit to the double white except for the pale lilac colour of the blooms. Once again claims have been made that it is centuries old but this is debatable.

Lilian Harvey Another Barnhaven with bright cerise-pink flowers and a yellow centre.

Lynleys Choice (New Zealand) Selected from Barnhaven seed, a free-flowering yellow.

Madame Pompadour A very famous old double described as bearing 'large double blooms of deep velvety crimson'. This plant, one of the most written-about of all doubles, was listed by Genders who said it originated about 1800 in France and was also known as 'Pompadour' and 'Crimson Velvet'. I believe the true plant no longer exists and has not done so for many years. A plant under this name was listed by a nursery in the early 1990s.

Marianne Davey Again probably from Barnhaven seed with shapely cream flowers.

Marie Crousse Although this variety was described in unflattering terms by Sacheverell Sitwell, it is a famous double given an Award of Merit in 1882. Two distinct clones were grown in the 1950s, one of a lilac-purple colour, heavily flecked with white, while the other was of a reddish-mauve colour with silver lacings and spots to each petal. Major Taylor grew the last form mentioned and was convinced it was not the Award of Merit plant. Flowers borne on long pedicels on very short polyanthus stems.

Mark Viette USA, from the André Viette nursery. A full carnation-like double with deep rose blooms on short polyanthus stems. A very floriferous, hardy and fragrant plant raised some years ago from Barnhaven seed.

Miss Indigo One of the most distinctive and best of the named Barnhaven seedlings. A dark bluish-purple with silver-laced petals. Very free-flowering.

Old Irish Sulphur A *vulgaris*-type primrose-yellow double, origin unknown but likely to be a sport of the wild primrose.

Old Rose (New Zealand) A double rose-pink from Bay Bloom.

Old Scottish Red The original clone, called 'Crimson King' was introduced by the Daisy Hill Nursery, Newry, County Down, in 1897. It was *vulgaris* type with bright, rosy-crimson double flowers. It is doubtful if the current plant is true.

Olive Wyatt Another Barnhaven with dark cerise-pink flowers.

Our Pat Discovered in the 1930s growing amongst a batch of *P. juliae* (or 'Wanda') at the Daisy Hill Nurseries, Newry, Northern Ireland, and named after the owner's daughter. It is a small-flowered *vulgaris* type, sapphire-blue double, and the bronze-tinted foliage shows the *juliae* influence

Penlan Cream Raised by Dr Jones in 1959 and sent to William Chalmers. It was still listed in 1991 although scarce and expensive. In a letter to Dr Jones in 1995 David Chalmers said he no longer had 'Penlan Cream' and knew of no other source.

Petticoat A *vulgaris*-type plant with white flowers. On the plants I have seen the flowers are not fully double. Freely available as it has been micropropagated.

Prince Silverwings A very famous polyanthus-type primrose originating at the Daisy Hill Nursery. The flowers are mulberry-coloured, each petal edged with white and having a conspicuous orange blotch at its base. Double, semi-double and single flowers may be produced. A well-known source of pollen and extensively used for hybridizing. Mrs Emmerson noted that open-pollinated seed often produced seedlings very similar to the parent.

Quaker's Bonnet See *Lilacena Plena*

Red Paddy ('Paddy', 'Irish Paddy', 'Crimson Paddy', *Sanguinea Plena*, or *Rubra Plena*) A number of very similar plants are listed under these names and *may* be the same or very similar clones. It was offered as 'Paddy' by the Daisy Hill Nursery in 1897. The usual description is of a plant with both *acaulis* and polyanthus flowers, of crimson purple with a white or silver edge to the petals.

Red Velvet A Hopley's variety with red flowers and bright green leaves and a red margin.

Regale (New Zealand) Bay Bloom a 'double rich mauve'.

Rhapsody Another free-flowering plant from Hopley's with mid-blue flowers.

Rose or Rosie O'Day A light rose-red shade.

Roy Cope Another Barnhaven seedling, a good vigorous red.

Sue Jervis This dull pink-coloured primrose is said to have been found growing wild in Shropshire. Some scepticism has been expressed as only yellow and white-flowered doubles have previously been reported growing wild. It was introduced by Bressingham Nurseries and is widely distributed. Apart from the colour the habit is remarkably like the double white which suggests a wild origin.

Sunshine Susie One of the best of the named Barnhaven seedlings, with masses of bright yellow flowers.

Torchlight A Hopley double with pale lemon-yellow flowers. RHS Award of Merit.

Tyrian Purple Another plant listed commercially in recent years thought extinct. Originally described as 'a superb variety, having a bloom the size of a florin. Vivid bluish-mauve colour with a trace of yellow in the centre.'

Val Horncastle A Barnhaven seedling with attractive flowers of a pale primrose yellow.

Victoria (New Zealand) Bay Bloom 'double powder blue'.

Winter White (New Zealand) Bay Bloom 'glistening pure white'.

6 THE GOLD-LACED POLYANTHUS

The laced polyanthus, unique amongst the primrose family, was one of the special flowers cultivated and exhibited by the English florists at early flowers shows – known as feasts – from the mid-eighteenth century. It should be noted that these plants were always referred to as 'polyanthus'. The term 'gold-laced' was not commonly used until the latter half of the nineteenth century, when the need arose to differentiate them from the developing garden polyanthus.

Gold-laced were most popular in the first half of the nineteenth century; this popularity declined and they were then less widely grown. Nevertheless, gold-laced were still grown in some numbers, especially by members of the National Auricula and Primula Society northern section, formed in 1873. The northern section developed from the Middleton Amateur Florists Society who held their 56th Annual Show at the Mason's Arms, Middleton, in 1872. At this event it was decided to reform the National Auricula Society, and the following year the first show was held in Manchester. A few years later, in 1876, the southern section was formed and

here again many members grew the plant. The midland section, not formed until 1900, made little contribution until the 1960s.

Countrywide at the height of the laced polyanthus's popularity, growing tended to be more concentrated. This was primarily in those parts of the North of England – around Middleton, Rochdale and Halifax – where the laced polyanthus had originated. Sacheverell Sitwell also mentions Falkirk in Scotland as a centre of activity. Nevertheless, John Barlow, a member of the southern section of the NAPS, writing in the 1976 *Centenary Yearbook* of the society, stated that the gold-laced polyanthus still enjoyed considerable popularity, throughout Great Britain and Eire, during the last quarter of the nineteenth century. Classes were provided at many horticultural and provincial auricula society shows. The decline of the gold-laced polyanthus during the late nineteenth century has been overstated in previous accounts, based mainly on the drop in numbers of plants exhibited. The *Gardeners Chronicle*, 27 December 1884, has the comment:

'The numerous enquiries that are being made about these seems to show that they are being grown much more numerously than is supposed. A few years ago it was almost feared that fine old named sorts were altogether lost, but here and there a grower in a quiet way held a collection, and time has enabled some sorts that were scarce to become numerous.'

The first really serious decline in numbers was caused by the First World War (1914–18). The report of the 37th Annual Show of the northern section of the NAPS, held in 1910, states that polyanthus were shown in great numbers, many of them seedlings. It does go on to say 'they do not satisfy a polyanthus lover's ideal; there were better varieties 30 years ago, and Mrs Brownhill was still the best flower of all.'

In 1913 the 40th Annual Exhibition had around 150 gold-laced, a considerable number never attained in recent years. It would appear though that many of the old varieties were scarce or had already disappeared, a source of much concern to the society.

The First World War had a catastrophic effect on the growing of laced polyanthus, as it did on the growing of its companion plant, the auricula. This was followed throughout the 1920s and 1930s by disastrous economic conditions; only brought to an end by the Second World War (1939–45). Unfortunately, the effects of the war further weakened the laced polyanthus. Nevertheless, it remained in cultivation, if scarce, and the story – given wide credence – that gold-laced died out in the UK and were reintroduced from America is untrue. The supposed demise of the laced polyanthus was based largely on the number of plants exhibited, but this told only part of the story. Later in this chapter I hope to persuade the doubters that the gold-laced remained alive and well, albeit tenuously, during the period of its supposed disappearance.

The laced polyanthus gradually developed from the ordinary polyanthus during the eighteenth century. The first polyanthus appeared in the early part of the seventeenth century. It was a hybrid plant, almost certainly the progeny of red-flowered cultivated forms of *P. veris*, the cowslip, and *P. vulgaris,* the primrose. The hybrid has been referred to as *P.* x *variabilis* but is more correctly called *P.* x *tommasinii.*

The early history of the laced polyanthus remains obscure but illustrations from the beginning of the eighteenth century indicate lacing was starting to appear. The second volume of the florilegium made for the Duchess of Beaufort at Badminton, in about 1710, has drawings depicting early forms of laced polyanthus. Joseph Bobart the younger sent to Badminton a silver-laced primula described as '*Primula veris limbis argentis*' and may also have sent the red polyanthus depicted in the first volume of the florilegium. In 1730 James Furber published what is generally considered to be the first illustrated nurseryman's catalogue. In it is depicted a laced red-ground polyanthus, rather surprisingly of hose-in-hose form, called 'Goldfinch'.

By the 1750s plants were being exhibited at florists' feasts, usually combined with auricula displays. It is not clear how fully lacing had developed but it certainly had developed by the 1780s. Full descriptions of the properties that should be present in a prize-winning plant, notably in a broadsheet discovered by the late Ruth Duthie, a historian of florists' flowers, were published by the Leicester Florist Society to assist judges in awarding prizes for the best carnation, auricula and polyanthus. The broadsheet was not dated but Ruth Duthie's researches indicated it was published in the early 1780s. During this decade the first illustrations of good-quality named varieties appeared.

Although its companion plant the auricula was widely grown on the Continent, this was never the case with the laced polyanthus. In the three volumes of Dr Trew's *Hortus* (1750–86) only one polyanthus is illustrated and this is purple with a silver edge, described as 'Auricula IV'. Most other French books from this period have none, the exception being P. Bessa's *Herbier général* of 1822, which shows three polyanthus, all with a suggestion of lacing. Ruth Duthie believed that the name polyanthus may not even have been in use in Germany at the time, as J. Kratz refers in 1861 to the polyanthus as '*P.elatior...*engl.Polyanthus'.

As stated, the heyday of the laced polyanthus was in the first half of the nineteenth century, when the florist movement was at its peak. The florists included both professionals and amateurs, rich and humble, including the famed weavers and miners of gardening folklore. At this time the florist movement had a very wide following amongst industrial workers, especially those living in Lancashire and the North and parts of Scotland.

During this period a very large number of varieties were raised, indeed the Rev William Hanbury, in his two volume work, *A*

Complete Body of Planting and Gardening(1770/71) wrote that he grew in his garden at Church Langton, Leicestershire, more than a thousand varieties! Hanbury gives one of the earliest accounts of what he called 'Shed or Prize Flowers', devoting a complete section to these plants, including the polyanthus and auricula. He describes the numerous florists feasts 'regularly held at towns, at proper distance, almost all over England'. Not all featured polyanthus; they were regularly exhibited at auricula feasts although the winning polyanthus was always accorded prizes of lesser value than those given to the auriculas. The involvement of weavers and other artisans features heavily in the literature of the nineteenth century but Hanbury was the first to record their involvement at this earlier date.

Alice Coats tells us that even before Hanbury, in 1760, Philip Miller wrote that 'the plant was much improved' and in some parts of England 'so much esteemed as to sell for a guinea a root'. One could hardly imagine many industrial workers or weavers, earning a few shillings a week, paying these prices – this indicates once again that the gold-laced polyanthus was a plant grown by the affluent. Many of these gentlemen would have employed gardeners to cultivate the plants although exhibiting them under their own names.

In Scotland James Justice of Dalkeith, a famous florist who was said to have the finest collection of auriculas and polyanthus in Europe, wrote in 1759 that 'the varieties (of the polyanthus) which are obtained each year by the florists… are very great.'

Abercrombie recorded, in 1778, that the laced polyanthus was 'one of the noted prize flowers among florists, many of whom are remarkably industrious in raising a considerable number of different sorts'.

In 1792 James Maddock, a native of Lancashire, then living at Walworth, London, published his *Florists' Directory*. Maddock was a noted florist in Warrington before moving to London, where his nursery offered an enormous range of florists' flowers. In it he lists eight flowers he considered worthy of the florists' attention, one of which was the polyanthus, which he describes in great detail. Maddock indicated that lacing, described as 'yellow' as it usually was by the early writers, had improved dramatically in the previous 50 years. He listed no varieties but refers readers to his annual catalogues for the names, colours and prices of the plants described.

During this period many annual florists' feasts were held throughout Great Britain. In the County of Kent for example, a long way from Lancashire, a large number took place, many solely for polyanthus, between 1766 and 1805 and continued some years thereafter.

By the early 1800s the gold-laced polyanthus had become a major craze, with a fanatical following. The quality had improved dramatically and the utmost care and attention was lavished on the flower. Old florists' magazines carry many articles, giving comprehensive details on cultivation and other aspects of growing and exhibiting.

Thomas Hogg, a nurseryman of Paddington Green in London, wrote his famous *Treatise on the Growth and Culture of the Auricula and Polyanthus etc* in 1812. This was followed by a supplement some years later with revisions. In his book Hogg listed

46 varieties of polyanthus 'of different tints and shades'. He describes the ground colours as being 'bright red or scarlet, a very dark crimson, and chocolate with brimstone or yellow-coloured eyes, and the edging of the same'. He then wrote: 'Its two most prevailing colours are a very dark reddish brown, and a bright red, of a crimson hue, edged with yellow of an orange or pale lemon colour. Some of the polyanthus so resemble each other, that if the tallies be removed, it is difficult for a common observer to distinguish them again.' Hogg also complains about 'dealers' sending out wrongly named plants.

A little book called *The Polyanthus,* published in 1844, gave a list of choice polyanthuses presumed to be still grown at the time. This list was printed in Sitwell's '*Old Fashioned Flowers*'.

There are 96 varieties with names that are typical of the time. Many plants are named after royalty or 'persons of consequence', while others have a martial ring. Several varieties appeared in the list – if still then extant (and Sitwell expressed a slight reservation on this point) – that were almost 100 years old. 'Duke of Wellington', 'Buck's George the Fourth', 'Black Prince' and 'Barnard's Formosa' are examples, with others dating from the Regency era – for example, 'Nicholson's Bang Europe'. Lists of these and many others were published regularly until the mid-1850s, when the craze began to abate.

The longevity of these early gold-laced cultivars is something that is often quoted by enthusiasts bemoaning the short life-span of present-day seedlings. This is another myth that was disposed of by John Barlow in the article previously mentioned. John identified nearly 300 named plants and only 69 of these appeared on the show benches over a period of ten years or more. Fourteen exceeded 20 years with a further 17 between 30 and 40. A mere five lasted 50 years and a solitary variety more than 60. Even so it has been rare for a seedling to last longer than five or six years during the last 50 years. As a result few plants have been named and no named cultivars established.

By the mid-1800s the standards that apply more or less unchanged today had been confirmed. The following extract, from *The Gardener and Practical Florist* (1843), was provided by David Hadfield, secretary of the NAPS (northern section) and is given in full:

> *The flower of the gold laced polyanthus like that of the auricula is formed of one petal only, but being divide at the edge, it appears like five or six petals.*

OF THE PIP

> *The single pip or flower should be perfectly flat and round, and be slightly scalloped on the edge, and three quarters of an inch in diameter.*

> *It should be divided in six places, forming six apparent flower leaves, each of which should be indented in the centre to make a kind of heart-shaped end; but the divisions must not reach the yellow eye.*

> *The indentures in the apparent flower leaves should be exactly the same depth as the indentures formed by these flower leaves, so that it should be known, by the form of the flower, which is the indenture; in other words, which is the centre and which is the side of the flower leaf, and all the indentures should be as slight as possible to preserve the character.*

> *The tube should be one fifth the whole width of the flower, and stand up at the edge, above the surface of the yellow eye.*

> *The flower should be divided thus – the yellow tube in the centre being measured, the yellow eye round the tube, should be the same width as its diameter, and the ground colour of the flower should be the same: or draw with the compasses, open one sixteenth apart, a circle for the tube or centre; open them to three sixteenths, and draw another circle for the eye, then open them to five sixteenths and draw a circle for the ground or dark colour.* ★ *beyond this circle there is a yellow lacing, which should reach round every flower leaf of the yellow eye, and down the centre of every petal to the eye, and so much like the edging that the flower should appear to have twelve similar petals. The end of these twelve should be blunted, and rounded like so many semi-circles, so that the outline of the circle should be interrupted as little as possible.*

> *The tube should be nearly filled up with six anthers, which are technically called the thrum, and the flower should not exhibit the pistil.* ★★

The edging round and down the centre of the leaves formed by the divisions, should be of even width all the way, and universally of the same shade of sulphur, lemon or yellow, as the eye, and there must be by no means two shades of yellow in the eye.

The ground colours should be just what anybody likes the best, but clear, well defined, perfectly smooth at the edge inside next to the eye, to form a circle; and outside: next to the lacing: a black or crimson ground, being scarce, is desirable; but the quality of the colour as to clearness, rather than the colour itself, constitutes the property.

OF THE PLANT

The stem should be strong, straight, elastic, and from four to six inches in length; the footstalks of the flowers should be of such length as to bring all the flowers well together; the truss should comprise seven or more flowers, and be neatly arranged to be seen all at once. The foliage should be short, broad, thick and cover the pot well.

OF THE PAIR OR COLLECTION

The pair or pan or more should comprise flowers of different and distinct colours, either the ground colour or the yellow of each being sufficiently different from the rest to be well distinguished. The whole should be so near the height as to range the blooms well together.

★This measure is for a flower only five-eighths of an inch in diameter, but it is the easiest to explain the proportions.

★★ Some Polyanthuses show the pistil only, and are called pin-eyed; they are considered useless.

Present-day rules have been somewhat simplified. It is interesting to see the comment about ground colour 'what anybody likes best'. As with the auricula, present-day ground colours are very restricted. In the polyanthus they are basically a very dark red that appears near-black, brown or dark chocolate and a lighter shade of red. Sitwell remarks that a great many of the early varieties were crimson, cherry-red, or pink 'as to their ground or body colour'.

Lancashire and Cheshire and parts of Scotland continued as centres of polyanthus growing in the early nineteenth century. Locally raised varieties like Buck's 'Marquis of Anglesey' and Nicholson's 'Bang Europe' commanded in 1836 prices of £1 a plant.

In the first volume of *The Florist* for 1848 is a report on the 33rd meeting of the Middleton Amateur Florists, held on 24 April at the Mason's Arms in Market Place. Winning plants included Maude's 'Beauty of England' (J. Heap), Pearson's 'Alexander' (Robert Lancashire) and Moore's 'Freedom' (J. Buckley). Buckley was a relative of the famous Fred Buckley of Macclesfield who grew the old English strain of gold-laced more than 100 years later. As was the custom, the raiser's name preceded that of the plant.

Among other varieties shown were Gibbon's 'Royal Sovereign', Hufton's 'Lord Lincoln' and Clegg's 'Lord John Russell'. The

Fig. 5. *Gold-laced Polyanthus* 'Cheshire Favourite'

comment was made that 'polyanthus were rather on the wane… [but] exhibition better than for several years past.'

In the same issue is a report on the Handsworth and Lozells Floral and Horticultural Society's show on 25 April, a predecessor of the NAPS midland section. The exhibitors were mainly nurserymen with Mayle & Co and Pope & Sons; winning most of the polyanthus classes. The Premier was 'Beauty of England', described as a 'dark ground', with 'Alexander' and 'Buck's George IV' 1st and 2nd in the single dark-ground class, all three shown by Messrs Mayle & Co. In the amateur class a J. Willmore was awarded Premier with 'George IV'.

In 1834 the famous illustration of Barnard's 'Formosa' appeared in J. Harrison's *Floricultural Cabinet*. This, from an engraving, showed a flower that more or less equates to current standards although the lacing is rather thinner and the pip somewhat larger than present-day varieties. We cannot be certain of course how much artistic license was used in drawing the plant. In those days the current vogue of 'warts and all' did not apply and photographs were still in the future.

By the 1860s a decline set in, with a great reduction in the number of spring-held shows. This affected all florists' flowers, some like the hyacinth and ranunculus disappearing from the florists' scene never to return. Nevertheless, it was not until 1861 that George Glenny, a well-known writer and powerful influence, published *The Culture of Flowers and Plants*. Glenny, a formidable individual, laid down his 'rules' which included a strict code of properties that the laced polyanthus should possess.

Even so, from then onwards the popularity of the laced polyanthus and other florists' flowers, declined as the lobby against 'artificial flowers', led by William Robinson, gained strength.

On 24 April 1877 the newly formed southern section of the NAPS held its first show at the Crystal Palace. Three classes for polyanthus were included but surprisingly competitors were not restricted to gold-laced varieties. Quality was considered very indifferent with 'many plants quite unworthy of being exhibited'. A plant of Smith's 'Duke of Wellington' gained a certificate for a Mr G. Smith.

By 1878 the classes had been revised, including one for six plants and until about 1890 the polyanthus was quite well supported. Well-known florists like Richard Dean, James Douglas Snr and Sam Barlow were the principal exhibitors. Dean and Douglas were both southern nurserymen while Barlow, a founder member of the northern section of the NAPS, was a prosperous businessman from Castleton, Lancashire. 'Cheshire Favourite' was one of the most successful varieties, while other winners included 'Duke of Portland', 'Earl of Lincoln', 'George IV' and 'Prince Regent'. In 1881 Sam Barlow was awarded First Class Certificates for 'Criterion' and 'John Bright'; his first-prize entry in the six-plant class included five varieties of his own raising. Barlow, one of the most famous florists, was consistently the most successful exhibitor during this period, his main challenger being James Douglas.

After 1885 things deteriorated and plants shown were mostly seedlings of 'poor quality'. By 1896 the six-plant class had gone and any improvement in the following few years proved fleeting. Some of the last named varieties to feature were 'George IV', 'Lancashire Hero', 'Middleton Favourite' and the famous 'Tiny'. After 1906 the southern section had no classes for gold-laced polyanthus for 23 years.

The northern section continued to lead the fight and the 1913 show had 150 laced polyanthus on the benches. A league table of the best varieties voted by the members for black grounds was: 'Mrs Brownhill', 'Tiny' and 'Exile' – first, second and third respectively. For red grounds it was: 'George IV', 'Nellie', 'Middleton Favourite' and 'King Alphonso' – first, second, third and fourth respectively. The comment was made that 'The gold-laced polyanthus were *as usual* [authors italics] past their best.' Mr Norman Brownhill won a cup for the best plant, a seedling that he named 'Mrs John Tonge'. A photograph appeared in the 1913 report and illustrates a plant unlikely to win an award today.

By 1921 things were dire, and G. D. A. Hall of Stockport, a keen gold-laced enthusiast, writing in *The Garden* of 5 March, states that 'In the Midlands and South to-day scarcely a plant of quality is to be found. It is only in the North that the flower can be seen each spring, and then only in a few gardens.' Southern growers were exhorted to make 'one more effort' with choice varieties and a 'novel' method of cultivation was suggested. This was to plant them in drills about 3 inches (75 mm) deep running east and west.

The current secretary of the northern section was John Tonge and Hall asked readers to send Mr Tonge a shilling, which would bring in return a list of names and addresses of all northern growers of gold-laced polyanthus, show auriculas and Alpine auriculas. An appeal was made to anyone knowing the existence of 'genuine old varieties' to let Tonge know the location. Hall went on to say 'the following ancient sorts are still to be found in the Manchester district: – "Sir Sidney Smith", "George IV", "Nicholson's King", "Exile".' Finally he named 'a few' of the lost varieties including 'Pearsons Alexander', 'Cheshire Favourite' and 'Beauty of England'.

This article smacked of desperation and indicated the problems that would persist during the next 40 years. Even so, in 1925, 53 mostly named plants were exhibited with 'Beeswing' Premier, and famous florists like William Grindrod and George Lord appear on the list of winners. The northern society continued to maintain a section, with eight classes for gold-laced polyanthus, supported by a small number of enthusiasts. Two in particular were James Antrobus of Wilmslow, and Tom Lovesay who was gardener to Colonel T. M. Brooks of Tarvin Hall, Tarvin, Cheshire. As war approached, these two are increasingly listed as the main winners and sometimes only exhibitors. Prior to 1940 T. M. Brooks is usually shown as the exhibitor and prizewinner but it was Tom Lovesay who was responsible. Brooks won the Gold-laced Polyanthus Cup 12 times between 1926 and 1938. His only failure was 1930, when the well-known grower Sam Etherington was successful. Even in the South C. J. Howlett and Richard Staward continued to show plants, although – as the yearbooks did not record varieties – we don't know whether they were named cultivars or seedlings. I stress once again that we are talking about exhibitors. It seems certain that an unspecified number of others, who did not exhibit, were growing gold-laced.

The northern show for 1939, slightly more than four months prior to the outbreak of the Second World War, had 40 gold-laced on the benches. 'Tiny', shown by Antrobus was Premier and other named varieties were 'Bonny Bess',' Dark Hillock', 'Dark Warrior', 'Beeswing', 'Danesfield', 'Wendy', and 'Alsace'. Captain G. L. Hearn, a prominent southern grower from Stevenage was first for 'three dark grounds' with 'Bonny Bess', 'Tiny' and 'Dark Hillock'. The only comment in the subsequent yearbook is that James Antrobus had won both the cup and Premier for polyanthus.

The first northern show after the end of the war was on 4 May 1946. Three exhibitors are listed: T. Lovesay, J. Antrobus and Captain Hearn! No names are given for the winning plants.

Tom Lovesay had now retired and was exhibiting under his own name, winning the cup every year from 1946–9. Antrobus followed him in 1950/51 and 52, his final cup success in 1955. Both these growers were now advanced in years. Tom Lovesay died in the 1950s, followed in 1961 by James Antrobus. They were true florists and a great debt is owed to them by their present-day successors.

Dan Bamford, of Middleton, a well-known northern florist, much revered in America, said that 'during the first war, many varieties disappeared, but during the last war there was wholesale disappearance.' It seems that possibly only three named varieties survived: 'Tiny', 'Beeswing and 'Daresfield'.

Bamford himself maintained a large stock of 'Tiny' until about 1956 – although he did not exhibit – when they were lost due to gale damage.

I now come to the controversial subject of the gold-laced's 'resurrection'. The story of how the laced polyanthus came to America and was then 'returned' to Britain has had wide publicity. It was said that R. H. Briggs, secretary of the northern section, sent practically the last remnants of gold-laced seed to Florence Levy (Florence Bellis) of Barnhaven who immediately began a hybridizing programme. Peter Klein of Tacoma, Washington State, obtained seed or plants from Barnhaven and began his own crosses. From these beginnings a fine strain was developed and seed supplied to a prominent southern grower, Dr E. Lester Smith. Dr Lester Smith had previously tried to obtain seed or plants from the North without success. Incidentally, Lester Smith also obtained seed from Dr F. Jordan in the USA, but it produced silver-laced flowers, frowned upon by the more orthodox of the older English florists.

Where did R. H. Briggs get the seed he sent to Barnhaven? The story has been told that it came from a garden (or nursery) bombed out during the war. The remaining few fragments were gathered up by the owner and given to Mr Briggs. The grower in question was James Antrobus and it is true that most of his plants were lost 'when a shell burst near his home'. I presume, if it was a shell rather than a bomb, this must have been an anti-aircraft shell that misfired. The source of the 'shell' story is Thomas Meek, then editor of the northern yearbook. In the obituary he wrote in 1961, Meek attributed the survival of the gold-laced to Antrobus and Tom Lovesay. He said that Antrobus 'still kept exhibiting Alpines and gold-laced polyanthus of his own raising' and this continued for some years after the end of the Second World War. The show results bear this out. Another comment was that 'Both he and Mr Lovesay were very generous with seed and plants to any interested beginner.'

Were there any other sources of gold-laced polyanthus remaining in the UK? Fred Buckley of Macclesfield, a famous auricula grower and the last in a long line of florists, maintained an unadulterated stock of the old English strain well into the 1960s. The late Dr D. A. Duthie knew him well in the latter stages of his life and was quite certain that his plants were the genuine article. Not long before he died Buckley threw out his gold-laced plants but fortunately Dr Duthie, who happened to visit him soon afterwards, hurriedly rescued them from the compost heap! Another well-known northern enthusiast, John Ollerenshaw, obtained some gold-laced in the 1960s from a close neighbour, who had been growing them in his garden since before the war. The neighbour had once been a member of the society but had dropped out.

In the South Richard Stanard of Ware wrote, in the 1946 southern annual report that 'I still have a strain of gold-laced… from a named collection sixty years ago… [and] keep these by selection and raising young plants.' Stanard was a prominent exhibitor between the wars as was Captain Hearn, who certainly still had 'Tiny' in the early 1950s and possibly later.

And so it goes on. Some years ago, when the controversy was at its height, David

Hadfield, who has been secretary of the northern section for over 20 years, carried out his own investigation. He discovered that many more people grew gold-laced than was apparent from the show results. A similar comment was made by Phillip Green, the midland section secretary at the time, and husband of Ethne Green, a prominent midland grower of gold-laced polyanthus. This remains the case today with many people growing gold-laced who never exhibit. I came across an example myself when asked to dispose of the plants of a deceased member, who had not exhibited, of the midland and west section of the NAPS. To my surprise there were a good number of gold-laced polyanthus, many of an excellent standard.

The purpose of the above has not been to denigrate the efforts of Barnhaven who have certainly done a great deal to increase the popularity of laced polyanthus. The Barnhaven plants can be summed up as a modern strain developed in America that stems from the old English strain. A comment to me about the Barnhaven strain, by an experienced grower, is that they are different to those that remained in the UK, and the lacing lacked the refinement of the homebred article. Most hybridizers of the present and recent past have crossed Barnhaven plants with their existing strains. As a result there is no disputing the majority of current plants have some Barnhaven blood. The lineage of strains offered by other seed merchants is unknown.

Following the end of the Second World War the three sections of the NAPS slowly recovered. A much reduced schedule of classes was introduced by the northern section with the midland and southern lagging behind. By 1958 Sir Robert Ewbank, in the North, and Dr Lester Smith in the South were showing a few plants raised from Peter Klein's seed. At the same northern show Fred Buckley exhibited plants from the old English strain and he shared the gold-laced polyanthus cup with Sir Robert Ewbank.

Since then many other enthusiasts have contributed to the gold-laced story. They included, in the 1960s, W. Lambert Smith of Sheffield, Mrs Ethne Green of Balsall Common, near Coventry, and Dr D. A. Duthie of Newcastle-under-Lyme. In the South the most notable growers were Dr Lester Smith and Mr W. Warriner who began exhibiting in 1960. Mr Warriner, American-born who later became a naturalized British citizen, was the most prominent southern grower for some years and a plant from his seed, raised by John Barlow, was named 'Warriner's Wonder', surviving for several years before finally expiring in 1978.

In more recent times we have had raisers like Dr Cecil Jones of Llanelli, the late Bernard Smith and Lawrence Wigley in the South. In the North the most prominent raisers have been John Ollerenshaw, Hubert Calvert and Les Kaye. Derek Salt, formerly of Donnington Plants, also made a contribution with his 'Oaklea' strain. Now some younger growers like Terry Mitchell, who lived close to Hubert Calvert, have taken up the challenge. Terry has begun by crossing Kaye plants with some 'Penningtons', given him by Hubert Calvert.

In the Midlands the contribution of Ethne Green has been mentioned while Gwen Baker also made a significant impact

for a few years. Ethne Green won the northern cup in both 1971 and 1972, with Gwen winning in 1978. Gwen, who lives at Wolverhampton, was easily the most successful midland exhibitor between 1976 and 1981, although she has not exhibited gold-laced in recent years.

In America Peter Klein made great strides in a short time but his death in 1958 brought this to an end. Other growers like Dr Fred Jordan, John Zanini, Agnes Johnson, and Cyrus Happy also contributed to the gold-laced story. Agnes Johnson had obtained 'Tiny' some time in the 1930s. Her gold-laced and those of Dr Jordan were being grown in America before Florence Bellis received seed from R. H. Briggs. Possibly remnants of these strains survive and have been used by other American hybridizers. Nevertheless, Barnhaven's contribution to the modern strains and the resurgence of the gold-laced polyanthus is considerable.

Currently Dr John Kerridge of Vancouver is a leading raiser of gold-laced in the APS. In New Zealand Dr Hammett and in Australia Dr Clark are important hybridizers of gold-laced polyanthus.

Dr Cecil Jones is well known for his gold-laced polyanthus called, like his other primroses, the 'Penlan strain'. His original stock were raised from Barnhaven seed obtained from America and no other blood has been introduced during the 30 years he has been raising gold-laced.

The initial seedlings, grown in the garden, had imperfect centres with incomplete lacing on the petals. The six best pin were potted up and crossed with a dozen thrum-eyed similarly selected. By continuous line breeding, the centres and lacing showed yearly improvement to the extent that Cecil was awarded Premier at the southern show for five successive years between 1968 and 1972. He estimates that approximately 5–10 percent of seedlings proved acceptable to show standards. In most crosses a small number of silver-laced would appear and these were discarded. Cecil had another Premier in 1983 and his Penlan strain were highly regarded. Seed was given to other growers and his plants have been crossed with other leading strains. Although his gold-laced hybridizing has been muted in recent years he still retains stock. Cecil stresses that his experience indicates the necessity for continuous raising of seedlings strictly bred to florists' standards. He was unable to keep the individual plants for more than a year or two, and quality soon declines without careful hand pollination.

The search for ground colours other than the shades of red that predominate interested Cecil almost from the start. He had obtained a plant from Miss Wynne about 1960 that she described as her 'Old Irish Light Blue Silver Laced Polyanthus'. This was considered a great rarity and cost him a small fortune. The flower, pin-eyed, was an attractive light blue with the lacing distributed as in a good gold-laced polyanthus. Miss Wynne told him that this plant had never set seed so he used a blue pin-eyed polyanthus to make the 'illegal' pin x pin cross. Various tribulations followed – the seedlings were a motley selection and most of a follow-up F2 generation died off. The project was almost abandoned until he read an article in the northern yearbook 1955 (Part Two). Although fantasy, this talked of gold-laced in a range of exotic colours, and had the effect of spurring him on to

further effort. A normal gold-laced polyanthus was used as pollinator to the best F1 plant remaining from the original cross. In the F1 generation several essentially blue gold-laced flowers appeared and were crossed with the best blue of the surviving original F2 seedlings. From these experiments plants were raised that, although silver-laced were otherwise very similar to true gold-laced except for the blue ground colour. The plants caused a considerable stir when shown but were eventually lost and the blue-ground laced polyanthus remains a memory. Unfortunately, no colour photographs were taken at the time. It is his view, based on this experience, that gold-laced with other ground colours are a real possibility. The way to do this is to cross a gold-lace with a blue, or other coloured polyanthus and take a large F2 generation. It may take several further generations to achieve the desired result. This is a challenge for younger growers to pick up.

Dr John Kerridge, of Vancouver, British Columbia, originally from Hampshire, has been growing and exhibiting gold-laced polyanthus for some years.

John has maintained the traditional standards and been very successful at the shows of the APS. He started growing gold-laced in the early 1980s, crossing plants obtained from various sources. One was from Vic Costley, a noted local grower. This plant was called 'Tiny' and resembled the famous British variety of the same name. Later some Barnhaven blood was introduced and the resulting seedlings line-bred for a number of years. As well as the best plants some of variable quality have been used, often producing excellent progeny. From his experience, John is not convinced that only 'best x best' produces an ever-improving strain. He even pollinates thrums and gets seed, although he has not compared the yield with the more traditional 'pin x thrum' crosses.

All his plants are grown in the open ground. As a result they are hardy and have survived temperatures as low as −14°C (7°F) without snow cover.

John divides his plants annually, admitting that this does cause problems when he wants to collect seed. He is of the opinion that the plants do better with annual division rather than letting them clump.

Hubert Calvert, a former secretary of the Wakefield and North of England Tulip Society began breeding gold-laced about 1963. His seed came from Thompson and Morgan and first results were disappointing, with nothing approaching show standards. Nevertheless, he persisted by crossing and recrossing the better seedlings until real improvement appeared in 1972. By 1974 a plant that was good enough to exhibit had flowered, and it was awarded first prize at the northern show. It was named 'Pennington Lady' and survived for more than ten years, although it was soon superseded by its siblings. Hubert was very generous in distributing seed both in the UK and abroad. By 1986 he had lost his stock of this strain but received plants back from Bob Taylor, editor of the northern section yearbook, to whom he had previously given seed. The 'Pennington' strain was considered by David Hadfield to be soundly perennial and distinct from anything else. The origin of Thompson and Morgan's gold-laced is unknown. Hubert was told that at one time they used to grow

varieties like 'Tiny' and 'Beeswing', so speculated that the Barnhaven and T & M strains might have a common ancestry.

In addition to 'Pennington' he raised a second strain. In 1973 Allan Hawkes, of striped auricula fame, sent him some gold-laced seed. The resulting three plants had soft, hairy leaves and the foliage was greyer than normal. The flowers, on slender upright stems, were six-petalled and fairly small, 12–15 mm (½ to ⅜ in), body colour light red with pale yellow centres and lacing. The plants, quite different from any he had seen, intrigued him, and enquiries to Allan brought the reply they were from the late Jimmy Long in the USA, who had obtained the seed from Barnhaven.

The three seedlings were crossed with 'Pennington Lady' with excellent results. The best, named 'Allanbert Red', won a first at the 1978 northern show. 'Allanbert' is an amalgam of 'Allan' and 'Bert', short for 'Hubert'. The plants with hairy leaves from the cross, about 8 percent, proved difficult to maintain and soon died, as did the parents. Nevertheless, they provided the foundations of the new strain and some very good seedlings resulted.

Hubert Calvert's plants have been used by other raisers of gold-laced polyanthus and his strain lives on in the gardens of several northern growers. Unfortunately, Hubert died in the spring of 1997. He made a significant contribution to the laced polyanthus story.

John Ollerenshaw of Hyde, Cheshire, has grown gold-laced for many years and still takes an active part in the northern section of the NAPS. In the early years he struggled due to the scarcity of quality stock but was then fortunate to be given two good plants, one red-ground the other black. Later he obtained others and said that his original stock came from three sources, Mrs Ethne Green, Mr A. L. Watkins of Stockport and a neighbour. Although he has said that none of these strains were remotely related to Barnhaven, in fact Ethne Green's were. I believe her original stock came from Dr Lester Smith whose plants were from Klein seed. John's strain is also perennial in habit.

Without denigrating the others, it can be said that the most highly considered raiser and grower of laced polyanthus in the North, and possibly the UK, in recent years is Les Kaye of Stocksbridge, Sheffield. Unfortunately, due to ill health, his growing has had to be curtailed. Les, who has also raised some excellent Alpine auriculas, and the yellow show self 'Golden Fleece', developed a superb strain, combining plants from Barnhaven, Calvert and Ollerenshaw. He is considered by good northern judges to have worked wonders with the laced polyanthus and exhibited some beautiful, mainly red-ground, plants. Photographs have appeared in the northern yearbook of some of these. His 'Kaye' strain has one significant disadvantage in that it is only biennial in habit, an unfortunate trait that caused him some anguish. As he grew them in pots, this may be the reason. Seed of the 'Kaye' strain has been widely distributed to others, both in this country and abroad.

The most successful breeder and exhibitor in the South, first winning awards as long ago as 1976, is Lawrence Wigley of Carshalton Beeches, Surrey. Lawrence, secretary of the southern section for over 20 years, has developed a fine strain of gold-laced polyanthus and his seed has been widely distributed.

Although his interest has extended over this lengthy period it was not until the late 1980s that he became serious. Lawrence makes a good point about the many so called 'strains' that have appeared over the years. Most have a common ancestry but carry the hallmark of the particular grower. His plants are 'no more or less a mixture than any of the others'. Plants used in his breeding programme include 'Penlan', 'Kaye', Barnhaven and 'a dash' of 'Oaklea'.

Lawrence, like John Ollerenshaw, grows his plants in pots, for a similar reason. The conditions in his garden are not suitable for open ground cultivation.

The above does not do justice to all who have contributed but it would need a book to cover the gold-laced story in its entirety.

Before carrying on, I should mention the controversial question of silver-laced polyanthus. The early laced plants were mainly silver-laced and gold lacing was a later development. Silver-laced plants eventually became unacceptable and are frowned upon, although at least one of the sections has a class for 'lacing other than gold'. Attempts to legitimize them have occurred from time to time but have largely failed. In many crosses plants with silver lacing appear but are discarded by purists.

Where is the gold-laced polyanthus now and what does the future hold? The modern renaissance of the laced polyanthus really began in the early 1960s. Since then dramatic changes have taken place, and what John Ollerenshaw has described as 'miserable, small, multi-headed, small flowered, thinly scaped exhibits of yesteryear' have been replaced by plants of a much improved quality. Generally, the centre and lacing are the same colour and the size of pip, habit and ground colours, although limited to black and red, are much improved. Purists say that remaining faults needing attention are the stained disc – which is a fault in many plants – and an increase in the size of the disc as a proportion of the pip. With a smaller disc the petals can appear overlong, with other faults being twisted petals and trumpet-shaped pips. These are counsels of perfection for the dedicated exhibitor.

At the spring 1996 midland show of the NAPS some splendid gold-laced in two distinct strains were exhibited. Chris Wood of Swadlincote showed very fine plants with a ground colour of near black. Form was excellent and they aroused favourable comment. Equally admired – shown by John Eddington of Rotherham – were plants with slightly larger pips and a distinct red ground.

Chris Wood's plants have evolved over the last three to four years by line breeding from Barnhaven gold-laced. The improvement he has brought about in such a short time is stunning. John Eddington began with seed purchased from Les Kaye and has developed plants that are longer-lasting. He attributes this to growing them in the garden rather than in pots.

These enthusiasts are carrying on the tradition of the old florists. During the history of the laced polyanthus, particularly in the last 100 years, the actual number of raisers has been small. Some of those mentioned are no longer active or less active than previously. As a result, the gold-laced polyanthus continues to survive on a horticultural knife-edge; although a hybrid, it is almost an endangered species. While it might be considered a plant for those of catholic tastes, it does have a unique charm. It is to be hoped that the successors to today's NAPS members will continue to grow and nurture them.

Even so the gold-laced is not a plant solely for the exhibitor. As I have said, many other interested gardeners have, and continue, to grow gold-laced polyanthus. It is an attractive and unusual plant for the garden and well worth growing by non-specialists.

7 THE GARDEN POLYANTHUS

It is widely accepted that the polyanthus arose from a cross between the primrose, *P. vulgaris* and the cowslip, *P. veris,* probably between garden forms, rather than wild plants. The uncertainty arises because there were, as now, two species and one hybrid primula growing in the wild with flowers in umbels; the cowslip, the oxlip *P. elatior* and the hybrid plant known as the 'false oxlip'.

The earliest-known illustration of a polyanthus appeared in the 1687 catalogue of the Botanic Garden of Leiden University in Holland. The plant portrayed was one grown by Jacob Bobart the younger at the Oxford Botanic Garden and was red-flowered. As portrayed it is of jack-in-the-green form with long pedicels and a whorl of enlarged bracts immediately below the umbel. During this period the Oxford Botanic Garden grew various coloured primroses as well as red and yellow cowslips. The coloured primroses were likely to have been forms of *P. vulgaris* subspecies *sibthorpii* and *P. vulgaris* subspecies *heteochroma*, both with flowers in shades of red or purple, introduced into England in the first half of the century. Crosses between

these plants and their progeny probably gave rise to the early polyanthus.

The most detailed account is acknowledged to be that of R. Miller Christy in an article *The Garden Polyanthus: its origin and history.* (*RHS Journal* 1924, Vol. 49, pp 10–24). To this I would add Ruth Duthie's article *The Origin and Development of the Polyanthus* (*The Plantsman* June 1984, Vol. 6).

One of the first mentions of a polyanthus-type plant dates from 1665 when John Rea, a nurseryman who lived near Bewdley in Worcestershire, described a red-flowered 'big oxlip' in his *Flora seu de Florum Cultura* or *Complete Florilege. Sir Thomas Hanmers Garden Book* (1659, published in 1933) also describes 'cowslips and oxlips', meaning plants with umbels of flowers arising from a single stalk. These descriptions suggest the plant that later became known as the polyanthus. Although the word 'polyanthos' (from the Greek for 'many flowered') was used at the time, it referred to other plants with umbels of flowers.

There seems little doubt that the

polyanthus originated in England; it was known on the Continent as the English flower, and may have been grown earlier without being identified as such.

By the 1670s the name 'polyanthus' was in general use, describing a plant that was distinct from either the primrose or cowslip. Colour remained in shades of red, and the plants were widely used in spring displays. At about this time the polyanthus was taken up by the florists of the day and became a cult flower rather than a garden plant. This was the gold-laced polyanthus, still quite widely grown, although much less so than at the height of its popularity, in the middle of the nineteenth century.

The beginning of the garden polyanthus, as we know it today, can be attributed to the famous Victorian gardener Gertrude Jekyll. In the late 1870s Miss Jekyll discovered a bunch-flowered primrose in a cottage garden near her home at Munstead in Surrey. The colour was a pale primrose 'something between that and white'. The following year she obtained a yellowish one 'much of the same character'. The plants were very poor to start with but were allowed to seed and the best seedlings were kept. Gradually from yearly selection the quality improved, although at this early stage of the polyanthus's history hand pollination, although well understood, was not a common practice. This is odd because as Roy Genders pointed out in his book *The Polyanthus* (1963), with gold-laced polyanthus it was carried out as a matter of course. Genders quotes 'Innovator', pen name for a famous florist, in the March 1835 edition of the *Floricultural Cabinet*, as saying 'that the raisers of seedling polyanthuses may be more

Fig. 6. The Leiden Polyanthus.

amply repaid for their trouble, I would suggest to them the propriety of manual cross impregnation.'

From these early beginnings Miss Jekyll developed the Munstead strain of yellow and white polyanthus, unquestionably the great grandparents of all modern strains. By 1896 the polyanthus was becoming popular as a spring bedding plant and, to the horror of some, she began to sell surplus plants. Later Carters took over development of the Munstead strain and brought about a quite considerable improvement, adding further colours. The Munstead strain is still remembered, while many of those that followed have disappeared without trace and are forgotten.

Meanwhile others took up the challenge, one of the first being Antony Waterer, who built up a strain of 'red colourings'. By crossing these plants with the whites and yellows of the Munstead strain other shades like crimson, magenta and a pinkish shade were added.

By the early 1920s the polyanthus was well established as a cut flower and bedding plant and many new strains had been introduced. Companies like Carters, Toogoods, Suttons and Blackmore & Langdon all produced their own strains to general acclaim and 'Giant' strains, with blooms 25 mm (1 in) across, were much in vogue.

Two companies stand out on the British scene. They are Suttons of Reading, now at Torquay, and the Bath firm of Blackmore & Langdon, now at Pensford, south of Bristol.

Suttons were one of the first to improve the polyanthus, working on it prior to the outbreak of the First World War in 1914.

Work was resumed immediately afterwards, especially on the 'Brilliance' strain. This came in shades of red and orange, and was introduced in the early 1930s, soon becoming the finest available. It was from seed of 'Brilliance' that Florence Bellis raised the famous 'Kwan Yin'. Suttons also raised several other excellent strains, including 'Fancy' and 'Superb', but the outstanding one, alongside 'Brilliance', was 'Triumph', introduced in 1960. My father, a professional gardener for over 40 years, mainly in private service, used to raise large numbers of polyanthus annually for bedding purposes. He must have raised many thousands and never wavered in saying that Suttons and Blackmore & Langdon's were the best. Suttons sold seed from their 'Giant' strain, as separate colour blocks. They sold seed from 'Brilliance', 'White', 'Crimson King', 'Superb mixed', 'Fancy Shades Mixed' and the 'Triumph' strain until quite recently. Unfortunately, Suttons merged with, or were taken over by another seed company and, although still trading, no longer develop their own strains. Suttons plants were used by Barnhaven and others, including Frank Reinelt of 'Pacific' fame and Suttons can claim to be the originators of many famous strains.

The firm of Blackmore & Langdon, better known in recent years for delphiniums and begonias, have produced their own strain of polyanthus for over 90 years. The company was formed in 1901 by James Barrett Blackmore, a publican at Twerton, Bath, and Charles Fred Langdon who was gardener to the Reverend Lascelles at Newton St Loe. The first catalogue was issued in 1903 and Polyanthus were 2 shillings and 3 shillings per dozen, while seed was sixpence and 1 shilling.

Soon after forming, the company began to raise polyanthus and has continued to do so ever since. The Blackmore and Langdon families intermarried and the company is now run by John Langdon and his wife, who are third generation and have three sons, also in the business. The raising of polyanthus is now a small-scale operation compared to the peak period in the 1950s and 1960s.

In common with others, the exception being Barnhaven, Blackmore & Langdon improved their strain by discarding unwanted plants and marking selected ones from which seed was saved. By this method improvements were made in the range of colours and general vigour, with special attention paid to freedom of flowering and upright habit. Even so, progress was not entirely satisfactory and around 1946 the decision was made to change to controlled fertilization – in other words, hand pollination – initially out of doors when the plants were in flower. After a year or two this was changed and the selected plants lifted and potted up, so that the operation could be done indoors with much better control. Allan Langdon, in a 1956 article in the RHS magazine, commented that he found it strange that comparatively little improvement in the size of flower, colour range and habit had been made until very recent years.

This can be traced to lack of hand pollination. Today hand pollination is a very expensive process and F1 seed, produced by this method, is priced accordingly. In the period that Allan Langdon referred to, labour was plentiful and cheap, so cost can hardly have been a major factor in its non-use. Nor

surely can the seed companies have been ignorant of the process. W. J. C. Lawrence in *Practical Plant Breeding* (1937), in discussing plant improvement, pointed out that no real progress could be made until the fact of sex in plants was recognized. He went on to say that the Assyrians and Babylonians knew there were two kinds of date palm, one bearing fruit (the female) and the other sterile (the male), and that artificial pollination was practised before 700 BC. Early in the eighteenth century, Camerarius, professor of natural history at the University of Tübingen, established the sexuality of plants. In the latter part of the same century the German Joseph Kölreuter demonstrated that species could be crossed artificially and proved that both parents contributed to the offspring. Kölreuter also drew attention to the importance of insects in pollination, previously quite unrecognized. Later Christian Sprengel discovered that most flowers are naturally cross-pollinated by insects.

In spite of the work by these three, the importance of hybridization, as a means of plant improvement, was only slowly recognized. Once Mendel's paper was simultaneously rediscovered in 1900 by de Vries, Correns and Tschermak, real progress in scientific plant-breeding began. Why then was hand pollination of polyanthus not practised until around 1946? It was suggested by Florence Bellis that this was due to translation difficulties, Mendel's original work being in German. This was comprehensively refuted by Cecil Monson in a reply to Mrs Bellis's article. Even so, English plant-breeders had not been idle, with experimenters like Thomas Andrew Knight and Dean Herbert practising hybridization with some effect at the beginning of the nineteenth century. None of this work appears to have involved primroses and polyanthus and we can only speculate, like Allan Langdon, on why hand pollination remained unused for so long.

With the change to controlled fertilization, rapid improvement came about. Langdon's blue and pink strains were introduced in 1954/5 and the reputation of their polyanthus was equalled only by that of Suttons' 'Brilliance' and 'Triumph' strains. At some stage seed of the 'Pacific' strain of polyanthus was received from Frank Reinelt. Plants were raised and introduced into the Langdon strain but this was done with caution after the fragility of these plants in hard winters became apparent. Nevertheless, some benefit did accrue from the introduction of 'Pacific' blood.

In the 1950s many thousands of plants were raised outdoors, but today a smaller number are grown under cover. The polyanthus is not quite so popular now as a bedding plant, probably due to the increase in the variety of other plants suitable for bedding, while the modern, large-flowered strains of primrose have largely replaced them as pot plants. Certainly the Blackmore & Langdon plants, in 5 inch (125 mm) pots, are very large and the market requirement is for a shorter more compact plant. Nevertheless, a well-grown bed of polyanthus is a marvellous sight.

Plants are available from the nursery in season, and seed is also sold in packets of mixed colours, apart from blue, which traditionally has been kept separate. On a visit to the nursery Mr Langdon showed me the machine that was used to clean seed,

including delphinium and begonia. This was bought second-hand by Charles Langdon prior to 1914 and is still in use today. It is a wood and metal box-like structure originally manufactured by an American company at Saginaw, Michigan. The legend on the side describes it as a 'Grain seed and Bean cleaner'. This illustrates the marvellous tradition of this company, which in 1995 was awarded its 60th Gold Medal at the Chelsea Flower Show. Several were awarded for displays of polyanthus.

Many other excellent strains were raised in the UK, none of which survive, except perhaps in the blood of some modern strains. Names like Carter's 'Sunset Hybrids', Clucas's 'Cluseed Blythe Maximum', Read's 'Festival', Hurst's 'Monarch', Watkins & Simpson's 'Giant Bouquet', Harrison & Sons' 'Kelmscott', 'Giant' and 'Barkby', Harold Harvey's 'Riviera', Hansen's F2 hybrids, Toogood's 'Giant Excelsior', Nutting & Sons' 'Giant Gold Laced', were some of the better-known but alas they have gone and so have most of the companies that produced them.

The United States of America has given us two of the most famous polyanthus producers of all, Barnhaven and the California company of Vetterle & Reinelt. Barnhaven are the subject of a separate chapter and are now located in France, while Vetterle & Reinelt are no more, although the famous 'Pacific' strain lives on.

Although Barnhaven are world renowned, commercially the 'Pacifics' are of greater importance than any other strain. They were celebrated for the very large, substantial blooms on sizeable plants, in clear, bright shades of yellow, red, white, blue, carmine and rose.

Frank Reinelt, originator of the 'Pacific' polyanthus, achieved worldwide fame as a great plant breeder and was also responsible for new strains of delphiniums and begonias. Reinelt was born in Czechoslovakia, very close to the monastery where Mendel conducted his genetic experiments. After the First World War he became head gardener to the Romanian royal family, emigrating to America in 1925. He began breeding polyanthus in 1927 with a collection of plants received from friends. They included whites and bronzes from Suttons seed, two blues originally from Ireland via Hugh Logan of Inverness, Scotland, and others from the garden of Sydney Mitchell, who grew his plants from English seed. Gardens in the San Francisco peninsula were explored and he obtained several interesting plants from the owners.

Klaus Jelitto says, in a letter to the author, that the Dutch 'Colossea' strain were also involved in the development of the 'Pacifics'. The 'Colossea' strain was raised by the firm of N.V. Sluis & Groot's, of Enkhuizen, Holland and seems to be the only European (other than English) strain to make any impact outside the Continent, at least in this early period. The 1951/2 polyanthus trials at Wisley included 'Colossea', raised and sent by an American company, Vaughan's Seed Store of Chicago. They were Highly Commended, 21 April 1952. The plants were described as very free-flowering and vigorous, with flowers 1-2 inches (25–50 mm) in diameter in trusses of 18 to 24. The colours included white, cream, yellow, brownish crimson, crimson and magenta.

Initially, progress was slow, with 5000 seedlings being raised annually, of which only a handful were retained, the rest ploughed under. This early period, covering ten years, included the Second World War and Reinelt almost gave up at times due to lack of assistance.

Eventually progress was made and production increased, after 1945, to 50,000 plants per year, rising eventually to 200,000 with increasing commercial sales. Six hundred plants were selected annually for hybridizing from a new generation each year. As the strain developed flower size increased to the point where some plants became difficult to sell, becoming very ungainly. Nevertheless, huge numbers were sold to other nurseries in bloom for resale, generating the revenue to continue developing the strain.

In a letter to Roy Genders, Reinelt said that he used the original 'Cowichan' polyanthus in his red strain, in order to brighten the colours, previously dull magenta. This is not quite correct. In one of her many articles, Florence Bellis said that Frank Reinelt visited Barnhaven and took back plants of 'Kwan Yin' ('brilliant flame-red'), to brighten up his reds. Her original notes are quite specific and she continues by saying he did use the 'Cowichan' later on 'but for a different purpose'.

Blues were also developed by crossing blue primroses with the best polyanthus. The first generations were purple, but eventually the clear blues that are a feature of the 'Pacifics' were fixed together with a big improvement in quality of bloom.

The downfall of the 'Pacific' polyanthus can be traced to the area where they were grown. Vetterle & Reinelt's nurseries were at Capitola, in California. I have visited

1. *Primula vulgaris* (courtesy J. Kerridge)

2. *Primula veris*

4. *Primula juliae*

3. *Primula elatior* (courtesy J. Kerridge)

5. 'Kinlough Beauty'

7. 'Dorothy'

6. 'Snowcushion'

8. 'Tomato Red'

9. 'Lingwood Beauty'

11. 'Enchantress'

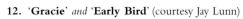

12. 'Gracie' *and* 'Early Bird' (courtesy Jay Lunn)

10. 'Blue Riband'

13. '**Jay Jay**' (courtesy Jay Lunn)

14. '**Nettie Gale**' (courtesy Jay Lunn)

16. '**Miss Indigo**'

15. '**Spring Sunrise**' (courtesy Jay Lunn)

17. *Rosetta double seedling* (courtesy J. Kerridge)

18. 'Dawn Ansell'

20. 'Ken Dearman'

19. Double mauve seedling

21. Ward seedling (courtesy J. Ranson via D. Salt)

23. Ward jack-in-the-green double
(courtesy J. Ranson via D. Salt)

22. Ward seedling (courtesy J. Ranson via D. Salt)

24. Ward seedling (courtesy J. Ranson via D. Salt)

25. Ward seedling (courtesy J. Ranson via D. Salt)

27. Penlan flaked double

28. Webster laced hose-in-hose polyanthus

26. Ward doubles

29. Webster yellow hose-in-hose polyanthus

31. Webster yellow jack-in-the-green polyanthus

30. Webster laced-edge jackanapes

32. Webster cream jackanapes

33. Rising Sun cowslip pantaloon

34. Webster cowslip/primrose hybrid pantaloon

36. Gold-laced jack-in-the-green primrose

35. Ward red jack-in-the-green primrose

37. Double gold-laced polyanthus

38. 'Katy McSparron'

39. The single green primrose

40. Feathered cowslip

43. Gold-laced polyanthus exhibited by R. Taylor

41. Wigley gold-laced polyanthus

44. Kerridge gold-laced polyanthus

42. Kaye gold-laced polyanthus (courtesy L. Kaye)   (courtesy J. Kerridge)

45. 'Barrowby Gem'

46. '**Crescendo mix**' (courtesy Ernst Benary)

47. '**Crescendo Bellarosa**' (courtesy Ernst Benary)

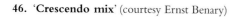

48. Barnhaven '**Chartreuse**'

49. Barnhaven '**Spice**'

50. '**Venetian Cowichan**'

52. Barnhaven '**Victorian**'

51. '**Garnet Cowichan**'

53. 'Yellow Cowichan'

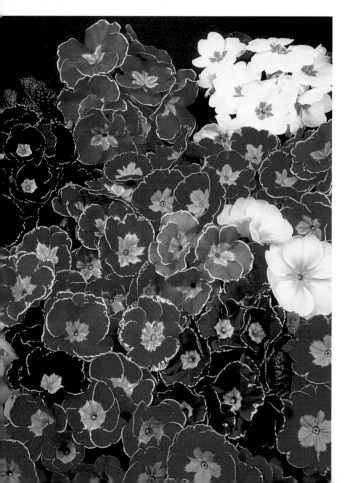

55. Large-flowered bi-colour primrose

54. 'Finesse' (courtesy Ernst Benary)

56. Spectrum strain '**Japanese Iris**' (courtesy K. Sahin)

58. '**Quantum**' (courtesy Colegrave Seeds)

57. '**Fascination Mix**' (courtesy K. Sahin)

59. '**Prominent Mix**' (courtesy Sakata)

60. The Sakata range (courtesy Sakata)

62. 'Danova' (courtesy Daenhfeldt)

63. 'Pageant Mix' (courtesy Daenhfeldt)

61. 'Wanda Supreme' (courtesy Floranova)

64. 'Bicolour F1' (courtesy Daenhfeldt)

California several times and am amazed that polyanthus were raised in such a dry, hot climate, although Capitola is only three miles from the Pacific Ocean. I mentioned earlier that Blackmore & Langdon received some 'Pacific' seed from Frank Reinelt and crossed some of the resulting plants with their own strain. This caused problems as it was noted that plants of the 'Pacific' strain did not like our cold, damp winters and tended to collapse. This occurred even when temperatures were not especially low.

With the popularity of the 'Pacific' strain self-evident the demand for seed became worldwide. The Californian company could not meet demand, and the large seed companies began to produced their own, mostly inferior, product. Seed was increasingly produced by open pollination because it was cheaper. Roy Genders quotes Mr Frank Holl, then in charge of seed production at Harrisons & Sons of Leicester, who found that 'unless the colours are separately grown under glass and hand fertilized, the whole strain quickly deteriorates.'

The success of the 'Pacific' was total for a time and I recall an occasion, around 1967, when driving towards Henley in Oxfordshire. On the outskirts of the town I saw a field full of 'Pacific' polyanthus in bloom. Customers were selecting plants which were then dug up. I stopped and bought some although many of the plants were not as good as expected. In conversation with me, the proprietors indicated they were not altogether happy and had complained to the seed suppliers. Needless to say by the following year the field was deserted.

This lack of reliability and suspect winter hardiness brought about the downfall of the 'Pacific'. A severe winter in the mid-1960s devastated outdoor plantings in the USA, leading to a loss of popularity from which polyanthus have never recovered. Whether this was the catalyst or not, a worldwide decline occurred in the 1960s and 1970s. No doubt there are a number of reasons, including ever-changing fashions and the introduction of many new bedding 'novelties'.

In 1968 Frank Reinelt retired and the famous Japanese Sakata Seed Corporation, established in 1913 by Takeo Sakata, took over the 'Pacific' strain. They had begun to produce 'Pacific Giant' polyanthus as early as 1959. Sakata have a worldwide presence, with major subsidiaries in Europe and America, and sell seed in 130 countries.

Sakata worked to restore the quality of the original, and pink shades were added in 1974. Although mainly intended for pot use, a 1995/6 wholesale catalogue describes them as 'the most highly recommended series for both bedding and pot crop'. The range is: bicolours, blue shades, pink shades, rose shades, scarlet red shades, white shades and yellow shades. They are certainly striking plants.

Of course, Barnhaven and the 'Pacifics' were not the only strains raised in America. Numerous others appeared, and disappeared, including McHenry's 'Midas Gold', Clarke's 'Colossal' and 'Pastel', Linda Eickman's 'Crown Pink' and 'Majestic', Alice Baylor's 'Sky Hook', Howard Lynn's 'Tyee', the 'Hood River' strain and several others.

As well as in Europe and America, polyanthus were raised in New Zealand and

Australia. In New Zealand several strains of good-quality polyanthus were produced, with names like McLaughins's 'Argyll', Sturmer's 'Warnley', Chittick's 'Hybrid', Wallis's 'Waterlight', Dean's 'Otago Superba', and Attwood's 'Giant'. Possibly the best-known New Zealand strains were Harrison's, 'Champion' and 'Tango Supreme' being the best-known examples. M. E. Leeburn, writing in *My Garden*, July 1957, commented very favourably, claiming the flowers were larger and more velvety than those of Blackmore & Langdon. In New Zealand the 'Tango' varieties were introduced, the name applying to a range of colours rather than any particular strain. These plants were in shades of orange, from chrome to a copper-bronze. Although all the above have disappeared, some hybridizing is still being done. In 1961 Noel McMillan began breeding polyanthus at his Ohinewai garden centre – called McMillan's 'Greenworld' – north of Huntley. The original stock was from selected 'Pacific Giants', showing colour variations, with the infusion of Barnhaven blood. From these beginnings a 'pot pourri of flower colours and forms' has emerged. They are known as 'Waikato' polyanthus and include stripes, stars, picotees and other multi-colour combinations. Flower form varies from ruffled petals to blooms that resemble rosebuds. These plants were offered as seed by Thompson and Morgan for some years as the 'Paradise' strain but are now freely available in New Zealand as 'Waikato'.

A development, known as the 'Veined' series, with striped blooms of blue, red and chocolate, have recently been introduced. Noel McMillan has raised other strains, 'Flashlight' with multicoloured blooms in almost iridescent hues, the 'County' series in darker, earthy tones intended to be grown in the home in small pots, in a similar manner to African violets. When new forms and colours are stabilized they are released separately and future scheduled releases are the 'Ruffles' and 'Rosebud' series, currently part of the 'Waikato' strain.

In addition to Noel McMillan's breeding programmes, Dr Keith Hammett has been working with Jack Hobbs of the Auckland Regional Botanic Gardens on a number of specific projects. They include gold-laced polyanthus, covered in a separate chapter, and getting brighter colours into the Barnhaven 'Cowichan' series. The Auckland Botanic Gardens have also been developing the 'Muted Victorian' Barnhaven strain, which Jack Hobbs is particularly interested in, and this has been ongoing for some years. A variation has been raised with a slightly darker edging to the bloom. It is nice to know that all is not lost to the 'big battalions', who are following the path dictated by their main market, that for pot plants.

Australia has produced some polyanthus strains, although fewer than New Zealand. The 'Gartford' strain, raised by Mr Fred Danks of Melbourne, was highly regarded with 'perfectly formed flower trusses on sturdy ten inch [250 mm] stems'. They came in a wide range of colours from peach-pink to blood-red. In more recent times Goodwin's 'Regal Supreme', huge polyanthus with enormous flower heads, were very popular in the 1970s and 1980s. This hand-pollinated strain was produced by crossing 'Pacific Giants' with Harrison's 'Tango Supreme'. Seed was sold throughout the world and was available in England for a few years.

Unfortunately, even Goodwin's no longer sell either plants or seed, so Australia has no indigenous strains, only those that are sold on the world market. While not intending to denigrate the large companies, who are doing an excellent job within their remit, it does seem a great pity that changes in the market have brought about the demise of so many original and distinctive strains. Unfortunately, the quest for uniformity, a word that crops up in many different spheres, has brought this about, with the pot-plant market demanding a different type of plant.

Nevertheless, although most of the breeding in recent times has been devoted to primroses, a few new strains of polyanthus have been introduced.

Pride of place goes to 'Crescendo', which is generally regarded as the best outdoor strain and has been described as a winter-hardy 'Pacific'. The 'Crescendo' F1 hybrid strain was introduced by Ernst Benary, the leading German seed company, first established in 1843 in Erfurt. 'Crescendo' was raised by plant breeder K. Wagner, who has been responsible for the Benary primrose introductions since about 1970. A range of colours was introduced over a number of years with 'Gold' first appearing in 1971/2 and the most recent, 'Bellarosa', a deep salmon, in 1986/7. The colours, in addition to those already mentioned, are 'Blue Shades', 'Pink & Rose Shades', 'Primrose', 'Bright Red' and 'White'. They are sold to amateur gardeners in packets of formula mixture by seedsmen and garden centres, and commercial growers can buy seed in individual colour groups. 'Crescendo' is a

magnificent strain and fully winter-hardy although the colour range is considered to be limited. Benary were awarded a Gold Medal at Mannheim in 1975 and Silver Medals at Stuttgart in 1977, and Bonn in 1979.

I saw some plantings of 'Crescendo' at a garden centre in Devon in 1995, and the plants were a wonderful sight – large clumps with many strong flower stems and brilliant colours. Young plants are often available through garden centres.

A relatively new company, beginning in 1971, S & G Seeds of Ormskirk, Lancashire – as well as offering seed of the F1 'Crescendo' and open-pollinated 'Colossea' polyanthus – have their own introduction, available as both young plants and seed: the F1 'Jackpot' strain. 'Jackpot' is described as 'an excellent variety with large flowers on, short, thick stems and wide colour range'. Although obviously suitable for the pot-plant market it is also recommended for outdoor culture 'Jackpot' is available in rose, deep yellow, yellow, light red, blue and white.

Royal Sluis, started by the Sluis family 125 years ago, is another famous company who breed primroses and polyanthus. They list one polyanthus type, the F1 'Hercules' strain. This variety has been developed for 'pot and pack' production and is very compact with short, strong flower stems and large flowers.

Daehfeldt introduced the 'Concorde' F1 series in 1995 which they describe as a 'winterhardy series with a compact habit and mulitiple flower stems'. There are ten colours with yellow and red/pink shades predominating. This is another dual-role polyanthus aimed at both the outdoor bedding market and autumn and spring pot-plant sales.

Colegrave Seeds is one of the largest suppliers to the commercial trade. Their splendid catalogue, running to 227 pages, lists a wide range of primroses and polyanthus. Colegrave are flower seed specialists and sell seed from most of the major producers. Colegrave currently sell three strains of polyanthus, primarily for pot culture and three for outdoor bedding. They highly recommend the 'Presto' strain for early flowering and also 'Largo', which has been bred to follow 'Presto' in flower. Both strains produce neat, compact plants with strong shortish stems, in a selection of popular colours. The third pot type is the 'Pacific' strain, which can be used for bedding in milder areas, providing drainage is good in winter and some protection is given against cold spring winds.

Highly recommended for outdoor bedding is 'Crescendo', which they describe as unsurpassed for really brilliant bedding effects. The other outdoor polyanthus strains are the 'Rainbow' series and the 'Southbank' strain. 'Rainbow' is described as a good hardy strain producing several florets on relatively short stems. A wide range of colours in shades of cream, white, yellow, orange, pink, rose, blue and scarlet. This is a very good strain and the photograph in the Colegrave catalogue, a bed of cream shades, is most attractive. 'Rainbow' is available from several retail seed companies. 'Rainbow' is an F1 strain bred by the British company Floranova. It is a mature strain with no current breeding work.

Colegrave's final strain, 'Southbank', is a mixture containing the basic colours and is obviously intended for mass planting, costing far less than the hand-pollinated F1 types.

Retail seedsmen all offer a restricted number of polyanthus, which often includes their own mixture, usually described as 'Superb', 'Large Flowered', 'Giant Exhibition' or something similar. They are normally open-pollinated mixtures selling at much lower prices as an alternative to the expensive F1 hybrids.

One recent development is the attempt, by Dr John Kerridge in Vancouver, to produce a large-flowered laced polyanthus for the garden. This has been underway for some years. He started with seed from the APS seed exchange labelled 'gold-laced polyanthus x polyanthus'. The resulting seedlings have been interbred, with pollen introduced from Barnhaven gold-laced to maintain the lacing. From the many seedlings, the best were selected for lacing, size and sturdy stems. John has consistently selected flowers with the darker ground, preferably black, with a bright gold eye and good lacing. He also introduced plants from a traditional 'gold-laced polyanthus x deep red polyanthus'. The seedlings have shown enormous variation but the general tendency is to a better overall plant with increased flower size. The flower size is now at least 25 mm (1 in) in diameter. The best two plants so far were pin-eyed, which doesn't matter for a garden plant. These crosses still produce a mixed lot of plants with a few that are very good. John hopes that continuous line breeding will eventually bring more consistency. A selected seedling from this breeding line has been tissue-cultured and introduced commercially in North America.

Up to now I have described polyanthus purely in terms of seed strains. Although never approaching the numbers of either *juliae* hybrids or gold-laced polyanthus, named varieties of polyanthus were once very popular and much sought-after plants. Probably the only surviving old variety is 'Barrowby Gem' and this, with the few other current named forms, is included in the lists of named plants. Sacheverell Sitwell mentioned several, all of which he described as 'rare' or 'very rare', including 'Old Irish Mauve & Silver', 'Old Irish Light Blue', 'Red Indian' and the 'Old China Blue Polyanthus'. Other old varieties were 'Quakeress' and 'Bartimeus', the latter described by Roy Genders as 'possibly the original crimson'. Genders, in *The Polyanthus*, lists some, but they are mixed up with smaller plants better described as stalked primroses.

One legendary plant was 'Beltany Red', origin unknown. Champernowne listed this in the 1950s with the comment 'ideal for bedding but unfortunately our stock in not large and we know of no other source.'

Margery Fish, in *Cottage Garden Flowers* (1961) describes a variety she was growing called 'Princess Charlotte', with a flower colour a mixture of soft pink, yellow and green – 'one of the old painted polyanthus'. Townsend listed 27 named polyanthus, including miniature sorts, in the 1950s. They included 'Princess Charlotte' and the gold-laced 'Beeswing'. Others were 'Prince Albert' ('purple-crimson, with a blush-blue candy stripe down each petal') and 'Princess Violetta' ('pure blue-violet, with a distinctive eye of deepest yellow, striped persimmon orange'). Interestingly these 'painted polyanthus' were not mentioned by Sitwell.

Champernowne raised a number of what they termed dwarf polyanthus or polyanthus

primroses. 'Blue Cockade', 'Czar', 'Hunters Moon', 'Raspberries & Cream' and 'Red Ensign' are examples and also those with the 'Buckland' prefix, such as 'Enchantress' and 'Primrose', but few survive. In any case, although polyanthus in form, these plants were generally much smaller and not really comparable to the large-flowered garden polyanthus.

The RHS at its Wisley garden has occasionally held polyanthus trials during the last 50 years. One such trial is underway in 1996 and has attracted a large and varied selection of entries. As it is a seed trial, the identity of the donors will not be revealed until the results are announced. Prominent amongst the entries are 'Crescendo',' Rainbow', 'Cowichans', 'Victorians' and 'New Century'.

What does the future hold? Polyanthus are still extensively planted as spring bedding plants, especially by local authorities. A well-grown bed in full flower is a lovely sight and few other spring-flowering plants can compare. Nevertheless, the heyday of the polyanthus was in the 1950s and 1960s, and the rise in the large-flowered primrose strains, most having 'Pacific' blood, has seen the demise of most of the strains mentioned earlier. We can only hope that this trend does not get completely out of hand. The garden polyanthus, a magnificent development of the original species, is a far superior garden plant to the large-flowered primroses of today. These latter plants, often not hardy, are intended as pot plants and are not really suitable for planting in the garden.

8 THE BARNHAVEN

STORY

Amongst the many companies producing seeds and plants of primroses and polyanthus one remains unique. Started 60 years ago on a smallholding at Gresham, in the state of Oregon, USA, it can truly be described as the 'enthusiast's seed company'. Despite relocation in the 1960s to Brigsteer, near Kendal in England, and more recently to Plouzélambre in France, with consequent changes of ownership, the ideals that developed from a humble beginning have been maintained despite increasing commercial pressures in a changing world.

The Barnhaven story is really about a remarkable lady who was born Florence Hurtig in New Orleans, 19 May 1906. Florence was of European origin, her grandparents first emigrating to Indiana in America, from the Baltic, in the mid-1800s prior to the Civil War. Later they moved south to New Orleans but did not stay there, moving to Oregon in 1910. In Oregon her mother grew market produce and Florence attended school, discovering an aptitude for the piano and training as a concert pianist. It seems she did not have an altogether happy childhood; once in an unguarded moment describing herself as being 'raised without love'. This experience translated into a lifelong reluctance to reveal, or discuss, details of her private life although she was always willing to talk about primroses 'until the petals dropped'.

Florence went to work at the age of 14, and after being secretary to a bank manager became involved in managing a theatrical company, the Toy Theatre Players of Portland. As manager she lived on the premises, a studio on the top floor of Portland's first bank building where the theatre business was conducted. When the theatre company collapsed she was unable to pay the rent and became very ill with a number of complaints, leading to a nervous breakdown. Fortunately, a friend came to the rescue and took her in. While still in very poor health and virtually destitute – she once guardedly said 'maybe because of it' – she married Lou Levy in 1933.

It was Levy who persuaded a wealthy acquaintance to let them move into an old decrepit barn, which they later called

'Barnhaven'. Florence recalled her first sight of the old barn in its enchanting setting on Johnson Creek, at Gresham, ten miles east of Portland. It was a cowbarn belonging to the big house on the hill, and after crossing the creek a lane led up to it. As she approached she had a premonition or feeling of destiny which never left her.

The barn was a tall rectangular building – one end close to the hill, the other sitting on the stones in the creek. Florence and her husband moved into the hayloft and had to make do with the most makeshift arrangements due to their dire financial state. The barn leaked like a sieve and had no windows or doors. The bed, a pile of straw boxed into the least leaky corner, had umbrellas over it. Old orange crates served as tables or bookcases, although she did bring her two cherished pianos, a cherry upright and a mahogany artist's grand. Bit by bit, the barn was improved, some of the improvements, like doors and windows, paid for by the owner. Finally, on 26 September 1937, water was piped into the kitchen area followed by electricity 'on November 23 1938 at 10.29 am'. In these days of prosperity for the majority, it is difficult to imagine a life as hard as this.

Outside, this harshness was replaced by a vista of natural beauty at the centre of which was the creek 'the real mistress of Barnhaven'. Wild creatures abounded – a family of otters lived in the bank across from the primitive southeast bedroom. In season, salmon could be heard spawning, splashing and thrashing throughout the night, below the northeast one. Deer would make their way upstream or downstream, browsing the mock orange and wild roses trailing in the

water along the banks. In winter the creek sometimes lost its tranquillity changing to a rushing torrent, with flooding that rose in a few hours and subsided in a few days. Florence was an interested observer of nature and delighted in the great variety of birds and animals that co-existed with her. Despite the difficult circumstances that brought her to this spot, she developed an attachment and love for it that never changed, even after she eventually moved away.

A considerable amount of land surrounded the barn. The creek area was about one acre (0.4 hectares), while the old apple orchard on the hill stretched to ten (4 hectares). The soil was rich and the adjacent valley lush with farmlands. Florence had, some time earlier, seen primroses in the English catalogues of a friend and it had been love at first sight, although at that time she had no money to purchase seed. At this time primroses were little known and little grown in America, with the bulk of the seed produced in England, by firms like Suttons, Blackmore & Langdon, Carters, Toogood and Thompson and Morgan. Then what she described as a 'miracle' occurred – 'a bit of luck and a bit of cash' – and she carried her seed order, sent to Suttons together with $5, through snow drifts to the nearest post office.

Weeks later, after an anxious wait, the seeds arrived and were duly sown the following spring. Although she was a pure beginner her natural talent was already evident and germination was excellent. This happened prior to her move to Gresham and she took the flats or boxes of seedlings with her. She planted out the resulting polyanthus seedlings under the alders along the creek at the back of the barn. At this time she was still walking with a stick and weighed less than 100 pounds, but working outside and cultivating the soil had a therapeutic effect and her health gradually improved.

A year later 1231 plants bloomed – the whites and yellows of the Munstead strain and the reds' of Suttons' Brilliance and Crimson King – to Florence each a priceless beauty and delight beyond imagining, although a far cry from the later developments.

Word soon spread and her first visitors arrived. She recalled her first sale was to a lady on the morning of 12 September 1936. She came at 8 o'clock and spent 50 cents. Of this 20 cents went for kerosene for the lamps, 4 cents for yeast and the balance for whatever else was needed most!

The idea of a mailing list came easily to Florence, as she had previously designed and produced hand-painted lists and delivered thousands to homes in the wealthy districts of Portland, when she worked for the theatre company. In the winter of 1939 she hand-painted 500 primrose folders, using green poster paper, two small bottles of poster paint – yellow and white – and a stencil. Half were posted on 4 April and by 10 April all the folders had been posted; a number of others were distributed at a garden club. Sales by then totalled $35.50, a considerable sum to her, all for the expenditure of little more than a dollar. This first catalogue created a style which was to be continued for 30 years of catalogues and advertising. Commercial considerations were secondary, no mention of price was made in the first list – she completely forgot to put prices in! The lyrical and somewhat romantic language that was to become a trademark of Barnhaven

literature was prominent. This style does not appeal to everyone, a kind of horticultural 'Mills & Boon', but it obviously struck a chord in America and indeed elsewhere because Barnhaven has become world famous.

A frequent visitor to Barnhaven in the early days was Dean Collins, formerly drama editor of the defunct *News-Telegram* in Portland, who by then had a garden page in the *Oregon Journal*. Collins had met Florence when she was involved in the theatre, and he and his wife often visited. He persuaded Florence, much against her will, to write a series of 12 primrose articles for the *Journal*. The articles led to the foundation of the American Primrose Society in 1941, Collins conceiving the idea of a society dedicated to primroses. In 1943, on the strength of the *Journal* articles, the Board of Directors asked her to become editor of the quarterly. She soon realized that she needed to augment her scanty knowledge. Visits to Oregon State University, some 90 miles away, enabled her to research RHS journals from Victorian times, as well as the Belgian and French equivalents, for articles on primulas. She recorded everything she could find, which took ten days, using a typewriter provided by the University, and this information – together with her rapidly growing personal experience – enabled her to contribute to as well as edit the quarterly.

She occupied this position for the next nine years, despite an expanding business and a young daughter to raise. One of the benefits of her editorship was correspondence and friendship with many of the famous British growers of the time, such as R. H. Briggs, Dan Bamford and Captain

Comley Hawkes. Florence Bellis (as she was to become in 1959), although not without critics, remained a towering figure in the APS throughout her life and is regarded with affection, admiration and awe even today some years after her death.

In the meantime the business developed. In the first batch of seedlings from Suttons seed appeared a 'Chinese red polyanthus' with a small, precision-stamped gold star and an almost black stem. It was named 'Kwan Yin' as its elegance of form and grace suggested China's goddess of mercy. This one plant was used to produce three strains of polyanthus, two of which are still current.

One of these is the famous eyeless 'Cowichan' strain offered for the first time, both as plants and seed, in 1949. Three generations of line breeding, using 'Kwan Yin' as the seed parent, were needed to produce what has become possibly the most famous strain of all. The 'Kwan Yin' strain was released in 1950 followed by 'Little Egypt'. Although many new types and colour combinations would come later the original 'Kwan Yin' polyanthus is the great grandparent of all the Barnhaven polyanthus strains.

From the outset Florence hand-pollinated, by emasculating her plants, and indeed claimed to have pioneered this method commercially. With large numbers of plants to deal with, she did not use brushes, hence avoided the necessity of constant sterilization. In the early days she often worked well into the night, pollinating by the light of a storm lamp and on one famous occasion got too close to the oil lamp, causing her underwear to smoulder! Later, as the business expanded, a team of three ladies did the pollinating

Apart from the 'Cowichan' other lines were being explored as the number of primroses increased. They were segregated, the colours improved by selection and hand pollination so that, by 1944, her 'Marine Blues', another show stopper, were fixed. The majority of other strains were fixed by 1950. They became known as 'Silver Dollar Primroses' because the size of each flower equalled or exceeded that of the then dollar coin.

The only outside blood used was from the pink seedlings raised by Linda Eichman. Linda was a nurse who lived and worked in Dayton, Oregon, 'one of those backyard growers' in Florence's parlance, a number of whom had sprung up in the Pacific Northwest area. Linda had purchased seed from Toogood's of Southampton, England, and raised two pink polyanthus seedlings, the best described as 'wild-rose', that were distinct colour breaks, although the plants were feeble. Not really knowing what to do, she made a long bus journey to Barnhaven to get advice, carrying the plants in a wicker basket. Advised to cross-pollinate then select and recross, she did so and soon fixed the wild-rose pink. Later coral and apricot shades appeared and two separate strains were fixed and immortalized as 'Crown Pink' and 'Warm Laughter'. Linda later sold plants and seed but gave some to Florence in 1947 who bred them into her lavender pinks. This led to the Barnhaven 'New Pinks', introduced in 1958, creating equally as big a stir as had the 'Marine Blues' 14 years earlier. It had taken ten years to breed the Eichman colours into the more vigorous and hardier Barnhaven stock but the results proved it had been worth the effort.

I mentioned earlier the 'Cowichan' polyanthus, perhaps the strain most associated with Barnhaven and Florence Bellis. Reams and reams have been written about it, generating more than a little controversy. As can easily happen, some of the historical information published – some circulated by Barnhaven – is not completely accurate, and the true story, from the late Sybil McCulloch who grew up in the Cowichan Valley, was published in the Summer 1992 *Quarterly* of the American Primrose Society.

I travelled through the Cowichan Valley in May 1995, a delightful region situated between two great trout and salmon fishing rivers on Vancouver Island in British Columbia – the Koksilah and the Cowichan, both emptying into Cowichan bay. This valley was largely settled by colonists from England many of whom crossed the prairies of America to Oregon and then went on to British Colombia, where the community is described as 'Anglo-Canadian'.

The 'Cowichan' primula arose in the small community of Cowichan Station roughly 30 miles from Victoria. It appeared in the garden of a Mr Neel, who had a reputation as a gardener and imported seed from England. Next door to Mr Neel lived a Major Knocker whose wife was a keen gardener. Plants were exchanged and Mrs Knocker was given a piece of Neel's primrose.

Major Knocker, described as 'a convivial soul', distributed plants to his friends and neighbours and one, Mrs Louis Norie, was given a plant of the primrose. Part of the controversy that subsequently resulted was due to the Norie children believing the plant originated in their mother's garden. Sybil McCulloch had a friend who once lived next door to Mrs Knocker. Mrs Knocker told the friend that the plant originated with Mr Neel in the 1930s.

From this point things became more volatile and bad feeling developed that still reverberates to this day. The dispute began when plants were offered at a sale as the 'Cowichan' primula. What happened was that a local nurseryman, R. M. Palmer of the Palmer Gardens, had obtained a plant or plants, multiplied his stock, then offered them for sale. The furore this caused was considerable and led to much bad feeling with people taking sides over the argument. The idea that a gift should be turned into a commercial proposition and renamed to boot, caused shock and outrage in the small community. This is a common practice with nurserymen and can cause annoyance to the originators of the plants, but it seems in this instance to have caused quite astonishing turbulence.

This is the plant that Florence Levy, or Bellis as she is more commonly called, obtained from Palmer's nursery or some other source. The original is not a robust grower, although the flowers are a good size, reddish-purple and eyeless. It has never been known to set seed but provides plenty of pollen. The leaves, next to the eye the most distinctive feature of the 'Cowichan' strain, have a reddish tint. I have deliberately used the present tense as it is now believed that the original clone, or something very close to it, is not extinct and survives in gardens on Vancouver Island. Indeed, in 1992 Dr John Kerridge saw clumps of a polyanthus with dark foliage in a Dr Verchere's garden in

Ladysmith, British Columbia. Dr Vechere, who was 90 and passed away a few months later, was able to tell him the history of the plant, the trail leading back to Palmer's nursery. John was given a piece which, on blooming, appeared identical to the one grown in the Victoria area for many years.

Sybil McCulloch asked R. M. Palmer's daughter, whom she knew well, some 20 years after the original events, whether the form she had recently been given was the true 'Cowichan', but even after all those years the subject was taboo. It does appear though that more than one form may have existed.

From this it has been agreed, by the British Columbia primrose growers, that the correct name for this famous clone is 'Cowichan, Neel Variety'.

Florence acquired a plant of the 'Cowichan' primrose nearly a decade after its initial discovery. By then, due to intensive vegetative propagation, the constitution had weakened and her plant flowered once, in 1942, before expiring. Fortunately, pollen was obtained and after ten years work a range of hardy 'Cowichans', soon to become world famous, were introduced throughout the 1950s and 1960s. With the small, neat, circular centre, solid self-coloured petals in a variety of lustrous shades, foliage of deep green, often edged or tinted bronze or purple, they are 'plants of distinction'.

By no means were Florence Bellis's achievements confined to polyanthus. Considerable progress was made with anomalous primroses, *juliae* hybrids, gold-laced polyanthus and finally the sensational Barnhaven doubles. This is covered in the chapters devoted to these individual plants.

By the early 1960s, after 30 years

dedication, her health began to deteriorate and she was advised to retire. Her first marriage had ended in divorce in the mid-1950s but she then met Bob Bellis, an Australian, when on a holiday in Hawaii paid for from the money won with a hybridizing award. They married in 1959 and it was a very happy union, although not destined to last many years.

When she decided it was time to retire the fame of Barnhaven was worldwide. The Barnhaven strains were highly marketable and some of the large seed houses would have paid considerable sums to gain control of them. Florence had never made much money and could have secured a solid financial base for retirement but, typically, chose not to do so. The hard-faced businessman might say she always lacked financial acumen, and this was the prime example of it. Others may take a different view and consider it a final act of sacrifice by someone who refused to let her principals be debased by pure monetary considerations. There are arguments to support both views. In any event, she chose to send 100 seeds of all her strains, with the message 'yours to keep or kill', to Jared and Sylvia Sinclair at Brigsteer in the Lake District of Cumbria, England. The Sinclairs had been customers for years and were now Barnhaven's European agents. Previously, they had mainly grown cut flowers for the local floristry market. Florence made her gift without any consultation – the seeds arrived 'out of the blue'. The Sinclairs were not altogether pleased by this development – they were reluctant to get involved in large-scale seed production. But they undertook it so successfully that in the following 20 years or more they raised the reputation of Barnhaven to new heights.

When it became known in America what was happening, consternation ensued. Offers poured in to Florence, the telephone ringing incessantly, with panic buying taking place. Many people were not at all happy and Florence was heavily criticized – in British parlance being virtually 'sent to Coventry', or in Jared Sinclair's words 'the corks popped out of the vitriol bottles'. Nevertheless, she refused to change her mind and 'did it her way', so that the tradition of Barnhaven would be upheld.

Florence retired with her husband to the Oregon Coast in 1966, both with heart trouble. Bob Bellis died soon afterwards and she was obliged, due to her financial situation, to work in a small health-food store until finally forced to retire for the last time. In and out of hospital, she managed to survive despite her predicament for a number of years, finally dying peacefully in her sleep on 15 November 1987. It is hard not to feel that there were many elements of tragedy in the life of Florence Bellis, a rather lonely and often misunderstood woman, and it is a pity her last years were not more comfortable. A final tribute might be that of Howard Lynn of the Lynn Gardens of Tacoma, Washington, raiser of the 'Tyee' strain of polyanthus, who wrote in 1952 'Besides a tremendous organizing ability, great skill as a writer, editor and lecturer, a scintillating personality, the lady had a plain genius for plant-breeding.'

The Sinclairs and Florence never met but carried on an extensive and lively correspondence and had many telephone conversations. When her 'bombshell' arrived and the decision to take over the Barnhaven operation was made, the Sinclairs hurriedly erected a pollinating shed and took other measures – like planting forest trees for shade – to create the conditions suitable for primroses and polyanthus. Then, in Jared Sinclair's words, 'her innermost secrets arrived and we were off.'

The climate in Oregon has been likened to that of the southwest of England. The tiny village of Brigsteer is situated in the northwest where winters are frequently much colder and the weather generally harsher, even though it is a very beautiful area. Jared Sinclair describes the local climate, in his famous collector's catalogue 8/85, as 'a frost pocket, a wind funnel, and, in high summer, a steaming casserole. When it is cold, it is colder than an Eskimo's kiss. When it is hot, the will to move wilts'! Mr Sinclair, a man of very colourful prose and an independent character in the tradition of Florence Bellis, carried on the Barnhaven way by pollinating carefully selected open-ground plants, lifted and planted in the pollinating sheds, open on all sides to the elements. When the pollinating season was over the plants were put back in the open ground to ripen the seed pods for July harvesting. A team of ladies did the pollinating, working under less than perfect, often very cold, conditions. This was again in the Barnhaven tradition to ensure that the strains remained hardy.

With the move to Brigsteer, Barnhaven went from strength to strength. Eleven new polyanthus strains were introduced and Florence said that each succeeding generation surpassed the last with 140 identifiable colour shades. Where else was it possible to buy polyanthus seed with names like 'Indian Reds', 'Chartreuse', 'Grand Canyon', 'Spice Shades', 'Carnation Victorians', 'Daybreak', 'Paris 90' to name a few?

By the mid-1980s Barnhaven had peaked, and the Sinclair's thoughts turned to retirement. At the time, the commercial development of primroses and polyanthus was reaching a new professional level. The enormous growth of the pot-plant trade was evident and Barnhaven plants had been used in many of these breeding programmes. Jared Sinclair did not care for the new large-flowered strains although he understood the logic and appeal.

When it became known that retirement was being considered, Barnhaven devotees were aghast and the many howls of protest persuaded the Sinclairs reluctantly to carry on for a few more years, until finally the decision was made that 1989 would be the very last year. I can remember the feeling this induced amongst customers, of which I was one. Although primarily intended as garden plants, Barnhaven polyanthus and primroses had been a major presence, for years and years, in the Vernales section at the shows of the national auricula and primula societies and also the American Primrose Society. The other seed strains on the market, although producing some excellent plants, simply did not have the range, diversity and attraction of Barnhaven. A 'black hole' loomed. Fortunately, this did not last for long before it became known that a lady named Angela Bradford, who had some connection with Barnhaven, was going to restart the business moving it, for financial reasons, to Plouzélambre in Brittany, France.

Angela, a professional academic librarian, who was a keen hobby gardener with an interest in old-fashioned flowers, first met the Sinclairs after her father and stepmother moved to Brigsteer in the early 1980s. When on a visit she happened to mention to her stepmother that she would like to acquire some hose-in-hose polyanthus. She was pointed in the direction of the Sinclairs, whom she met and became friendly with. Whenever possible she and her husband visited the Lake District and in her words 'the Sinclairs taught me the trade'. The years passed and like so many people in these difficult times she found work becoming more onerous and less satisfying. The green fields and tranquility of the countryside beckoned. The Sinclairs talked about retiring and the thought of her taking on the mantle of Barnhaven arose. They pointed out the difficulties and asked whether she really knew what she was taking on. Angela admits, at the time, she didn't, although convinced it would be enjoyable.

The decision made, the problem of finding and financing a suitable property arose. The high property prices prevailing in the UK almost caused the project to founder. A lucky set of circumstances intervened. Angela's husband, who is a translator, wanted to spend more time in France to keep his language up-to-date. On a holiday in 1989 it became obvious that house prices were much cheaper in France and suitable properties, smallish houses with about an acre of land, were quite common.

In January 1989 the decision was made. Angela was on an academic staff contract and required to give a terms notice so the move to France took place on 18 January 1990.

The house chosen was a typical farmhouse, four miles from the sea, in the small village of Plouzélambre.

Permission had to be obtained from the French authorities to run a horticultural business and this was duly granted. The first seeds were sown in March 1990 in a compost recommended by a local grower. This proved totally unsuitable and Barnhaven 3, as Angela christened the company, almost foundered at the first of many hurdles. Nevertheless, she persevered despite finding that growing primroses commercially was an entirely different proposition to helping experienced people like the Sinclairs, or growing them for a hobby. Soon her first seed list was issued and this has steadily expanded in the last four years. Most of the famous Barnhaven strains are now being offered.

In the last years prior to the Sinclairs' retirement some deterioration took place in quality. This was certainly the feeling of several regular customers, both in the UK and America, and the gardening journalist, Graham Rice, commented on it in his book *Hardy Perennials* published in 1995, expressing the hope that, with the move to Brittany, the trend would be reversed.

It is to be hoped, that in time, Angela Bradford at Barnhaven 3 will gain the same reputation and respect accorded to her illustrious predecessors, Florence Bellis and Jared Sinclair, at the height of their fame.

In summary, seed from Barnhaven has produced tens of thousands of wonderful plants in a variety of different types. In his final catalogue, Jared Sinclair referred to the lack of recognition for the pioneers who had surrendered a large part of their lives to create the polyanthus as known today. He was no doubt referring to both Florence Bellis and himself, possibly others like Frank Reinelt. Barnhaven was never a money-making operation but has made a great deal for others. Double primroses from Barnhaven seed have been produced in huge quantities by micropropagation and sold across the world wherever primroses are grown. This has happened to a lesser extent to some of the 'Cowichan' polyanthus. In none of these instances have the originators profited. All of this was perfectly legal and Barnhaven themselves could have made a great deal more money if they had adopted a purely commercial approach. That they chose not to do so meant poor financial rewards but it also produced a range of unique primroses and polyanthus that have enriched the gardens of primrose growers the world over.

9 COMMERCIAL PRIMROSES

While development of the polyanthus reached a peak in the 1950s and 1960s commercial plant-breeders were working on improving the primrose.

Polyanthus had become very large and were not ideal as pot plants. A shorter more compact plant was required for a burgeoning market in spring pot plants.

By the 1960s numerous pot-plant strains had been introduced, many emanating from the Continent, especially Germany and Switzerland. Examples included 'Vatter's Strain', 'Biedermeier', 'Amulett', 'Premiere' and 'Grandiflora'.

A Swiss breeder, Herr Bonsack, in the early 1960s, is credited as having created the base for the modern types, breeding from the 'Aalsmeer', 'Potsdam' and 'Pacific Giant' strains; later he began the process that led to the 'Wanda hybrids', perfected by Niederlenz.

This trend continued in the 1970s and 1980s, with many strains introduced of F1 *acaulis*-type plants having large brightly coloured flowers. They were mainly the result of crossing primroses with polyanthus

and often had short polyanthus stems.

Monsieur Clause, at Brétigny-sur-Orge near Paris, was the major breeder and producer in the 1970s and 1980s and Brétigny was considered, in Mr K. Sahin's words, '*The* place of pilgrimage for all people concerned with commercial primroses'.

The modern commercial strains are all based on Frank Reinelt's 'Pacific' polyanthus strain. Mr Sahin visited Capitola in the mid-1960s and saw the strain in its best original form with colours and colour combinations not known today. The only drawback was the polyanthus form – it was not the desirable stemless type favoured by the European and Japanese growers.

The pot-plant market for primroses took off. Millions are now sold annually throughout the world, and a number of highly professional companies are engaged in the business of developing and producing new strains to meet the demand. Primrose seed is small and light and a gram can contain between 900 and 2000 seeds. At a retail cost of around £250 a gram (£7000 an ounce) seed is more valuable than gold! The

UK was once the major seed-producing centre, with over 350 companies engaged in this activity during the 1950s. Only a handful remain, one being Bypass Nurseries of Marks Tey in Essex, formerly the centre of such activity.

In January 1995 I visited Colegrave Seeds, at Adderbury near Banbury, Oxfordshire. Colegrave are one of the largest wholesale flower seed companies in the United Kingdom and I interviewed John Gibson, Seed Director, and Alan Miles, Marketing Manager. John Gibson also showed me the primrose trials in a large glasshouse – hundreds of plants flowering freely in mid-January!

John and Alan explained the dynamics of the market. The primrose market extends over six months, between October and March. This requires early, mid-season and late-flowering varieties, as no primrose blooms for six months. Two basic markets exist, one for pot plants, requiring a larger plant and flowers, and one for baskets, where a smaller, more compact plant is needed. Although primroses have always been regarded as fairly long-lived perennials, these pot strains are intended as annuals, to be discarded and replaced by newly purchased plants the following year. Many of these new strains are only half-hardy and will not flourish in gardens unless the climate is mild. These developments are something that gardening 'purists' find hard to accept, but the commercial success speaks for itself. Whatever one's views on this point, there can be little doubt that some of the new strains are very striking. The self colours are brilliant while some of the new bi-colours are very attractive indeed. The unfortunately named

'Wanda hybrids' produce a whole range of very attractive plants and have become very popular in the last few years.

Much breeding activity is underway with primroses, and many people, in several countries, are involved. It is a highly scientific and precise approach that aims to provide plants that behave in exactly the manner required. Flowering plants, of a uniform character, must be ready for the market when required. At one time most of this breeding and seed harvesting took place in the UK but this has changed, as it is easier to produce seed abroad in more reliable climates.

Who are the companies involved and what do they offer? One of the best-known is the Japanese company of Sakata, who have become very well known outside Japan in the last 40 years, although in business since 1913. I should point out that primroses, important though they are, remain only a part of the wide range of flower types that Sakata and competing companies offer.

Apart from the 'Pacific' polyanthus, covered elsewhere, Sakata sell three strains of primrose, all F1 types. They are the extra-early 'Pageant' series, the early 'Prominent' series and the semi-miniature 'Lovely' series. 'Pageant' and 'Prominent' are available in a wide range of colours and bi-colours, 13 and 11 respectively. The 'Lovely' series are smaller, more compact plants in seven shades. These three strains are for the pot-plant market and no mention is made in the literature about growing outside.

A few years ago Sakata marketed a range of miniature primroses that they called Julian hybrids. At least five types were listed in the 1988/9 catalogue. They were 'Hybridas', 'Bicolors', 'Cheerleaders', 'Gold Ridges' and

'Cherriette'. These plants were semi-hardy and intended for small pot-plant culture. For a while they were widely offered by retail seedsmen and became quite popular with primrose enthusiasts, resembling *juliae* hybrids with more brilliant colours. I asked Mike Hull, of Sakata Seed Europe, about their demise. Mike said that they had not proved a commercial success and so regrettably are no more, although I notice Thompson and Morgan are offering, in the 1996 catalogue, a juliana mini-strain that looks very similar.

An American company, Goldsmiths Seeds, Inc., has a good reputation, and I spoke to the chief plant breeder, Jan Sijm, who is based at Goldsmith Seeds Europe, at Andjik in the Netherlands. Colegrave regard his strains very highly and plantings of 'Quantum' and 'Gemini' were in the trials. 'Quantum' is early season and available in nine colours, while 'Gemini' follows in ten colours. Both were very attractive, with excellent uniformity, quite the best of all the strains on trial. The flowers, although large, were not oversized, and Goldsmith also recommend both strains for outdoor bedding in mild-winter climates in protected areas.

Ernst Benary, established in Erfurt, Germany in 1843, have been plant-breeding for over 150 years. Mr K. Wagner has been responsible for the primrose breeding since the beginning of the 1970s, and as well as the famous 'Crescendo' polyanthus raised 'Pacino' and the *acaulis* (*vulgaris*) strains 'Premiere', 'Ernst Benary', 'Laurin', 'Finesse', 'Finale', 'Joker', 'Fama', and the juliana strain 'Valentin'. 'Valentin' was a miniature primrose similar to the Sakata julianas but is no longer grown. The range is 'Fama', 'Ernst Benary', 'Finesse', 'Joker', 'Lucento' and 'Finale' – all

F1 hybrids. The 1996 introductions are 'Lucento' and 'Joker'.

'Lucento' is a mid-late-season variety with eye-catching colours, clear pink, salmon pink, amaranth, apricot, bright red, deep red, violet and canary-yellow. The yellow centres are smaller and less obvious than many of the other *vulgaris* strains and this accentuates the very attractive, luminous, colours. 'Lucento' will undoubtedly become very popular. Colegrave's describe 'Lucento' as being reminiscent of the Wanda type but not quite as hardy.

'Joker' is of the type that people either love or hate, a 50/50 mixture of clear and bi-colours. The flowers are very large with separate colours of carmine with eye, cherry, violet with eye and red and gold. This is a mid-season variety and will certainly appeal to those who like these multi-coloured primroses. In 1996 and 1997 I took particular note in the spring of the primroses on sale at local garden centres, and the bi-colours were selling very well. It was interesting to note the very large quantities on offer, an indication of their popularity and the size of the market.

Another major player is the Danish firm Daehnfeldt. This long-established company was originally oriented to the home market but has grown into one that is highly international. They have perfected the performance of primroses by using vitro-propagated clones for their F1 hybrid seed production and have a reputation for high quality.

Originally, the only primrose strain offered was Dania but this grew over five to six years, with four more series added. The first Bicolour F1 was in 1987, followed by

Danova in 1989. This latter grew to 20 colours. In 1993/4 the Grande F1 was introduced, followed by Daniella F1 in 1995 for late sales. Until then the focus had been on early to mid-season varieties for the Danish market.

The star is Danova F1, an early-flowering variety, in a very wide range of colours and shades. Bicolour F1 is as described, with seven bicolours identified as Meteor, Dione, Sinope, Elara, Leda, Rhea, Calypso and Triton. They cover a mix of rose, pink, purple and yellow shades. Grande F1 is a huge-flowering plant, even earlier than Danova in white, yellow, light rose, purple with white edge and burgundy. The original Dania F1 series is still available, a mid-early plant, large-flowered in the standard colours including blue. Finally, Daniella F1 is a late series comparable, in quality, to Danova. The colour range is restricted to six colours, including an attractive apricot.

Future plans are to improve the quality of the range offered, especially with regard to uniformity and plant habit. Daehnfeldt say that new unique colours will be introduced replacing some existing ones.

Royal Sluis, started some 125 years ago by the Sluis family, were bought in 1995 by Petoseed, the vegetable section of George Ball Inc. of America. During the 125 years of their existence they have majored mainly in the breeding and sale of vegetables. In recent years development of ornamental plants has increased, and this includes primroses. David Wales, the Ornamental Sector Manager, in a letter, says that the UK market demands a range of varieties giving a variety of attributes. They are colour range, flower type, compactness, flowering period, clean habit,

acceptable germination and good vigour. This would appear to be the case throughout those areas of the world where these pot-type primroses are grown.

Royal Sluis's commercial range includes varieties from a range of breeders. They also have an exclusive arrangement with a German breeder, Hans Voss, with whom they have worked closely for 15 years. This co-operation has resulted in the following F1 varieties:

'Anjulette' A miniature type with a wide range of both foliage and flower colours, ideal for bowl work.

'Belinda' An exceptionally tidy and compact, mid-season variety with a basic colour range.

'Paloma Plus' The latest update of the popular 'Paloma' rang, with a wide and varied colour range, a mid-early variety.

'Confetti' Similar to 'Paloma' but a mixture of bi-colour and pastel shades.

'Springtime' A late-season variety with a particularly wide colour range for this period.

'Pola' A hardy recent introduction with a standard colour range directed specifically – and this is most interesting – at the outdoor bedding market.

'Revue' A 1996 introduction, a mid-season strain of more robust habit with a standard colour range. 'Revue' is described as a 'very predictable' variety, therefore simple to produce.

David makes a number of interesting points about the present market and possible future trends. Commercially, one of the overriding factors is price. The cost of seed, young plants and the finished product is continually under pressure. Alan Miles of Colegrave's made the same point about price, with the purchaser not prepared to pay more than about 65 pence for a flowering plant. Enthusiasts have always been ready to pay higher prices for something they really want, but unfortunately they represent a tiny percentage of the gardening public.

It is also noted that more and more people are using these plants in the garden and in tubs on patios. As David Wales says this could well create a demand for hardier varieties that are more robust and weather-resistant with a wider range of flower and leaf colours. I subscribe to this seeing the numbers of these pot-type primroses planted in gardens in my village. I find them unattractive grown in this way and perhaps a different type of plant is required for garden use. A few hardy strains are still offered by the retail seedsmen, and Barnhaven have both *vulgaris* (*acaulis*) and juliana types for outdoor use. However, as already said, the polyanthus is a far superior garden plant except where space is at a premium.

The Dutch company of K. Sahin, Zaden BV have always been keen to develop new types and colour combinations. A special development is a range of large-flowered hardy *vulgaris* primroses for outdoor use. Although they currently list only two strains – F1s 'Spectrum', and 'Picotee' – both cover an exceptionally wide range of types and colours. The 'Picotee' range of bi-colours are individually named, with examples being 'Lollipop', 'Peaches in Cream' and 'Frangipani'. 'Spectrum' has an amazing range of types and colours covering the whole 'spectrum'. There are laced, bi-colours and

standard forms, at least three distinct groups in the one strain. Once again each is individually named, except 'Fascination' which covers five separate combinations. Sahin seem a very innovative company and are currently working on a range of large-flowered hose-in-hose primroses and polyanthus in a comprehensive colour range.

S & G Seeds of Ormskirk, Lancashire, in addition to polyanthus also offer several primrose strains developed by the S & G/Sandoz group. They are F1s 'Peseta', 'Lira', 'Corona', 'Ulrike' and 'Tina'. Other non-F1 varieties are 'Sterling', 'SG90' and 'Peer Gynt'. 'Peseta', 'Lira' and 'Corona' are early, early mid-season and mid-season respectively. They come in a wide range of colours and are intended for the pot-plant market. 'Ulrike' is an interesting variety with bi-colour flowers in a range of pastel shades. 'Tina' is another bi-colour with a colour range from plum to pale pink.

A relatively new British company is Floranova, based at Foxley in East Anglia. Floranova was established in 1978 to breed key species of bedding plants for the UK and international seed trade. This company is research-based and has already established a reputation for innovation in bedding and pot-plant breeding. Seed is produced at Foxley and also in both the northern and southern hemispheres. This ensures year-round production as Floranova's seed is sold throughout the world. Sales of plants and seed to nurserymen and growers throughout the UK are made via an integral subsidiary, Elite seeds.

The range from Floranova are the F1s 'Festival' and 'Pirouette' and three open-pollinated types, 'Wanda Supreme',

'Masquerade' and 'Dreambird'.

'Festival' is a standard early mid-season, December-to-January primrose with a range of colours that continue to be increased and upgraded. 'Pirouette' is a most attractive bi-colour mixture of yellow, pink and orange shades. It is a miniature, bearing some superficial resemblance to the original Sakata juliana strains. It is classed as a miniature, but the flowers are still almost 50 mm (2 in) across on plants 100–125 mm (4–5 in) high. This type is mature, with no current breeding work. 'Masquerade' and 'Dreambird' are both open-pollinated types intended for late flowering – the end of February onwards.

The pick of current offerings must be 'Wanda Supreme'. This is a reselection of the earlier 'Wanda hybrid' seed strain, with improved uniformity and vigour. The original 'Wanda hybrid' seed strain was developed at the Niederlenz Horticultural School in Switzerland about 25 years ago, and development continues. This was started by crossing *juliae* hybrids together but since then many others have been involved and other blood, including some Barnhaven 'Cowichan', has been introduced. The problem with the 'Wanda hybrids' has been lack of uniformity. Nick Belfield-Smith, responsible for plant-breeding at Floranova, confirms that breeding better vigour and uniformity into the 'Wandas' proved difficult. In 1995 I noted polyanthus stems on several plants – hardly Wanda-like! Nevertheless, Floranova's 'Wanda Supreme' are considered the best, of those at present on offer, of what is a fascinating and interesting series.

Nick Belfield-Smith says that Floranova are primarily concerned with introducing high value F1 hybrids but are increasingly being asked to come up with more competitive open-pollinated lines. They have a number of projects underway exploring more innovative ideas, with a view to creating value-enhanced products that are of a unique or unusual nature. This sounds intriguing and we await future developments with interest.

The above does not cover all available strains by any means. Other companies who offer primroses include Adolf Ebbing-Lohaus, Chrestensen, Elidia, Farmen, Flecke Saaten Handel, Mauser, Meisert, Miyoshi, Roggli, Schäfers, Sluis & Groot, Takii, Thorberger and Wyss.

Adolf Ebbing-Lohaus are one of the largest German producers of both seeds and seedlings. They have a large range with some interesting new colours and colour combinations. Chrestensen and Flecke Saaten Handel are also German, Chrestensen formerly an East German company.

Elidia is a large French producer, mainly for the French market, strains include the early flowering 'Flamina Mixed' and 'Rapid Mixed'.

Semi Farmen, an Italian company based in Naples, have been responsible for a number of original new colours and patterns. Their strain is heat-tolerant and popular in Mediterranean climates for both pot and bedding use.

Meisert are well known for their very late-flowering primroses; a good financial product for the grower.

Miyoshi, a Japanese company, have a wide and special range with interesting colours including the 'Higo' primroses, much to the taste of the Japanese because of the upright flower habit. Another Japanese company is Takii with the 'Soprano' series.

The Swiss firm of Roggli, better known for pansies, offered an interim type primrose-polyanthus range in the 1970s and 1980s, in a limited but bright colour range. Samen Mauser are also Swiss and market the original 'Wanda hybrids' while offering other strains like 'Easter Joy' and 'Winter Melody'.

Schäfers are a German breeder-producer who are not well known outside Germany but have an important position in the domestic market.

Sluis & Groot, another Dutch company, are a major breeder and producer of very commercial pot-plant types with a basic colour range but a reputation for high quality.

Thorberger exhibit very large-flowered *vulgaris*-type primroses at German exhibitions which Mr Sahin thinks may be due to a special cultural regime, as others who have grown the strain get normal-sized flowers.

Finally, the famous old Swiss firm of Wyss were the originators of the first picotee types derived from the 'Victorian' polyanthus. Mr Sahin says they also bred the first 'true' green primroses.

In 1996 the Colchester-based seed supplier Moles Seeds carried out a cold-house primrose trial in which some of the strains described, as well as several others, took part. An article in *Horticultural Week*, 4 April summarized the results. One, from a Dutch independent breeder, Herman van Mierlo, is the 'Polka' range, described as 'outstanding' in Mole's trials. It seems the list is endless, but it must be remembered that competing companies are producing mainly similar products that bear a close resemblance to one another. Also some of the companies are small, while to others primroses are a minor part of their business.

There are, in addition to the 'Wanda hybrids', some others that are intended for outdoor use. The Jelitto Seed Company of Swarmstedt, Germany, offer the F1 Bergfrühling hybrids, a winter-hardy strain in shades of blue, pink, red and yellow. This originated by crosses between *P. vulgaris* hybrids, in separate colours, and two different forms of *P. juliae*. Jelitto developed this strain and registered the name in 1985. Plants are smaller, about 75 mm (3 in) high, with flowers up to 37 mm (1 ½ in) diameter. They are closer to the *juliae* hybrids and bear some resemblance to the 'Wanda' types. In England seed and plants are available from Fieldhouse Nurseries of Gotham, near Nottingham.

The 'Husky' strain, in shades of scarlet, white, rose, pink, yellow, orange, gold and blue, was produced for outdoor use and is recommended for bedding. Colegrave say that 'Husky' was bred especially for UK winter conditions and is the primrose equivalent of the 'Crescendo' polyanthus. Personally, I would always prefer a good polyanthus for garden planting, and for limited spaces a smaller-flowered primrose, like the Berfrühling or Wanda; though this is purely a matter of personal taste.

Barnhaven also offer a wide range for outdoor planting. The *vulgaris* (*acaulis*) include yellows, reds, whites, blues, pinks and a variety of other hues with names like 'Osiered Amber', 'Casquet' and – a 1995 introduction – 'Harmony', described as a new mixture of pastel shades including blues, pinks and mauves. I prefer the stronger colours, like 'Tartan Reds' and 'Candy Pinks' and find some of the paler shades less attractive, not living up to the descriptions in fact, again a matter of personal taste.

The juliana strain from Barnhaven has a good reputation and at its peak was the best *juliae* type on offer. Initially they were not available from France but by 1992 some colours had reappeared. The cushion forms are only available, in the 1995 list, in yellow and blue with Angela Bradford commenting that red was proving difficult to fix. The stalked or miniature polyanthus strains, 'Fireflies' and 'Footlight Parade', together with separate red and yellow shades are listed.

Jelitto and Barnhaven are retail companies, so seed can be purchased directly from them whereas the others described sell to the trade. There are numerous well-known and slightly less well-known retail seedsmen who sell a limited range of primrose seed, usually including at least one 'exclusive' mixture. Those strains on offer tend to fluctuate year by year, with some disappearing and new ones appearing. For this reason I am reluctant to go into detail about what is on offer.

As it is one of the largest companies, offering a wider range than most, I contacted Thompson and Morgan and enquired about their future plans. A letter from the chairman, Keith Sangster, told me that T & M currently have 'a broad breeding programme' which includes both primroses and polyanthus. He says that 'uniquely for a commercial company we will not be looking for material that can be sold as pot plants but… looking for and developing new colours in hardy Polyanthus and Primrose

types.' Mr Sangster further says, in his letter of 27 March 1996, that 'we are still two to three years off offering our first product.' We await developments with interest.

What does the future hold in the commercial field? Naturally the companies involved will not discuss current and forthcoming projects in this highly competitive field, other than in general terms. They are constantly testing each other's products and headhunting of key staff from rivals is not unknown.

The ultimate aim is to develop a race of highly uniform, free-flowering plants with exceptional vigour, a large and brilliant range of colours and complete reliability. Seed must germinate as near 100 percent as possible on a timescale that allows flowering plants to be ready exactly when needed.

I asked Colegrave's whether these astonishing developments in commercial primroses had been market-driven. Their reply was this was partly the case, but considerable effort has gone into gaining acceptance of plants that have little resemblance to the original wild parents. The vast numbers sold bear witness to the success of the strategy and each year even greater numbers are sold at garden centres and other retail outlets.

In studying plants on sale in the early weeks of 1996, I saw that the most noticeable features were the enormous flowers, monstrous in some instances, and the brilliant – dare I say – garish colours. The balance of some does not look right, with huge flowers dumped in the centre. I know that not all are like this, and I was very impressed with Goldsmith's 'Quantum' strain in Colegrave's trials – rather more restrained than some others. The 'Wanda' seed strains are also attractive although even here the flowers are getting larger. There are many primrose lovers who question these developments, much preferring slightly smaller flowers and a better balanced, more natural-looking plant. We shall have to see what the future brings.

10 CULTIVATION

PRIMROSES

Roy Genders wrote in *Primroses*, 'they are amongst the easiest plants to grow… given a little attention will flourish in almost any type of soil and in any part of Britain.' He conceded that doubles required rather more exacting conditions and cited his own experience in growing 50 different doubles over a 12 year period in his own garden.

The wild primrose is often quoted as an example of this ease of growth. Hecker (1971) says, 'Our native primroses and cowslips can be found… in almost any kind of soil, in sun or shade… unaffected by the coldest of winters.' He does go on to say that the largest plants are to be found in the warmer and damper parts of the British Isles, 'especially in the West Country and Ireland'. Barbara Shaw (1991) says, 'Primroses… are not difficult plants,' and as one of the holders of the National Collection writes from recent experience.

Graham Rice has an interesting chapter on primroses in *Hardy Perennials* (1995). In discussing the difficulties in growing named clones, especially doubles, he blames drought and vine weevil as 'the two reasons that

primrose-growing in Britain has been in a state of crisis'. This is the first time that the problems that many experience in growing these plants have been stated so bluntly. While agreeing in principle, I suspect there are other reasons.

The general conditions that primroses require are well known: a moist but well-drained fertile soil, containing ample humus in a partially shaded position. Ideally the plants are exposed to early morning sun but shaded for the remainder of the day. In dry periods they must be well watered and regularly top-dressed with some form of humus. Garden compost, hen manure mixed with peat, sedge peat, leafmould, horse and cow manure, mushroom compost, chaff, spent hops, seaweed and various other materials have been recommended at one time or another. We now have substitutes, including pine bark and some proprietary 'mulching' mixtures. Whatever mulch is used it must be well rotted, especially so in the case of animal manures.

Reading of past disasters, when large losses of plants were incurred, the main cause seems to have been drought, often in association with high temperatures and a degree of neglect.

With primroses, like some other plants, the apparent ease with which they were grown in the past causes some to study the old writings in order to discover the lost 'magic formula'. Personally, while interesting, I think this is a wasted effort as present-day conditions bear little resemblance to those of even 50 years ago. If one goes back even further, 100 or 200 years, then we might be living on a different planet. The population of the UK has increased enormously, with buildings taking up more and more land, while the motor vehicle has replaced the horse. One consequence of this is that gardens have been getting smaller – many are now like the proverbial postage stamp. Another factor is pollution in its many forms. Mrs Eda Hume, writing on growing doubles although admitting to having lost all her plants, in an appendix to Sacheverell Sitwell's *Old Fashioned Flowers*, says 'Small town gardens have little chance of success. I am now so built up all around me, buses passing, leaving exhaust fumes and petrol smells, and road dust, I would never attempt them again.' She was writing in 1939, so one wonders what she would make of today's conditions! Mrs Pam Gossage, one of the National Collection holders, has a rural garden, a few miles from Yeovil, in Somerset. She has lived there for many years and told me that even the farmyard manure from the farm next to her is no longer the same.

The number of people who have large gardens, ideal for primroses, are in the minority. They do still exist, but few enthusiasts of my acquaintance have one. How many gardeners do you know who have an old apple orchard for instance? This was the preferred site for primroses in the distant past with the plants growing beneath the apple trees. Shady banks and ditch gardens are other sites that have been quoted, but once again who is lucky enough to have such luxuries? Most of the old orchards have been concreted over and are now part of housing estates. This means that, in order to grow and enjoy these plants, different growing techniques may be necessary. I am referring to named clones rather than seed-raised plants. In the latter case, seedling vigour provides a good show for two to three years even in less than perfect conditions, and the plants can be grown in a similar way to garden polyanthus.

Where conditions are suitable – a mature garden with good fertile soil and ample shade – then the orthodox methods work well. Good drainage is essential and the soil must contain plenty of humus, the ideal being well-decayed farmyard manure that has been kept under cover, and half-rotted leafmould. The bed in which they are planted should be well dug initially, double digging is the old method, to a depth of at least 300 mm (12 in). Farmyard manure is incorporated in the bottom layer with the half rotted leaves in the top 50–75 mm (2–3 in). Farmyard manure varies, some of it is nearly all straw, and if it has been kept in a heap exposed to the elements then most of the goodness will have been leached away. The term leafmould is often misinterpreted. The black decomposed residue, dug from woods, is properly known as leaf soil, not mould. The best plan is to collect leaves in the autumn, ideally beech or oak, and put them slightly damp into black plastic binliners. The bags are tied, a few holes made

Fig. 7. Propagation by division.

in them, and placed in a shed or garage corner for nine to 12 months. This is quite long enough. The partially decomposed leaves are then put through an electric or petrol driven shredder. The resulting shredded leaves are perfect for composts or top dressing of precious plants. When collecting leaves the law must be observed and leaves not taken from places where such activity is forbidden. It is still possible, in many parts of the country, to obtain at least small quantities of leaves legally. Care should be exercised in collecting from the side of roads because of possible contamination. If one does not have access to a shredder – it is possible to hire one – then the leaves must be kept rather longer, another year or so. When suitably decomposed they can be sieved and crumble to the touch.

If farmyard manure and decayed leaves are not available then substitutes will have to be used. It is still possible to get horse manure from many riding stables. Some even give it away, while others make a small nominal charge. Mushroom compost, made with horse manure, is also acceptable. Up until the advent of the motor car, horses were the usual mode of transport. One would assume therefore that horse manure was readily available, and used in much greater quantities than cow manure to fertilize gardens. I think this was the case until well into this century.

Spent mushroom compost contains chalk, but as primroses are not recognized lime-haters can be used. I was able to grow primroses on the hot dry chalky soils of Oxfordshire by adding liberal supplies of humus, although they are not so long-lived.

Shade is another essential condition, filtered shade being the ideal. Small deciduous trees or shrubs are suitable shade-providers. Primroses flower when the branches are still bare. The leaves start appearing in late spring and give cover during the hot summer months. They also provide a mulch and humus with autumn leaf fall. This is what happens with the wild primrose – nature's way. Another means of providing shade in more open positions is by growing herbaceous plants or perennials amongst them. When these plants make their summer growth, the primroses are shaded from the heat of the sun. Annuals can be used for the same purpose.

Assuming your primroses are happy, they will eventually increase making large clumps. If left, most have a tendency to die out in the centre and should be divided, usually after two years. Those with *juliae* blood increase by stolons which root as they spread. They are the easiest to divide, but others make separate crowns which can be gently 'teased' apart, in the old phrase, to form new plants. The time to divide plants is when they are ready and the time of year is suitable. This is a broad statement but means there are no hard and fast rules. A lot depends on where one lives and on weather conditions. In the South of England early autumn is probably the best time and it should never be attempted during hot, dry periods. Past growers have given all sorts of conflicting advice, but they lived in a different era.

The actual process is simple and involves separating the new crowns from the old rootstock, which is discarded. Often they can be pulled apart. If the clumps are particularly large and tough, one old method is to use two hand forks back to back to prise them apart. A hand trowel is also useful and can be used to carefully separate divisions while the plant is still in the ground. The division is lifted with ample soil around the roots and will establish very well. A knife can be used although the old growers, primarily talking about gold-laced polyanthus, said you should never take a knife to them.

The cut or torn surfaces should be dusted with green or yellow sulphur before replanting into a previously prepared bed. Shortening the roots to about 100 mm (4 in) and twisting off the larger leaves down to 75 mm (3 in) is often recommended. I am not convinced that this is necessary although Barbara Shaw does it. The crucial factor is that care should be exercised when dividing the plants. Another thing to avoid is making too many divisions. The resulting plants are small, have insufficient roots and foliage, and are difficult to establish. I have received named primrose plants from some commercial growers that were literally tiny pieces and, despite every effort, refused to grow.

The divisions should be replanted into their new positions and given a thorough watering. They must not be allowed to dry out and should be well established before winter sets in, with sufficient new root growth to anchor them against soil upheaval caused by frost. They can be treated with a suitable fungicide after replanting, to prevent rot developing in the centre, a real possibility at this stage. A mulch is also beneficial but take care not to smother the plants.

DOUBLE PRIMROSES

Although similar in most respects to that for single primroses, cultivation of doubles requires more skill. While they were grown in great numbers in the eighteenth and nineteenth centuries, it seems cultivation was always troublesome apart from the common white, lilac and yellow varieties. *The Gardener's Chronicle* for 8 April 1882 has the following comment: 'If some one were to rise up who could inform us how to treat the beautiful old double crimson primrose...

they would do a substantial service to practical horticulture.' This refers to 'Madame Pompadour', and in the same issue E. Jenkins writes 'it should never see a ray of sun or feel the frost and must be kept incessantly moist.' An earlier issue, 11 Dec 1880, says 'That these charming spring-flowering plants should be favourites is not to be wondered at, but that they are difficult to cultivate is a truism.' Then, referring to growing them in pots: 'The general complaint is that the plants dwindle away to nothingness, and a kind of rot passing up what is termed the "carrot" causes a decay.' In the 22 November 1884 issue, Hy Johnston writes: 'I find no difficulty in propagating or growing this class of plant, as I have been successful with them for many years.' The magazines response was to ask for her method of cultivation.

In the 1950s the nurseryman T. A. Townsend sent out a special growing mixture with each plant of 'Madame Pompadour', claiming to have discovered 'a method of growing this more satisfactory'. Not long afterwards a supplement to the catalogue had this comment: 'Money can be lost very easily with these. I lost £85 on Madame De Pompadour. Discarded now. Rose Du Barry, too, proved hopeless.'

The previous few examples illustrate that the double primrose is a capricious plant that has always caused both delight and despair to its adherents. During this century there have been several instances where gardeners, both amateur and professional, have claimed they were 'easy' plants and waged campaigns to persuade the less successful that this was so. A notable example was Major Taylor of Glazeley Gardens. He grew many thousands and put on large displays to promote the plants. Glazeley Gardens was at Bridgnorth in Shropshire and the plants were grown in a field. Major Taylor dressed this field with large quantities of 'chaff', the remains of rotted straw, which was then rotovated. The reason he used straw was because he could get it from the local farmer, who was reluctant to let go of his manure but quite happy to get rid of the chaff. Despite Taylor's efforts the reputation for difficulty continued. Others like William Holt in Dorset grew a large number and similarly claimed they were 'not difficult'. Examples of this are fairly frequent, and one can divide the growers of doubles into two camps, roughly 'optimists' and 'pessimists'. Even so it is not unusual to discover that successful growers suffered large losses, sometimes almost their entire stock.

William Holt's method was interesting. He maintained that the secret was to keep splitting and replanting, although cautioning against too small divisions. He also discarded most of the foliage and cut off the long roots, the idea being to keep the plant working. Plants were grown in two 24 ft x 14 ft (7.2 m x 4.2 m) shade tunnels, structures of metal hoops covered with Netlon greenhouse shading. In these he grew 1100 doubles, and a friend, who visited him and bought plants, attested to the health and vigour of his stock. The soil in which they grew was very soft and sandy and the plants could literally be lifted from the soil without need of trowel or fork.

William used sedge peat, a black soil-like peat which was available locally. This is quite different to the lighter-coloured and fibrous moss peat used in composts. He dressed the soil with at least 1 cwt (25.4 kilograms) to 2 sq yards (1.7 sq m). Although his soil was light, drying out quickly, he dug in coarse grit and finished with a dressing of bone meal. Phostrogen, a high-potash powdered fertilizer, was dusted on the beds twice during the summer. The plants were sprayed with systemic fungicides and insecticides at regular intervals. He was also adamant that plants should never be allowed to dry out, especially in summer.

The great Reginald Farrer said that doubles required 'A very stiff, rich greasy soil (with no stint of liquid manure for which they are insatiable)'. Certainly doubles are gross feeders and need a richer soil than the single primrose. They have a tendency to flower themselves to death and spent flowers should be removed to prevent rot developing, which then spreads to the rest of the plant. A good mulch after flowering is essential, and a liquid feed beneficial. Barbara Shaw recommends manure water 'the colour of good ale'. This is obtained by soaking manure in a container of water which is then diluted before applying. You may not wish to do this and there are several excellent liquid fertilizers that give equally good results. I like Maxicrop liquid seaweed, and there are other suitable high-potash feeds. The Devon nursery Champernowne recommended lawn mowings as a mulch and used hoof and horn meal as a substitute for farmyard manure. The list is endless and a hundred and one different solutions can be quoted from previous writers going back more than 200 years.

It is puzzling why some varieties succeed and others fail. About 30 years ago I was visiting relatives in the Tyne Valley near Newcastle. My uncle had a large general nursery at a small village called Mickley. On idly poking around, I found some left-over double lilac primroses that had been literally dumped on the ground. They had rooted into the soil, and while not exactly thriving were growing. And this is one of the varieties that dates back to the nineteenth and possibly eighteenth century!

GARDEN POLYANTHUS

Garden polyanthus are easy to grow and will tolerate a wide range of conditions. They are relatively short-lived, mostly two to three years before being discarded, and provide a brilliant array of colours for spring bedding. Selected plants, especially some of the Barnhaven strains, may be divided and maintained for longer, but in general this is not done as it is so easy to raise them from seed.

Plants can be purchased ready for planting in their final positions, or raised from seed. If raised from seed the seedlings must never suffer from lack of moisture during the summer, otherwise growth may be seriously retarded. They can, when large enough, be planted out in suitable weather from early September onwards; in milder climates it may be possible to plant as late as December. Proper preparation of the soil will ensure the best results but they will give a good show even under less favourable circumstances.

Providing the roots remain moist, the best position is an open one in full sun. Plants in semi-shade grow larger but may not flower quite as freely. Nevertheless, a small group of three of four plants, preferably of the same colour, look very good in a partially shaded

position.

Polyanthus require a fertile soil, moist but not waterlogged, and a mulch should be carefully worked under the leaves and around the crowns in early March.

GOLD-LACED POLYANTHUS

A great deal has been written on the cultivation of the gold-laced polyanthus reaching back over 200 years. As a florists' flower, elaborate instructions were issued for its cultivation, and to repeat them would probably deter all but the most hardened enthusiast. As usual, the old growers' advice should be taken with a pinch of salt, as some of the elaborate procedures and weird composts are quite unnecessary. There is not sufficient space to go into such detail here, so I will summarize the main points.

To begin with gold-laced are not quite as hardy as garden polyanthus. They are smaller, have softer foliage and are less robust. The conditions they require are similar to those of the choicer primroses. In harsher climates, if grown outside, they need protection in winter from frost and east winds, as well as excessive wet. It was the old practice to grow them in raised beds, and they were covered in winter with frames or cloches. The plants were lifted in spring, potted up for exhibition and replanted afterwards.

There is some difference of opinion about the best way to grow them. The northern growers maintain that pot culture is anathema and that plants must be grown outside in the old way and given protection where necessary, potted up for exhibition and replanted afterwards. This is disputed by others who have been obliged to grow them in pots. Pot culture is similar to that described for primroses and works for some growers. It does appear, though, that careful open-ground culture may prolong the life of individual clones.

Only a small number, usually including all the main hybridizers, exhibit these plants. For the majority I would regard the gold-laced polyanthus as an easy plant to grow although relatively short-lived. For the would-be exhibitor there are frequent articles, in the NAPS and APS yearbooks, that go into greater detail.

GROWING IN POTS

It is not my intention to dissuade people from growing primroses, either named single clones or any sort of double. They are amongst the loveliest of small garden plants and well worth the effort. They can be grown in the garden, but the named clones and doubles need specially prepared beds and regular attention. Where gardens are unsuitable, either due to size, soil or aspect, there is an alternative.

Primroses can be successfully grown in pots or containers and not just for short periods. They make a delightful conservatory or cold greenhouse plant and provide masses of bloom for several weeks or longer in late winter and spring. This is the case with the large-flowered pot strains that flood the garden centres in the early part of the year. It can also be done with named varieties and home-raised plants.

Generally, the view has been that long-term pot culture is unsuitable, and plants kept in pots soon deteriorate. I would have agreed with this until fairly recently. Margaret

Webster grows nearly all her plants in pots, around 300 at any one time, and has individual clones that are over eight years old. She grows them in soilless compost in plastic pots and repots in August to avoid problems with vine weevil. It is true that she grows mainly seed-raised plants, but she has clones – like the green-flowered primrose – which are given the same treatment.

Kay Overton at Dursley in Gloucestershire has been delighting members and visitors to the NAPS southern and midland shows for several years. Kay exhibits all types of primroses and polyanthus and they are always beautifully grown. Like most of us, she started with the old named varieties and spent a small fortune collecting them. Growing proved difficult and they were not long-lived. She does still have a few and notes that 'Dorothy', which came from the late Mary Mottram's garden in North Devon in 1987, grows very well and has spread to many friends' and neighbours' gardens!

Kay grows most of the Barnhaven strains and has, over the years, received lots of seed from the ever-generous Dr Cecil Jones. Her present-day plants have either Barnhaven blood, 'Penlan' or both.

Kay's garden is on a north-facing, 3-in-1 slope – a frost pocket in winter, baked dry in summer and subject to mud slides when very wet. All her attempts at growing in the open failed so she turned to container culture. She follows Jared Sinclair's advice and grows everything in black plastic polythene bags. Plants for show are put into pots about three to four weeks prior and brought into the greenhouse. The polythene-bagged plants remain outside throughout the year and are kept in dappled shade. In normal summers she finds that watering is rarely necessary. She incorporates lots of grit into her compost and also top-dresses with at least 20 mm (¾ in). This is due to the damp shady conditions with the main problems waterlogging and root rot. Kay admits she suffers losses in winter in these uncovered plants but most survive.

I also grow many primroses in pots. My present home was purchased new some 16 years ago and the unmade garden had an appalling mixture of builders rubble and subsoil. After two years hard work it was planted but the soil is poor for primroses and space is at a premium. Trees and shrubs do well but smaller plants struggle. Primroses flourish for a year or two then dwindle away. The old named clones are hopeless. At the moment I have about 300 primroses in pots. They are grown in plastic pots of various sizes. The largest plants are in 8 inch (200 mm) pots, the smallest in 3 inch (75 mm) pots. Two of the plants in the larger pots are a semi-double lilac and a pink-flowered double 'Garryard'. These plants, *juliae* doubles, were raised nine years ago and have survived in pots ever since. Divisions planted in the garden dwindled away. The compost is John Innes No. 3, bought fresh from Smiths of Green Ore, Somerset, and mixed with extra grit and humus. I have been using Cornish grit, potting-grade bark from Cambark and shredded leafmould as the added ingredients. The result is a more open, coarser mix than that of the John Innes formula which comprises 7 parts sterilized loam, 3 coarse peat, 2 sharp grit plus base fertilizer. With annual repotting, rather like auriculas, it seems perfectly possible to

maintain a good collection in pots.

In winter, pot-grown plants are vulnerable. I once lost 24 beautiful doubles, half of them pink, half blue, to frost. The plants were growing in 5 inch (125 mm) plastic pots in Levington compost. They were in a cold greenhouse on the bench. In January a sudden freeze occurred which lasted two weeks. The plants went limp and failed to recover. Similar plants in the garden were unharmed. Now in winter, I put all the pots together on the greenhouse floor, a glass-to-ground Alton. No more losses have occurred.

While not ideal, pot culture can achieve good results and give great satisfaction.

MICROPROPAGATION

In earlier chapters, tissue culture or micropropagation was mentioned. This laboratory-based technique is used extensively by specialist companies for the mass-production of plants. Micropropagation involves the production of plants from very small plant parts, tissues, or cells grown aseptically in a test tube or other container, with a rigidly controlled sterile environment and nutritional programme. Commonly known as tissue culture, the process was used for research in scientific laboratories for many decades before being applied to the commercial propagation of plants. The most advanced method is called meristem culture and can produce virus-free plants. Meristems are the growth points of the plant and even in affected plants are often free of virus. Embryo flower-bud material can be used to produce similar virus-free plants.

One effect is to rejuvenate plants that

have deteriorated due to virus infection. The other is the opportunity to mass-produce in a way that is not possible with normal vegetative propagation. This has occurred with primroses, particularly the doubles. A number of others like 'Lady Greer' and 'Guinivere' are also mass-produced by this method.

While commercially important, meristem or tissue culture is a complicated and very expensive laboratory procedure and not within the scope of the average amateur gardener.

NORTH AMERICA

In general, enthusiasts in the primrose growing areas of North America have much larger gardens, and my impression is that the plants grow very well, better than in the United Kingdom. More named clones survive, and several that have died out in the UK are still being grown, although correct identification remains a problem. Why is this? I can only think that conditions, with a much lower density of population, are the main reason, although there is no doubting the enthusiasm and expertise of members of the APS. In addition, named primroses have been very popular during the last 50 years and remain so, whereas they have had their ups and downs in the UK.

In places, winter conditions are much harsher than we normally experience, and plants are given protection by covering with pine branches and other materials. Floods also seem to be an ever-present risk in some areas.

Dr John Kerridge of Vancouver grows his primroses on Saltspring Island, some three hours away by Ferry. Despite the plants having to fend for themselves, the conditions obviously suit them and they flourish.

The northwest Pacific states of Oregon and Washington enjoy a climate somewhat similar to the southwest of England. The adjacent Canadian province of British Colombia is another good primrose area.

Surprisingly, parts of Alaska, notably the southeast coastal region, harbour a strong band of enthusiasts. Mr John O'Brien Snr of Juneau writes that while the climate 'is often too cold and miserable for the gardener... the primroses love it.' Mrs Cheri Fluck, also from Juneau, says that the worst problem is the winter freeze, and prized plants must be covered or very well mulched.

AUSTRALIA AND NEW ZEALAND

In Australia the best growing areas are in the southeast, with Tasmania and Victoria having the most suitable conditions. Other good areas where primroses are grown are the mountain districts of New South Wales, southeast Queensland, Canberra and the Adelaide Hills in South Australia.

From Dr Vincent Clark's letter it would seem that climate and growing requirements in Woodend, Victoria, are very similar to parts of the UK and North America.

New Zealand is a long thin country with a varying climate and a variety of soils. Some districts are far more suitable than others with cool moist conditions in spring and autumn. Summers are not excessively hot and winters are mild. Dr Hammett writes 'the seed strains do not over summer well... so are treated as a short term annual.'

11 HYBRIDIZING

Plant-breeding began in the sixteenth century by collecting seed from existing plants with no real system or plan, as the sexuality of plants was not known.

Early in the nineteenth century, plant-breeders, influenced by experiments in controlled pollination by J. G. Koelreuter, began to select both parents for hybridizing. The early plant-breeders did this by isolating the plants and hoping bees would do the rest. Crossing like with like was introduced and later hand-fertilization, which gave more control. Despite a lack of scientific approach, many beautiful ornamental plants were raised, as existing illustrations of the work of breeders prior to 1900 show. This is something that should be considered by amateurs, who may be discouraged by the complexity of genetical science.

It was only in the early years of this century that systematic plant-breeding began, following the discovery of a paper in 1900, first published in 1865 by the Natural History Society of Brun. This was written by Johann Mendel, by then known as 'Brother Gregor', an Augustinian monk who was president of the society.

In 1851 Mendel went to the University of Vienna to study mathematics, physics and the natural sciences, which he did for ten years before returning to the abbey at Brunn. There he began to teach, also working in the kitchen gardens. Mendel had read Darwin's ideas on the origin of species prior to publication and was inspired to begin his experiments with garden peas, which he did for the following eight years. His results laid the basis for the concept of genetic inheritance.

Copies of Mendel's paper were almost certainly sent to both the Linnean Society and the Royal Society in London but despite this remained neglected for another 35 years. Mendel was elected Abbot of Konigskloster in 1868 but only published one more work, in 1869, entitled *On Hieracium (Hawkweed) Hybrids obtained by Artficial fertilization.* Mendel, who died in 1884, was very disappointed that his work had not been recognized but remained confident that eventually this would happen.

Others were working in the world of

Fig. 8. Hybridization.

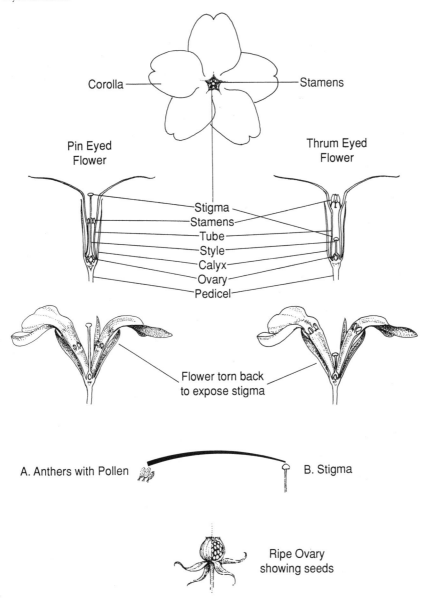

Corolla — Stamens

Pin Eyed
Flower

Thrum Eyed
Flower

Stigma
Stamens
Tube
Style
Calyx
Ovary
Pedicel

Flower torn back
to expose stigma

A. Anthers with Pollen   B. Stigma

Ripe Ovary
showing seeds

Genetics but it was not until de Vries, Correns and Tschermak published papers at the turn of the century, based on conclusions reached by Mendel 35 years earlier, that the mystery of inheritance was solved. The German Botanical Society published de Vries' paper *The Law of Inherited Characteristics* in 1900, in which particular reference was made to Mendel's paper. From this work the science of Genetics was born and enormous strides have been made in plant-breeding, bringing about great improvements in cereals, vegetables and flowers. The modern science of molecular biology, particularly its discovery of DNA, has and is taking Mendel's work further and further.

The value of Mendelism to primroses and polyanthus is shown in present-day strains, producing spectacular plants bearing little if any resemblance to the original species. Some regard these modern strains as 'the epitome of the hybridizers art', while others think the charm of the primrose has been lost in the search for bigger and better flowers, allied to strident colours. Some time ago I read a comment by Herb Dickson, a leading figure in the APS and a nurseryman in Washington State, 'never get too far from the species'. This struck a chord, and I believe Mr Dickson is right. We have got too far from the species and in many instances have lost the charm of the plant, as well as perennial habit and hardiness. I noticed this year that several of the F1 strains were described as 'needing protection in winter'. It is appreciated that the general gardening public, at whom these plants are aimed, may not agree. Jared Sinclair once wrote, of the juliana strain he developed, that there was little demand for the tiny sorts.

As far as the amateur breeder is concerned, he or she need not be put off by the complexities. In many instances F1 crosses are sufficient to give good results and rarely does one need to go beyond F2 or F3 crosses, whatever may be said to the contrary.

Someone may ask, why bother with all the available commercial seed strains? My reply is that the possibilities for hybridizing primroses and polyanthus are considerable. Some knowledgeable enthusiasts have suggested that we have only just scratched the surface. When *P. juliae* was introduced it was crossed with *P. vulgaris*, *P. elatior* and *P. veris*. From these basic crosses arose most of the named hybrids like 'Wanda', while others

were chance seedlings. The difference today is that, while we still have the species, the range of potential partners is colossal. Many of the commercial strains, from Barnhaven to Berfrühling to 'Wanda hybrids', contain lovely plants. There are some excellent colours in polyanthus strains like 'Rainbow' and 'Crescendo'. Selecting plants and crossing with either *juliae* or *elatior* will produce some very interesting seedlings. You can cross back to the selected parent or cross the F1s together, depending on the objective. I have crossed primroses for many years in a fairly unscientific way, yet have raised many lovely plants. They are certainly far easier than auriculas.

The reason for crossing the species with the modern strains is twofold: first, to maintain the charm and habit which has been lost with the large-flowered commercial pot-plant strains; second, to try, especially where *P. juliae* is used, to produce a perennial plant that can be divided and increased – this has also been lost with the majority of modern strains, many of which behave almost as annuals.

POLLINATION

The mechanics of pollination are easy with single primroses and polyanthus. Doubles are slightly more complicated and will be covered later.

It is advisable to select a pin-eyed plant as the seed parent with a thrum-eye as the pollen parent. By doing this – nature's way, although some thrums do self-pollinate – success is almost guaranteed. The mechanics are simple. All one has to do is transfer pollen from the thrum-eyed plant onto the stigma (i.e the upper part of the pistil) of the seed parent. The pistil is the entire female organ of the flower and includes the stigma, style and ovary. With minimum effort anyone can do this, all one has to do is follow a few basic rules. It is possible to cross thrum with thrum and pin with pin. This is frowned on by more orthodox plant-breeders, but might be necessary where it is desired to cross two special plants. It should only be used if all else fails.

When crossing, certain conditions are necessary. The pollen must be ripe and the pistil or pin of the seed parent receptive. Most hybridizers own good magnifying glasses with which to examine the flower. The pollen ripens usually just as the flower is opening. The stamens have a smooth appearance which changes to a fluffy one when they burst and release pollen. This can be seen under a magnifying glass. The pin, usually when the flower is half open, should have a moist appearance, which indicates that it is sticky and ready to receive pollen. Flowers that are old are less likely to 'take' and it is better to pollinate when they are young and fresh. Pollen can remain viable for some time and there are ways of storing it to ensure it does. The drier the pollen is kept, the longer it lives. W. J. C. Lawrence in *Practical Plant Breeding* (1937) gave details of the viability of pollen in many species, some as long as a year, although primulas were not listed. He recommended that anthers about to burst are selected, put in a screw of tissue paper, then placed in a small corked receptacle (tube or jar), at the bottom of which is some calcium chloride. The calcium chloride absorbs all the moisture in the sealed tube. The only reason for keeping

pollen like this would be if one wanted to make a cross where the seed parent flowered later than the pollen parent. This is unlikely to be necessary with primroses.

Pollen can be transferred in several ways. One common method is by using a fine camel hair brush. The problem with this is that the brush must be thoroughly cleaned and sterilized after each pollination, usually by dipping in methylated spirits, and then dried. This takes time and causes delay. Another is to use fine-pointed tweezers and pick off the ripe stamens one by one; then gently touch them to the stigma. Pollen can also be transferred straight from the flower. In this method the petals are carefully torn open, folded down and outwards so that the stamens stand proud. Held between finger and thumb the stamens are brushed gently against the stigma and shaken slightly. In all three of these methods the process may be repeated several times to ensure a good covering of pollen. Several pips can be pollinated if desired and the remaining flowers removed. When the process has been completed, the stigma is examined under the magnifying glass to check that pollen is adhering to it. If pollination was successful, the green stigma will have a yellow tinge and the grains of pollen can be seen. Once done pollinated plants should be isolated and even covered in some way to prevent accidental pollination by insects. Margaret Webster stresses the importance of preventing this from happening and goes to considerable lengths to avoid it. If the blooms are covered, care must be taken that the fertilized pips are not damaged. There are several variations on the above methods, but the aim is the same in every case, to transfer pollen from one plant to another.

Once plants have been pollinated they should be segregated. If the cross has taken, the footstalks and ovary will remain green. Failure is indicated by a premature browning and shrivelling. The seedpod will swell and when ripe, usually after several weeks, the footstalk or stem will turn brown. The seedpod also turns brown and eventually splits, then opens right up. Watch the seedpods carefully and remove them when the splits appear. Put them in a clean saucer or other receptacle until the pod dries out, when it will deposit seed onto the saucer. Carefully remove any remaining seed from the husk before disposing of it. Unless seed is to be sown immediately it can be stored for up to a year or even slightly longer without viability being affected. This must be in cool dry conditions in small envelopes or packets or even small jars. I put my seed, in packets or small containers, in an old ice cream carton (1 litre − 1 ¾ imperial pints, 2 US pints) with the lid on, kept in the fridge not the freezer. The seed must be completely dry and so should the envelopes or jars − any moisture and they go mouldy. I recently sowed some eight-year-old Barnhaven seed and 25 percent germinated. Keeping seed as long as this is not recommended.

SOWING THE SEED

Primrose seed, like that of other primulas, must be kept cool. Heat is not necessary and indeed can be detrimental. Primroses are affected by a condition known as heat induced dormancy. This occurs if the temperature exceeds 20°C (68°F), causing the seed to become dormant and preventing germination. Generally, primroses are easy to raise and nothing complicated is necessary to achieve this. There are various methods and some growers have their own pet ways.

Seed should be sown in early autumn, soon after ripening or the following late winter/early spring. Opinions vary, but either sowing time gives good results.

Personally I always use a good fresh soilless seed compost, usually peat with added perlite. There are several on the market that give good results. I have not tried the more recent composts with peat replaced by coir or other materials. Experience with soilless composts indicates that they give much better results than conventional loam-based seed composts. This seems to be a majority view.

Barnhaven produced an excellent leaflet on raising from seed. They recommended loamless composts but advised against late summer/autumn sowing. The reason for this is the danger of frost-heaving disturbing the small seedlings. This assumes they are planted outside, though, and is not a problem in trays in a cold greenhouse. Where the climate is particularly harsh, it is probably wiser to sow in early spring.

The procedure is as follows. Fill the pots, trays or other receptacles to more than half a centimetre (within a quarter inch) of the top. Sow seed thinly and leave uncovered. Primrose seed must have light and should never be covered. Water thoroughly using a *very fine* rose, and stand receptacles on bricks or boxes allowing free air circulation all round. Invert an empty tray or pot of similar size over the sowings. Make sure this will not come off by stretching a piece of porous material over the receptacle or placing a large stone or brick on it. This assumes that the trays are placed in a safe position outdoors, out of direct sunlight, and protects them from the elements. In a greenhouse the possibility always exists that a burst of sunshine will raise the temperature to dangerous levels, bringing about heat induced dormancy. The seed must NEVER be allowed to dry out. Drying out is probably the major reason for poor germination or lack of germination.

Although I have followed the above procedures with good results, my current methods are slightly different. I fill the trays, gently level the compost and water by standing in 20–50 mm (one or two inches) of water. This must be done carefully, otherwise the peat compost can be forced out of the tray. As the compost absorbs the water, add a little more until moistened throughout. The trays are removed, allowed to drain for 20 minutes, then the seed sown on top. In the last year or two I have put a thin covering of vermiculite over the seeds. Vermiculite is a porous material that allows light to penetrate. Finally, a mist spray is given to make sure the surface is fully moist. The vermiculite covering reduces the chances of drying out, and of mould developing on the seeds. Finally, the trays are placed in a large unheated propagator with a plastic top. The vents are left open with an inverted brick over them. I normally put the propagator outdoors, raised on bricks, in a north-facing position shielded from the sun. This method has brought good results with no obvious problems. The watering is done by immersion because roses on most watering cans have too coarse a spray. Unless you are very careful, the compost is disturbed and seed washed around.

If successful, germination of spring sowings takes place within 2–7 weeks. This varies year by year depending on the weather conditions. When the first seedlings appear, if you are using the inverted-pot method, the covers should be removed. Lightly cover them with compost and keep just moist. If too wet, there is a serious danger of damping off. Use a suitable fungicide if damping off occurs. Prick the seedlings out, when the first true leaf develops, into trays, approximately 18 to a standard seed tray. In recent years cell trays in a range of sizes have appeared and they are a good alternative. When sufficiently large, the seedlings can be planted out in the garden or singly into 3 inch (75 mm) plastic pots. If in pots move again when the roots start coming out of the drainage holes. Plants can be potted on into 5 inch (125 mm) or larger pots as necessary.

SINGLE PRIMROSES AND POLYANTHUS

The standard method of crossing pin with thrum is best, although pin x pin and thrum x thrum are feasible. I have successfully crossed two pin-eyed plants, 'Tawny Port' and 'Enchantress'.

Crossing thrum-eyed plants is more difficult and not really recommended. Here the flower of the selected seed parent is carefully cut back, using fine scissors, to reveal the stigma. Pollen is then transferred by one of the methods described earlier. On pin-eyed plants the stamens are lower in the tube below the stigma. To obtain pollen the petals are carefully folded back, the pin removed, and the stamens should be accessible. Some plants have very narrow tubes and it is difficult to reach the stigma without causing damage.

The possibilities for the keen amateur are wide with both primroses and polyanthus. I stress 'for the amateur' because he or she is not bound by the rigid requirements that dominate the commercial market. Unusual, attractive and interesting plants are easily raised.

When *P. juliae* was introduced, extensive hybridization took place with the other members of the primrose family. Hundreds of hybrids were raised and a large number given clonal names. Most have disappeared and much verbal 'wringing of hands' has taken place over this. Many enthusiasts, both past and present, spent considerable time and effort trying to trace these old varieties with very limited success. Only a handful survive, and – when looked at objectively – few have merit. Those still grown are lacking in vigour and may be affected by virus, although some have been 'cleaned up' by meristem culture. The glowing descriptions were written in a different era.

We still have the original species, in fact more so with some of the exciting subspecies of *P. vulgaris* and *P. elatior,* now correctly identified. In addition, there is a range of modern hybrid primroses and polyanthus in a vast array of colours and types. Thus the original hybrids could be recreated and new and exciting ones raised. To some extent this has already been done in North America by members of the American Primrose Society, less so elsewhere.

Interest in the then new *P. juliae* was staggering. Many individuals and organizations, both in the UK and on the Continent, crossed it to raise new hybrids. In England the John Innes Institute, now the John Innes Centre based at Norwich, conducted extensive breeding experiments over an eight year period beginning in 1919. A record was made of this work and is contained in six notebooks, running to 400 pages, held at the centre.

Much is highly technical and only of interest to botanists and geneticists. There are some points that are pertinent to plant-breeders who are using the species for crossing. To quote from the notes 'in *acaulis–juliae* hybrids, the *juliae* flower colour is dominant… in *elatior–juliae*, and *officinalis–juliae* hybrids, the *juliae* flower colour is recessive.' *Acaulis* refers to *P. vulgaris* and *officinalis* to *P. veris*. It is well-known that the biggest problem with hybridizing *P. juliae* is the dominant magenta colour. Perhaps less well-known is the dominance of the yellow colour in both *elatior* and *veris*. In some crosses between *elatior–juliae* coloured flowers were produced in the F1s leading R. J. Chittenden to conclude that *elatior* might be heterozygous for the colour inhibitor.

The work at the institute was summarized by C. Leonard Huskins in a paper in the RHS *Journal* in 1929. The following extracts are of interest:

> *The size of the hybrid families in which* P. juliae *was involved was limited, however, by irregular or delayed germination, which occurs in selfed seed of pure* P. juliae. *With either pure* P. juliae *or any of its hybrid descendants, it was found that some of the seed would germinate almost at once, while others would lie dormant in the seed pans for*

any period up to several years.

In his summary Huskins restated some general observations on the species crosses:

> *Thus the thrum style is dominant to pin in all crosses either within a species or between any of them… the pedunculate character of the inflorescence whether on the cowslip, the oxlip or the polyanthus is dominant to the single-flowered condition of either the primrose or* P. juliae. *The semi-glabrous character of P.* juliae *is dominant to the very hairy condition of all the other species used; the orange-coloured eye of the oxlip is dominant to the yellow eye of either the primrose or* P. juliae… *the anthocyanin coloured flower is dominant to either the white or yellow flower of any species except where an inhibitor is present, as in most oxlips.*

As well as species, crosses were made with polyanthus 'Cloth of Gold' and various jack-in-the-green, green primroses and hose-in-hose. No details were given about these latter experiments but are presumably covered in the notebooks.

To conclude, the possibilities are still considerable with single primroses and polyanthus, limited only by the imagination and flair of the hybridizer.

ANOMALOUS PRIMROSES

Most of what has been said about the ordinary primrose applies to the anomalous forms. One or two points need emphasizing. First they are easy to raise. Both jack-in-the-green and hose-in-hose characteristics are dominant, meaning that seedlings appear – up to 25 percent – in the F1 generation. This makes it all the more surprising that so few are grown. It has been suggested that little seed arises from such crosses. I haven't found this to be the case, and Margaret Webster's plants produce masses of seed. Seed is available from several commercial sources, notably Barnhaven and Craven's of Bingley, West Yorkshire.

Enthusiasts like Geoff Nicolle and Margaret Webster in the UK and Peter Atkinson in America have recreated many of the old forms. Brian Coop raised a series of very nice hose-in-hose some years ago, when he was my near neighbour in South Wales. Brian's mother Stella is still growing plants from those days. Margaret Webster has plants that are over eight years old, and they have been grown solely in pots. Interest in these unusual forms is still considerable and plants always attract attention when exhibited. Dr Vincent Clark says there is a lot of interest in Australia for primroses and polyanthus that are 'different'. He calls his nursery the 'Jack in the Green Primula Nursery'.

Jacks are raised by crossing a jack-in-the-green with a normal primrose or polyanthus. The same applies to hose-in-hose. To create pantaloons, jackanapes and other variations, begin by crossing jacks with hose-in-hose. The possible colour combinations are many and varied.

DOUBLE PRIMROSES

It takes a little more trouble to raise double primroses, but once again it is relatively easy. Although many doubles were raised in the early part of the twentieth century, the process was shrouded in mystery. Many must have been put off by the supposed difficulties, and it was not until the 1960s, both in the UK and America, that articles appeared explaining the mechanics of the process. It was known in the early 1900s that varieties like 'Arthur du Moulin' produced pollen, and indeed was the 'father' of the Bon Accord doubles, but nothing appeared in print about the actual process.

The problem with doubles is twofold: finding pollen in the first instance and having to raise an F2 generation from the F1 single seedlings. Select a pin-eyed plant as the seed parent and take care to pick one with good characteristics. This refers to quality of flower, size, colour and general habit of the plant. The pollen parent should be a true double rather than a semi-double, but some fairly indifferent plants have produced very good offspring. There is a tendency to use semi-doubles because they produce ample pollen. In instances where I did this, the proportion of true doubles was low, with semi-doubles more prevalent.

The problem is finding pollen. The flower has to be pulled carefully apart. The stamens, if present, are at or near the centre, attached to the lower part of the petals. You may find only one, sometimes several, but it can be a frustrating exercise. The fuller the flower the less likely you are to find pollen. This is a problem that has taxed all raisers of doubles, including Barnhaven. The finest doubles I raised produced no pollen. Nevertheless, keep looking and eventually pollen will be found, sometimes only one stamen. In some cases the stamen refuses to ripen or burst and no pollen is shed. If kept in a dry state, the

pollen may ripen in a day or so. Some past raisers have gone to great lengths to ripen such stamens. Although I have not tried, there are ways of persuading a reluctant double to produce pollen. This involves starving the plant so that, thinking it is dying, it will try to ensure that its genes are passed on by producing pollen. Towards the end of flowering, some plants produce flowers that are less double and may have some pollen. It is really a question of perseverance. If you keep looking some pollen will be found but it may not be from your first-choice plant.

Once pollen is found it is transferred to the stigma of the selected seed parent using one of the methods described. Once again make sure the blooms to be pollinated are receptive.

The seedlings of the F1 generation will all be single, unless of course the seed parent has some double genes. Two methods of producing doubles are now possible. The orthodox one, often recommended in the past, is to cross two F1 seedlings together, selecting a pin and a thrum. You can cross thrum to thrum and pin to pin but avoid this if possible. Crossing F1s together will produce up to 25 percent of double seedlings. I stress 'up to' because it is not automatic and the percentage may be lower. The other method is to pollinate the F1s with double pollen, any double pollen will do – it doesn't have to be the original parent. This latter method has been frowned upon, the perceived wisdom being that the quality of the resulting doubles will be poor. I don't think this is a problem that need concern us, as no obvious difference in quality is apparent in plants produced by the two methods. The benefit in using a double to pollinate the F1s is that the percentage of seedlings will be between 25 percent and 50 percent. I have read articles, notably from Barnhaven, where it has been said that a percentage of F2 singles come double in the second year. This is not something that has ever happened in my crosses, although I appreciate my efforts are small-scale by comparison.

As well as normal doubles, jack-in-the-greens have been raised, originally by Peter Klein in the USA and Cecil Jones in the UK. Major Charles Taylor may have had one earlier but the origin is unknown. The widely available jack-in the-green double 'Dawn Ansell' produces some pollen, while single jacks can be pollinated by ordinary doubles. Either way, double jacks should appear in the F2 generation.

I asked Margaret Webster whether she thought double pantaloons were possible. As far as I know, none have been raised but Margaret sees no reason why not.

Raising doubles is a fun thing and the sense of expectation and excitement, when the F2 seedlings begin to bloom, is considerable.

GOLD-LACED POLYANTHUS

Although I have grown gold-laced in the past and do so at present, my personal experience in breeding them is minimal. Fortunately, I know or have known many present and past raisers of these plants. The gold-laced is unique amongst primroses in that plants are bred to florists' standards, rigid rules that are 'fixed and unalterable'. Old florists like Dan Bamford would proudly write that the 'old growers' might only keep

one seedling in a thousand. This is enough to put anyone off but fortunately things have moved on. Modern hybridizers would expect to get around 5 to 10 percent of show standard seedlings from selected crossings, perhaps 5 percent being the more likely figure. Many of the other seedlings are attractive and well worth keeping by those who grow them purely for pleasure.

Although crosses of thrum to thrum are made, as in auriculas, this is not mandatory because both thrums and pins are produced. Indeed it is a fact that many pin-eyed seedlings are of very good form, and so are used as seed parents. While individual raisers have their own ideas of what constitutes the perfect parents the general rule is to cross those plants closest to the ideal. Peter Klein, the famous American raiser, made great strides in improving gold-laced in a few short years. He thought the best parents were the second-best plants, a perceived wisdom of the old florists. John Kerridge also subscribes to this view.

Experience with gold-laced indicates that, without hand pollination, the standard quickly deteriorates. Equally, a careful breeding programme soon produces a significant improvement. Raisers like Cecil Jones and Hubert Calvert, starting with fairly unpromising material, achieved very high quality after ten years. Chris Wood has made considerable progress in only three to four years.

As well as maintaining the existing standards possibilities exist with other ground colours and hybrids with the garden polyanthus. Cecil Jones raised blue grounds of a good standard, so it can be done. All we need are some creative hybridizers.

12 PESTS AND DISEASES

Problems with primroses tend to be few, with one or two exceptions. In the garden in suitable conditions and with regular attention, problems – with the exception of vine weevil – are relatively minor. In pots this may change, but providing the plants are outside during the summer months only the vine weevil is a major threat.

PESTS
Birds

Some small species of birds, notably house sparrows and blue tits, may destroy the flower buds. Sprays exist that make the buds unpalatable but a simple solution is to use black cotton. A single strand stretched between two sticks, 50 mm (2 in) above the flower buds, along each row or group of plants, is usually sufficient.

Greenfly Aphids (various species)

Greenfly make their appearance in early spring. Providing action is taken when first noticed, this is a minor pest that does not trouble primroses in a significant way, apart from the danger of introducing virus. A spray with a suitable systemic insecticide, or one containing the newer Bifenthrin, will keep them under control.

Black Vine Weevil (Otiorhynchus sulcatus)

The vine weevil is a serious pest of many garden and pot plants and attacks primroses both in the garden and in pots. Several species of weevil will attack primroses but the vine weevil is the most common. Plants grown in peat-based composts are especially likely to be attacked. Vine weevil prefer to lay their eggs near to host plants in pots and containers of some sort, rather than in more open sites. Although they attack plants in the garden, the problem, although worrying, is less severe. They love primroses and polyanthus of every sort and I once discovered over 20 grubs in a 6 inch (150 mm) pot of double primrose. A layer of grit or small gravel will discourage egg-laying and reduce infestation.

The adult beetles are 9–10 mm (about a

third of an inch) long, dull black with small, light brown patches on their roughened wing cases, giving them a speckled appearance. They have elbowed antennae and cannot fly, walking very slowly. They are excellent climbers and often found at considerable heights, even on ceilings in houses. Their eyesight is poor but they locate the host plants by smell. The adults do not attack the roots but cause unsightly damage by eating irregular notches, normally u-shaped, from the margins of the leaves. When this type of damage is seen on primroses the grubs are certain to follow!

In the greenhouse the adults may emerge in autumn but are more often found in late March to May. In the garden they are active during the summer months and will attack plants growing in the soil, but with less obvious effect. All adult vine weevils are female, although it has been claimed that males do exist. Each female can lay up to 1500 eggs, of which approximately 600 hatch, over a period of several months with the peak in June and July.

The minute eggs are laid on top of the soil or compost and the grubs burrow down after hatching. At this early stage they are at their most vulnerable. The grubs devour the roots, and even a single grub causes damage, although it will not kill mature plants. When several are at work, most notably in pots but also in the garden, the root system can be severely damaged, although the fibrous rooted primrose, providing it is already well established, seems able to survive most attacks. Seedlings are particularly at risk and grubs will sever the roots.

When fully grown, the grubs are about 10 mm (a third of an inch) long but appear

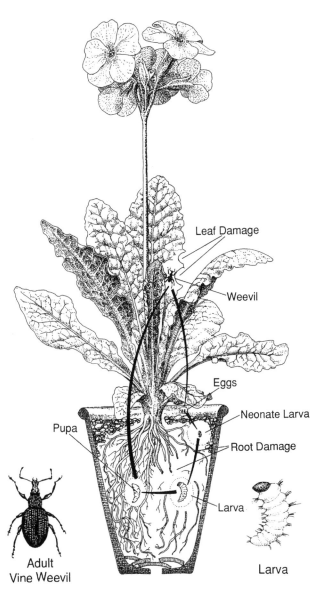

Leaf Damage

Weevil

Eggs

Neonate Larva

Root Damage

Pupa

Larva

Adult Vine Weevil

Larva

Fig. 9. The life cycle of the vine weevil.

shorter, as their bodies are curved. They are plump, creamy white with a pale brown head, and have no legs. They pupate in the soil, and some adult features, such as legs, antennae and wing pads can be seen on the pupae. Larval damage occurs mainly in autumn and spring, when the grubs are becoming fully grown.

The problem with vine weevil is that the grubs, especially when fully grown, have a considerable tolerance to insecticides. All the effective or partially effective products that could be incorporated into the soil or compost are either banned or under threat. HCH, also known as BCH (Benzene Hexachloride), which gives some control, is no longer approved for mixing in composts. Several pesticides were effective as drenches, at recommended spray strengths. Now, unless the label specifically states this is approved, to use them in this manner is a technical breach of the law.

Some new pesticides are being developed, but the cost of registration in the UK is very expensive and complicated. As a result, chemical companies are reluctant to go through the process of obtaining approval for sale to amateurs. New professional products have been developed that work well. One such, now widely used, is 'suSCon Green' which is 10 percent Chlorpyrifos, formulated as a slow-release granule to give two years or more control over vine weevil in composts. Another professional product is 'Cudgel' which is very effective when used as a drench. These products are not for sale to amateurs and it is illegal to use them. The ludicrous thing is that many of the plants sold in containers by garden centres and nurserymen now contain suSCon Green.

When planting or repotting the unsuspecting amateur is handling soil which contains these chemicals.

At the present time many of the existing chemical controls have either been withdrawn, will soon be withdrawn, or are under threat. If this is for environmental reasons or concerns about health risks to people, then no one can seriously argue against it. None of us want dangerous products to be marketed, but it seems that commercial considerations are at the heart of some of these withdrawals. At the very least, it is the duty of the chemical industry, in cooperation with the government of the day, to provide the amateur grower, of which there are millions, with products that allow him or her to safeguard valuable plants.

The only alternative for the amateur grower is biological control with the nematodes *Heterorhabditis megidis* and *Steinernema bibionis*. They are supplied as millions of nematodes in concentrated granules which are mixed with lukewarm water. The resulting solution is applied as a drench outdoors during April/May and August/September. In containers or greenhouses the danger period extends from February to May and August to November. Therefore *at least* two treatments are necessary, covering the early and late periods. Some doubts have been expressed about the effectiveness of nematodes in the garden. Graham Rice in *Herbaceous Plants* says they are 'useless'. The problem is partly temperature. Nematodes are only active between a soil temperature range of 10°C–21°C (50°F–70°F) and the soil must not be dry. In pots, a loose compost, such as peat or peat substitute, is preferred if the nematodes are to move freely. The nematodes enter the vine weevil grubs' bodies and release bacteria which cause a fatal infection. The grubs die and the nematodes feed on the bacteria in the decaying bodies. These nematodes also kill sciarid fly larvae as a bonus. The problem is that when the grubs are eliminated the nematodes die, and a fresh hatching of weevil eggs may start the process again. Drawbacks are the need for quite precise temperature and humidity control and the need for grubs being present in some numbers for the nematodes to seek them out. I understand that work is proceeding on developing new formulations that are effective at much lower temperatures, down to 2 °C (35 °F). This will certainly help the amateur, but cost is a cause for concern.

Amateur packs of nematodes are available for approximately £12–£40 from several sources. The pack can be stored for a short time in a refrigerator but as they are living animals, with a short shelf life, must be used as soon as possible after receipt. A £12 pack will treat the equivalent of 250 3-inch (75 mm) pots or 5–10 sq m (6–12 sq yards).

One product, 'Biosafe', is supplied in suspended form and not activated until mixed with lukewarm water. Once it is activated, you must use it within three hours, although the original pack life has now been extended to several months. Biosafe is primarily recommended for outdoor use and is claimed to kill several other soil pests in addition to weevils.

Some control of adult weevils is possible by spraying or dusting permethrin, pirimiphos-methyl or HCH, applied to the foliage and soil surface at dusk. The effectiveness of these chemicals is variable.

The latest liquid insecticide, 'Polysect' from Solaris, is based on Bifenthrin and is classed as a 'non-hazardous' chemical. 'Polysect' is essentially a contact insecticide but also, because of the way it works, partially systemic. This welcome new product is proving very efficient against red spider and flying pests like greenfly and whitefly. Possibly it may also prove to be effective against adult weevils. It is expensive, but it does work and is cheaper than using nematodes.

Red Spider Mite *(Tetranychus urticae)*

This is another pest, which together with vine weevil, has become a major problem in recent years. It appears mainly where plants are grown in greenhouses, but it will attack primroses grown in the garden and especially in pots. Gold-laced polyanthus are particularly vulnerable. The reason is almost certainly the run of hot dry summers we have experienced, providing conditions in which they thrive. In addition, the pesticides that are recommended for control are not very effective and the mites are difficult to eradicate. Nevertheless, it is worth persevering with sprays, varying the type of insecticide used and paying particular attention to the underside of the leaves. Systemic insecticides work better than contact sprays. In the brief period since 'Polysect' was introduced its effectiveness against red spider has been highly encouraging.

Red spider, which is not a spider at all, is difficult to see with the naked eye, but its presence is indicated by a yellow mottling of the leaves. In very bad infestations the leaves turn almost white, then brown, as the sap is sucked from them. A plant that has been attacked has an unmistakable appearance which is soon recognized. The mites cluster on the underside of the leaves which should be examined under a lens for signs of the tiny white webs. Among them the minute yellow mites with dark patches either side of the body, will be detected. The mites are less than 1 mm ($\frac{1}{20}$ in) in length but increase rapidly in numbers, each generation taking approximately two weeks at 20°C (68°F), less than a week at 30°C (85°F). Each adult mite can produce more than 100 eggs over a three-week period and large populations can develop in a short space of time. During the autumn the mites become deep red in colour and leave the plant to hibernate in cracks and crevices. They overwinter without feeding and emerge the following spring to begin again.

A biological control for red spider is available: this is the predatory mite *Phytoseiulus persimilis*, originating in South America. With a pear-shaped, shiny red body it is slightly larger than the spidermite. Once introduced, the predator searches out the mites and will consume many hundreds of them during its life cycle of 6–12 days depending on temperature. A typical cost is £5.95 for a standard pack of 200 predators, capable of treating 16 sites. The largest pack – costing £16.95 – contains 2000 predators and will treat 160 sites. Once again, temperature is very important and also timing, as once the mites are consumed the predators die. The predators should only be introduced when daytime temperatures exceed 10°C (50°F).

Probably the best way to control red

spider is to prevent the conditions occurring in which they thrive. Plants in pots should be removed to a cool outside shady position between May and October.

Whitefly (Trialeurodes vaporariorum)

Whitefly is only a problem when plants are grown in greenhouses, where – in hot dry conditions – an infestation spreads rapidly. This is also the case, to a lesser extent, with leafhoppers and thrips. Biological controls are available and Bifenthrin sprays seem effective, but the real solution is to move the plants outside immediately after flowering. Gold-laced polyanthus are particularly vulnerable when grown in greenhouses.

Slugs and Snails

In the garden, slugs and snails are a major pest and can ravage primroses if left unchecked. The effect of these pests seems to vary from one garden to another and some plants are not attacked at all. The small metaldehyde or methiocarb pellets can be used to control them or a metaldehyde spray. Methiocarb would seem to be the most effective control but has the unfortunate side effect of killing ground and other beneficial beetles.

Some people do not like using these pellets, due to possible dangers to wildlife and pets from eating poisoned slugs, so they should be used with extreme care. Small children may also pick them up. The old-fashioned method was to search for them amongst the plants and hand pick.

Recently a new biological control has been introduced called 'Nemaslug'. The standard pack (£12.95) treats 25 sq m (30 sq yards) and the nematodes seek out the slugs, which when infected are inhibited from feeding in three to five days. Slugs are killed on and below the soil surface and the treatment is effective for six weeks.

DISEASES
Fungal Diseases

Various fungal diseases may attack primroses and polyanthus but are not common. If primroses are grown in the same position for a number of years a condition known as primula wilt can occur but it is rare. It has been suggested that the reason for the sudden collapse of plants, notably double primroses, may be due to a fungus disease. With the withdrawal of the most effective fungal sprays this problem may escalate.

Botrytis cinerea

This, the most common disease, is a grey mould which grows on dead or decaying leaves. The fungus will invade the plant through a decaying leaf, or the spores may establish themselves on living tissue. Once started, the fungus spreads rapidly and if not treated will cause the death of the plant. The start of the disease is easy to detect, as the affected tissue turns soft and black with an unpleasant odour. As it develops, the affected parts are covered with a grey mould, from which fine white spores rise when the plant is handled. Treatment consists of cutting away the decaying parts to firm tissue and cauterizing with methylated spirits or one of the sulphurs. Providing treatment is given in time the plant will normally produce fresh

growth from the undamaged parts.

The best remedy is to ensure that conditions encouraging the growth of fungus do not arise by removing dead leaves and flowers. Good ventilation for plants growing in greenhouses or conservatories is another must.

Virus Diseases

The majority of viruses are transmittable, usually by aphids or other sucking insects, such as leafhoppers. One of the attractions of meristem culture is the possibility of eliminating virus. Primroses and polyanthus can be affected, most commonly by cucumber mosaic virus. It is likely that the demise of many of the old varieties was due, at least in part, to the build-up of virus infection. Some plants will be infected from time to time. They are recognized by stunted, distorted and/or blotched foliage, and any showing such signs should be destroyed at once, if possible by burning.

Chlorosis

This is a term used to denote the abnormal paling or yellowing of the leaves. It results from the failure of the plant to produce chlorophyll, the green colouring matter. It can be a result of poor cultivation, either under or overwatering, or unfavourably high temperatures. Generally, it is caused either by nutrient deficiency, usually iron, or by an excess of lime in the soil. If cultivation is not to blame for the yellowing of the leaves, then lack of iron is the main suspect. This is easily remedied by watering with a solution of sequestrene or Maxicrop plus Iron at the recommended dilution rates.

APPENDIX 1

SOCIETY ADDRESSES

National Auricula and Primula Society

Midland and West Section. Secretary:
    P. G. Ward, 6 Lawson Close, Saltford,
    Bristol, BS18 3LB.

Northern Section. Secretary:
    D. Hadfield, 146 Queens Road, Cheadle
    Hulme, Cheshire, SK8 5HY.

Southern Section. Secretary:
    L. Wigley, 67 Warnham Court Road,
    Carshalton Beeches, Surrey, SM5 3ND.

American Primrose Society

Recording Secretary: Dorothy Springer, 7213
South 15th, Tacoma, Washington, 98465
USA.

Dansk Primula Klub

Secretary: Vagn Jensen, Danmarksvej 43B,
2800 B, Lyngby, Denmark.

APPENDIX 2

NATIONAL COLLECTIONS

Primula (sect Primula)
Mrs Pam Gossage,
Oakenlea, West Coker Hill,
Yeovil, Somerset, BA22 9NG.

Mrs A. M. Jackson,
Paddocks, Shelbrook, Ashby-de-la-Zouch,
Leicestershire, LE65 2TU.

Mrs B. N. Shaw,
Tan Cottage, West Lane, Cononley, nr.
Keighley, Yorkshire, BD20 8NL.

Consult the latest edition of *The National Plant Collections Directory* (NCCPG), available from The Pines, c/o Wisley Gardens, Woking, Surrey, GU23 6QB, for any changes to collection holders.

APPENDIX 3
SOURCES OF SUPPLY

The best way to find sources of available named plants in the UK is to consult the current edition of *The RHS Plantfinder*, published bi-annually by The Royal Horticultural Society. This also gives details of international plant finders, of which there are quite a number.

Primrose seed is available from a wide variety of sources. The various alpine plant societies throughout the world have seed exchanges that often includes species primrose seed. The American Primrose Society has an excellent seed list covering a wide range. Both the National Auricula and Primula Society and the Dansk Primula Klub issue seed lists.

Retail commercial sources mentioned in the text are:

Barnhaven Primroses Langerhouad, 22420 Plouzélambre, France. (United Kingdom, 25 Warstones Crescent, Penn, Wolverhampton, WV4 4LQ). The largest range of primrose and polyanthus seed including anomalous, gold-laced polyanthus and 'Cowichans'.

Cravens Nursery 1 Foulds Terrace, Bingley, West Yorkshire, BD16 4LZ, England. Rare and unusual seeds including anomalous cowslips, gold-laced polyanthus and double primroses.

Field House Alpines Leake Road, Gotham, Nottingham, NG11 OJN, England. Bergfrühling, Wanda hybrids, laced polyanthus etc.

Jelitto Staudensamen GmBH PO Box 1264, D-29685 Schwarmstedt, Germany. Bergfrühling hybrids.

Rosetta Jones E. 170 Dunoon Place, Shelton, Washington, 98584 USA. Double primrose seed.

Thompson and Morgan Poplar lane, Ipswich, Suffolk, IP8 3BU, England. A good range of primrose and polyanthus seed.

There are of course many others.

GLOSSARY

anther The part of the stamen bearing pollen, also called thrum.

anthocyanin The pigment responsible for the pink, red, purple and blue colourings in flowers.

calyx The cup formed by sepals, modified leaves protecting the developing bud and later round the base of the individual flower.

capsule The seedpod, which dries and splits open when the seeds inside are ripe.

chlorophyll The green colouring matter of plants, essential for photosynthesis.

chlorosis A disorder where chlorophyll is absent from the margins of the leaf, usually caused by mineral deficiency, especially iron.

chromosome A multiple-folded chemical strand comprising thousands of genes. It only unfolds, becoming visible under a microscope, when cells divide.

ciliate Meaning 'fringed with hairs', usually applied to leaves.

crenate Having rounded teeth, usually used to describe leaves or the tube of the flower.

corolla The collection of petals forming the flower.

dentate Toothed, usually applied to leaves.

dominant One of two alternative characters in plants, visible in the progeny when both are inherited.

F1 Botanical shorthand for first filial generation, normally applied to hybrids.

gene A unit in the chromosomes of a plant or animal, determining one character in the adult plant, e.g. a gene for doubling, a gene for virescence.

genus A subdivision of a family of plants, a collection of wild species of plants that have many features in common. Primroses are members of the genus *Primula*.

glabrous Without hair or glands.

ground colour The ring of colour immediately next to the centre in a gold-laced polyanthus pip, usually black, brown or red.

heterozygous Where both genes of a gene-pair are different, and therefore the plant will not breed true. F1 hybrids are heterozygous for many gene-pairs.

homozygote See Zygote.

hybrid The progeny of a cross between two different but related species, showing a diversity of features derived from both parents. A hybrid rarely breeds true, the offspring showing further diversity.

inflorescence The flowering part of a plant; either the individual florets or group comprising the flowerhead.

line breeding The practice of breeding from related seedlings, of recrossing the progeny of two parents, thus concentrating good genes and also bad ones.

mutation A change in the genetic make-up of plants and animals passed on to future generations, often called 'a sport'.

node The place, often swollen, where the leaf stalk meets the stem, or where buds and side shoots grow from the stem.

out-cross Breeding outside a pure line, introducing fresh genes to try to create a different line of breeding.

ovary The part of a flower where fertilized seeds develop.

pedicel The individual stem supporting each flower in a truss, also called a footstalk.

peduncle The main stem or stalk of a truss of flowers.

petal The individual coloured parts of the flower, together forming the corolla.

petiole A leaf stalk.

petaloid 'Resembling a petal', used to describe parts of flowers altered from their normal function to resemble petals, often found in double flowers.

pin-eyed A flower in which the female style and stigma are visible in the throat or centre and are above the stamens which are lower down. In gold-laced polyanthus such a flower is disqualified and cannot be exhibited.

pistil The entire female parts of a flower, including the stigma, style and ovary.

pollen The yellow powder made by the anthers, the male sex cells of a flower, transferred naturally or artificially to the female pistil, subsequently fertilizing the seed.

recessive An inherited character not apparent in the plant which inherits it although it may reappear in future generations.

rhizome The part of the plant where food is stored and from which the roots and shoots arise.

scape The flower stem that rises from the crown of the plant, carrying the buds and later the flowers.

selfing Artificially pollinating a plant with its own pollen.

species A collection of individual wild plants that breed true.

stamen The male reproductive organ of a flower, being a fine stalk or filament and the anther or pollen sacs, attached in primroses to the petals.

stigma The pad resembling the knob of a pin at the top of the style, that receives the pollen.

stolon A shoot that runs along the ground, rooting and producing a new plant at the tip.

stoloniferous Producing stolons.

style The hollow tube joining the stigma and ovary down which the pollen tubes grow to fertilize the seed.

systemic A type of insecticide absorbed into the sap of a plant, rendering it poisonous to biting and sucking insects. Systemic fungicides help to prevent fungal attack.

tomentose Furry: densely covered in short fine hairs.

transpiration The loss of water vapour from leaves by evaporation.

thrum-eyed A flower in which the stamens are visible in the throat of the flower, usually hiding the 'pin' or stigma.

tube the narrow channel down the centre of the flower, containing the sexual parts, the pin and the thrum.

virescence (or **phyllody**) Abnormal greenness of petals, under genetic control and hence inherited by seedlings.

zygote Scientific name for an embryo or offspring. More often mentioned as a homozygote (with the same type of a given gene inherited from each parent) or a heterozygote (with a different type of a given gene inherited from each parent).

BIBLIOGRAPHY

Arends, G. *My Life As Gardener and Plant Breeder* (German Text), 1951

Bagust, H. *The Gardener's Dictionary of Horticultural Terms*, Cassell, 1992

Bellis, Florence. *Gardening and Beyond*, Timber Press USA, David & Charles UK, 1986

Blasdale, W. C. *The Cultivated Species of Primula*, University of California Press, 1948

Bobart, J. *Catalogus Plantarium Horti Medicic Oxoniensis*, 1648

Bradley, R. *New Improvements of Planting and Gardening,* 1724

Coats, Alice. M. *Flowers and their Histories,* 1956
The Quest for Plants, Studio Vista, 1969

Coats, P. *The Story of Flowers Plants and Gardens Through the Ages*, Peerage Books, 1956 (originally published by Weidenfeld & Nicholson as *Flowers in History*)

Douglas, J. *Hardy Florists' Flowers*, 1880

Duthie, R. *Florists' Flowers and Societies*, Shire, 1988

Elliot, C. *Rock Garden Plants*, Edward Arnold & Co., 1935

Emmerton, I. *A Plain and practical treatise on the culture of the Auricula, Polyanthus etc.*, 1816

Evelyn, J. *Directions for the Gardener*, 1687

Farrer, R. *The English Rock Garden*, Nelson, 1919

Federov, A. A. *Flora SSSR*, volume XVIII *Primulaceae*, Engl. transl. Jerusalem 1967

Furber, R. *Twelve Months of Flowers*, 1730

Genders, R. and Taylor, H. C. *Primroses and Polyanthus,* Faber & Faber, 1954

Genders, R. *Primroses*, John Gifford, 1959
The Polyanthus, Its History and Culture, Faber and Faber, 1963
Collecting Antique Plants, Pelham Books, 1971
Scented Flora of the World, Robert Hale, 1977

Gerard, J. *The Herbal, or General Historie of Plantes*, 1597
Catalogue of Plants, 1599

Gilbert, S. *The Florists' Vade-Mecum*, 1682

Glenny, G. *The Culture Of Flowers and Plants*, 1861

Halda, J. J. *The Genus Primula in Cultivation and the Wild,*
Tethys Books, 1992

Hanmer, Sir T. *Garden Book*, 1659 (published in 1933)

Hanbury, R. *A Complete Body of Planting and*

Gardening, 1770–71 (two volumes)

Harvey, J. *Early Gardening Catalogues,* Phillimore, 1972

Haysom, C. G. *Florists' Auriculas and Gold Laced Polyanthus,* Collingridge, 1957

Hecker, W. R. *Auriculas and Primroses,* Batsford, 1971

Herbert, J. *Floricultural Cabinet,* 1847

Hermano, P. *Horti Academici. Lugduno-Batavi Catalogus,* 1687

Hibberd, S. *Field Flowers,* 1870

Hogg, T. *Treatise on the Growth and Culture of the Auricula etc.,* 1812. Edition with supplement, 1833

Jacques, F. *Florists' Auriculas and Gold Laced Polyanthus,* NAPS (northern), 1985

Jelitto, L. *Die Freilandprimeln,* 1938

Köhlein, F. *Primeln,* Eugen Ulmer, 1984

Lawrence, W. J. C. *Practical Plant Breeding,* George Allen & Unwin, 1939

Leith-Ross, Prudence. *The John Tradescants,* Peter Owen, 1984

Macwatt, J. *The Primulas of Europe,* Country Life, 1923

Maddock, J. *The Florists' Directory,* 1792. An edition with improvements by Samuel Curtis, 1810

Mansfield, T. C. *Alpines in Colour and Cultivation,* Collins, 1942, revised 1945

Mcquown, F. R. *Plant Breeding for Gardeners,* Collingridge, 1963

Miller, P. *The Gardener's and Florist's Dictionary,* 1724

The Gardener's Kalendar, 1732

NCCPG, *The Magic Tree* (republished as *Devon Garden Plants*), Devon Books, 1989

Nelson, C. *An Irish Flower Garden,* 1984

Parkinson, J. *Paradisi in sole, Paradisus terrestris,* 1629

Phillips, R., and Rix, M. *Perennials* (Vol. 1), Pan, 1991

Rea, J. *Flora, seu de florum cultura,* 1665

Rice, G. *Hardy Perennials,* Viking, 1995

Richards, J. *Primula,* Batsford, 1993.

Primulas of the British Isles, Shire, 1989

Robinson, Mary A. *Primulas: The Complete Guide,* The Crowood Press, 1990

Shaw, Barbara. *The Book of Primroses,* David & Charles, 1991

Sinclair-Rohde, Eleanor, *The Scented Garden,* Medici Society, 1931

Sitwell, S. *Old Fashioned Flowers,* Country Life, 1939

Smith, G. F., Burrow, B., and Lowe, D. B. *Primulas of Europe and America,* Alpine Garden Society, 1984

Smith, W. W. and Fletcher, H. R. *The Genus Primula: section vernales.* Trans. Bot. Soc. Edinb, 1948

Tanner, H., and Tanner, R. *Woodland Plants,* Impact Books, 1981

Taylor, G. M., and N. Prizeman, *Old Fashioned Flowers,* John Gifford, 1946

Taylor, Jane. *Collecting Garden Plants,* J. M. Dent, 1988

White, J. W. *The Bristol Flora,* 1912

OTHER SOURCES

A large number of articles were consulted. The yearbooks of the National Auricula and Primula Society and the American Primrose Society quarterlies are major sources together with the RHS *Journal* and issues of *The Gardener's Chronicle* and *The Garden.* They are not the only ones but remain the most important.

The old northern-section yearbooks of the NAPS have most on gold-laced polyanthus, the old APS quarterlies and southern-section yearbooks the most on primroses. The history and development of Barnhaven plants is fully documented in the yearbooks and quarterlies, mostly by the proprietors. The APS produces an excellent index and so does the midland and west section of the NAPS. An index for the northern section yearbooks is available from the secretary on computer disc. A good selection of early APS quarterlies are still obtainable.

For RHS journals and early gardening magazines the Lindley Library is the best source.

I was also fortunate in being able to consult a large number of old catalogues.

PLANT INDEX

Note Only plants are listed in this index; for that reason, cultivars are not listed with apostrophes.

GENERAL INDEX